Investment Insight: Allocate or Concentrate

Joseph M. Maas

CFA, CFP®, CLU®, ChFC®, MSFS,
CCIM™, CVA, CM&AA, ABAR

Merrell Marketing, LLC
Bellevue, WA

Merrell

Printed in the United States of America.

Merrell Marketing, LLC, Bellevue, WA

www.synergy-am.com

Library of Congress Cataloging-in-Publications Data

Maas, Joe

Investment Insight: To Allocate or Concentrate

ISBN

Disclaimer

This book is presented solely for educational purposes and is not intended to represent or be used as an exhaustive financial resource. The information contained in this book is made available for illustrative purposes, explaining only the basics of investment planning.

The author and Merrell Marketing, LLC, emphasize this material is not offered as financial, legal, accounting, or other professional services' advice. It is highly recommended you seek the services of a competent professional before making any decisions regarding your business or personal finances.

Best efforts have underscored the writing of this book, but the author and publisher make no representations or warranties of any kind and assume no liabilities of any kind with respect to the accuracy or completeness of the contents, and specifically disclaim any implied warranties of use for any particular purpose.

Neither the author nor Merrell Marketing, LLC, shall be held liable or responsible to any person or entity with respect to any loss or incidental or consequential damages caused, or alleged to have been caused, directly or indirectly, by the information contained in this book, or disruption caused by errors or omissions, whether such errors or omissions result from negligence, accident, or any other cause.

The case studies and any references are fictional, and any likeness to actual persons, either living or dead, is completely coincidental. The investment case studies represented in this book were created to show only the highlights of how an investor might choose to make investment decisions.

The reader is advised to consult with a professional financial advisor who has experience with guiding clients and making investment choices relevant to an individual's financial situation.

Dedication

This book is dedicated to our Lord and Savior Jesus Christ, and my loving wife Molly, my precious children Madison and Andrew, my mother, Anne Maas, and in loving memory of my father, Henry Maas.

About the Author

Joseph M. Maas

CFA, CFP®, CLU®, ChFC®, MSFS,
CCIM™, CVA, CM&AA, ABAR

Meet Joe Maas, an esteemed financial professional with an illustrious career spanning over three decades. As the Chief Investment Officer and lead portfolio manager at Synergy Asset Management LLC (SAM), Joe is dedicated to providing comprehensive investment management services to a diverse clientele comprising individual investors, business owners, and financial advisors.

Joe's expertise is anchored in a multifaceted approach that combines deep fundamental and economic analysis, in-depth industry research, consultations with his network of industry experts, and a keen application of quantitative methods and technical analysis. Within his role, Joe doesn't limit himself to the analysis of existing investments; he also dedicates himself to assessing prospective opportunities, all with the aim of preserving his position as an industry thought leader and staying at the forefront of the investment industry's evolution.

Behind Joe's extensive knowledge of the financial industry is an unrelenting drive to continuously expand his understanding of investment management. This quest for excellence has led him to achieve certification from distinguished organizations and attain a host of globally recognized professional designations. Among these achievements, Joe proudly holds the prestigious Chartered Financial

Analyst (CFA) Charterholder designation, a testament to his mastery in the investment profession.

In addition to a CFA Charterholder, Joe is a Certified Financial Planner® (CFP®) and Chartered Financial Consultant (ChFC), equipped to offer comprehensive advanced financial planning services. His diverse skill set extends to life insurance and estate planning as a chartered life underwriter (CLU®). He also excels as a certified commercial investment member (CCIM®), demonstrating his prowess in the realm of commercial and investment real estate. In 2000, Joe earned his Master of Science in Financial Services (MSFS) from The American College, further solidifying his expertise in the field.

Beyond his proficiency in investment and financial planning, Joe brings a wealth of expertise and hands-on experience tailored to the distinct requirements of business owners. Joe holds the coveted title of Certified Valuation Analyst (CVA) and boasts accreditation in business appraisal review (ABAR). Furthermore, he brings to the table his expertise as a Certified Merger and Acquisition Advisor (CM&AA), a skill set honed in the intricate world of purchasing and divesting middle-market companies, with revenues spanning from $5 million to $500 million.

Joe Maas is more than just a financial expert; he is a visionary leader deeply devoted to assisting clients in navigating the complexities of the financial world, aiming to help them achieve their financial goals to the best of his abilities.

Certified Financial Planner Board of Standards, Inc. owns the certification marks CFP®, CERTIFIED FINANCIAL PLANNER™, and federally registered CFP (with flame design), in the U.S., which it awards to individuals who successfully complete CFP Board's initial and ongoing certification requirements.

This Book is for You

...if you are a private investor wanting to know more about true diversification...

or are interested in seeking higher return through focus investing...

or you are a professional investment advisor wishing to more proficiently guide your clients toward achieving their unique investment goals.

Private Investors:

This book will help you decide which investment strategy is right for you: asset allocation and diversification or focus investing. There is much more about these two investment styles than the popular media portrays, and since you are serious about investing for your financial future and well-being, reading this book will help you determine the style that suits you best. There is a hook, however, and here it is: Is it possible to have the best of both worlds by blending these two very different investment strategies...protecting your investments while accelerating your returns? This book shows you how!

Professional Investment Advisor:

Your position is unique, heavy with the responsibility of your clients' financial health and the impact your service has on their lifestyle and future. The more you learn about true asset allocation, diversification, and focus investing, the more capably you'll guide your clients' decisions toward the financial independence they want. The surprise this book offers is that these two very distinct investment styles can be blended to provide your clients with the protection they require and the growth they expect.

This book reveals what every investor desires...
how to have both risk protection and accelerated returns.

Other Books from Merrell Marketing

Available Now

Exit Insight: Getting to "Sold!"

401(k) Insight: Getting to "Retired!"

Real Estate Insight: Creating Wealth Through Real Estate Investing

Advisor Empowerment: Getting to Independent

Investment Insight: To Allocate or Concentrate

New Books Coming Soon!

Marketing and Sales Insight: Getting to Conversions

Money Insight: The Art and Science of Managing Money

Crypto Insight: How to Manage Electronic Assets

Synergy Asset Management, LLC

Synergy Asset Management, LLC (SAM) is an SEC registered investment advisory firm.

Our core specialty is providing comprehensive and integrated precision investment management services for individual investors, business owners, and financial advisors.

Synergy's 360° experience uniquely positions us to understand your needs, concerns and aspirations—and offer the tools and investment solutions to help grow your portfolio.

Serving as a trusted partner, we provide objective guidance and proven expert solutions based on a thorough understanding of your specific situation and goals. As our client, you will benefit from a collaborative relationship that addresses — and anticipates — your needs. We follow a disciplined process that provides a structured approach while allowing customization to your circumstances.

Acknowledgments

We wish to personally thank the following people for their help with creating this book:

Special thanks to Frank Roman for consistent general support, and as an integral contributor to Merrell books.

Roccy DeFrancesco, Jr., JD, CAPP™, CMP™, a vital collaborator, contributor, and unwavering supporter of the SAAM™ model. Your impact is invaluable.

Todd Jessup, Ryan Rippy, and Jason Zalarick for your contributions with the content and with your expert leadership.

The Synergy office staff for your hard work, insightful advice and continually helpful commentary.

Our editor, Dr. Daniel Levine; your expertise, enthusiasm and dedication were invaluable, as ever.

Lindsay Lush for always providing excellent cover design direction.

Olivia Hobson, your dedicated services with the technical layout and file processing are appreciated!

Synergy's valued clients, who inspire us to keep moving forward and provide meaning to our work.

Synergy Asset Management's RIAs and IARs ... You have made the Dream, for all of us, come true. Thank you!

Foreword

By Tim Nyland, CFA

Investment Insight: To Allocate or Concentrate is the fourth book by Joe Maas of Synergy Asset Management as he exposes one of the best kept disciplinary frameworks in the asset management industry, the concept of "Precision Investing". Precision Investing suggests that for many, perhaps the other side of the allocation coin is worth a closer look?

Consider for a moment what portion of your portfolio would you be able to pry away from traditional asset allocation models if you were willing to increase risk to achieve a more rapid accumulation of wealth. Furthermore, what if I told you that this increase in risk was going to be the result of a 'focus' on specific assets within a specific class that are more likely to have higher rates of return? Everyone from the infamous value investor Warren Buffett, to Hedge Fund legend Leon Cooperman, uses some level of focus investing to exploit their edge and generate alpha for their investors.

Most private investors and many professional investment advisors think of asset classes in terms of the big five; stocks, bonds, real estate, commodities and alternative assets. Mr. Maas takes you on a journey through focus investing and how it can be applied across all 22 commonly accepted asset classes. Mr. Maas outlines the entire disciplinary framework of Precision Investing that is synonymous with Synergy Asset Management. Everyone from private investors to professional investment advisors can benefit from this behind the scenes look at this discipline of 'blending' asset allocation and diversification together with focus investing to help all achieve financial independence.

My personal equity allocation targets a 70% core diversified weight coupled with a 30% focused, 6 stocks macro tilt. What will be appropriate for you? What will be appropriate for your clients? Prepare to learn one of the best kept disciplinary frameworks on Wall Street.

Isn't it time you looked to the other side of the coin?

—Tim Nyland, CFA

Table of Contents

Introduction to Disciplined Investing

When you have finished reading this introduction, you will:

- Possess a beginning understanding of the two basic types of investment strategies
- Acquire a good foundation for the intentions of this book through an overview of the more salient concepts
- Be aware of the realistic opportunity and compelling value of investing with precision while increasing your wealth and attaining the financial results you choose
- Understand how the SAAM™ program can help your investments grow
- Have an informed understanding of risk and return as the two opposing forces of investment philosophy and the investment process
- See the value of segmenting your investments in "buckets" for short-term, mid-term and long-term use

When you invest your money, you want two things to happen: you want your money to stay safe, and you want it to grow. Most people prefer financial safety more than they desire the risk that comes with high growth strategies. With Synergy Asset Management you can have both at the same time.

There are several basic concepts to know, which may already be familiar. These concepts are briefly outlined below so you can more clearly see the intentions of this book.

Riding Bulls and Taming Bears

Figure 1: The Two Sides of the Investment Coin

We take a dynamic global approach to managing money at Synergy Asset Management. We are active managers without constraints, and our main goal is to ride bulls – optimizing upside capture – while simultaneously taming bears – minimizing downside capture. Our approach revolves around building diversified portfolios that seek reasonable returns with reasonable risk over reasonable time periods.

In the world of finance, the pursuit of wealth often resembles a coin toss, with the green bear side representing caution and the red bull side symbolizing opportunity. These two sides of the coin serve as a powerful metaphor throughout this book, helping us unravel the intricacies of investment strategies and financial misconceptions.

Just like when you flip a coin 100 times, when it lands on heads roughly 50 times and on tails about 50 times, the world of investing presents two sides: bulls and bears, risk and return, stocks and bonds, risk-on and risk-off. While we all wish for the coin to consistently land on the "up" or return side, seeking rewards without risk is an unrealistic expectation.

In truth, the core principle of investing lies in the delicate balance between risk and return. To attain returns, some level of risk must be embraced. The greater the risk, the higher the potential for gains, and vice versa. Avoiding risk entirely also means missing out on opportunities for returns. The goal is to achieve that elusive equilibrium, akin to the coin landing on its edge, where risk and return are both optimally managed. This is the ongoing mission of our portfolio management approach.

The bear side of the coin signifies the use of safe money strategies, providing protection and mitigation in bear markets. On the other hand, the bull side of the coin represents the utilization of risk-on investments, such as stocks, for participation in bull markets.

The Investment Framework

As we journey through this book, we will delve into fundamental concepts that underpin our investment philosophy, which include Focus Investing, Asset Allocation, Active and Passive Management, Fundamental and Technical Analysis, the Investment Policy Statement (IPS), and The Investment Framework. These pillars guide our approach to wealth management, helping us navigate the complex world of finance.

We will emphasize the significance of considering a multitude of fundamental factors, ranging from value, profitability, growth, volatility, size, leverage, and many others, to technical factors and related tools and techniques. Both sets of factors form the building blocks of our investment strategy, and it's crucial to understand that no single factor or indicator reigns supreme in all circumstances. Instead, various factors come into play at different times and within distinct market conditions, making our approach dynamic and adaptable to ever-changing economic landscapes.

In addition to these foundational concepts, we will also explore the complexities of market and economic cycles. Understanding how these cycles impact investment decisions is crucial for success in the ever-evolving world of finance. Market cycles, driven by factors like inflation, interest rates, corporate earnings, and Federal Reserve actions can significantly influence investment strategies. Economic cycles, characterized by periods of expansion and contraction, shape the landscape in which investors must navigate.

Asset Allocation Versus Focus Investing

There are two primary investment strategies. One is asset allocation, and the other is focus investing. These two methods can be regarded as the two sides of a coin. Asset allocation seeks to manage risk, while focused investing seeks to maximize return. The dynamic is always the interplay of risk and return; the greater your money is at risk, the higher the return.

Similarly, the lower the risk, the lower the return. Some investments favor return-generating characteristics, while others favor risk-management characteristics. Finding the right combination of these two types of assets for your portfolio is the factor that consistently leads to your clients' success. Monitoring your portfolio and adjusting its assets on a continual basis is another important feature contributing to our clients' satisfaction.

Simply stated, asset allocation is the selection of investments that diversifies, or spreads, your investment funds among different classes of assets with the purpose of reducing risk. In traditional asset allocation, a well-diversified portfolio will include mixes of asset classes that are fundamentally different (have a lower correlation), providing diversification; as one asset class declines, others may offset the decline by increasing in value. Asset allocation is based

on a process that applies a mathematical analysis called the Modern Portfolio Theory; Harry Markowitz won a Nobel Prize for his work in this field. The analysis he developed identifies the best mix of selected asset classes for achieving anticipated return rates with the least possible risk. This range of selected investments is shown as a curve on a graph, and is known as the efficient frontier.

Figure 2: Asset or Focus Investing.

HEADS	TAILS
Asset Allocation	**Focus Investing**
A **risk management** approach	A **return seeking** approach
Returns are average	Returns are higher & lower
Accepts return to minimize risk	Accepts risk to maximize return
Spreads money over a broad set of asset classes	Seeks to place more money in fewer assets
Provides diversification	May provide diversification

Figure 3: The Efficient Frontier.

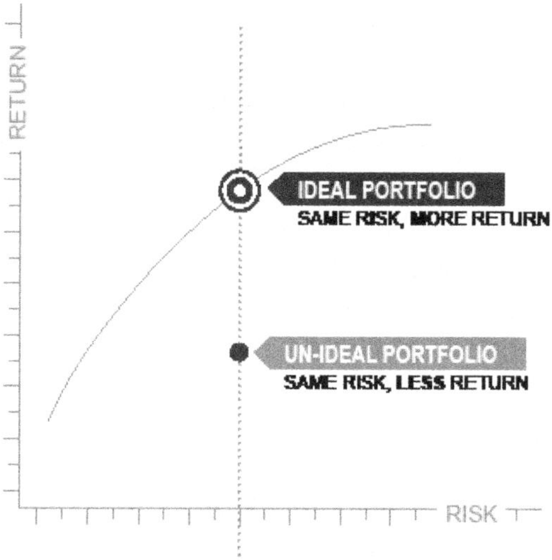

This chart is an example of how you calculate the relationship between risk and return, identifying the optimal mix of portfolio choices to attain a desired rate of return with the most limited level of risk. Investors differ in the level of risk they feel comfortable accepting, so the efficient frontier becomes a customized choice based on an investor's preferences.

Focus investing views the market in a different manner. In focus investing, the investor seeks to place more money in fewer assets with a higher mathematical probability for a successful outcome. The investor accepts the concentrated risk because of the potential for higher returns, provided that a carefully structured plan is in place to close the position when the features that made the investment attractive begin to erode. This allows the focus investor to enjoy the rewards of high expected returns while still maintaining the benefit of some diversification.

Academic studies show that investors can reach optimal diversification by holding as few as 15-20 stocks. This is the point at which all the risk specific to individual stocks has been removed. What remains is market risk, frequently referred to as beta. Warren Buffett is a proponent of the focus investment style.

Figure 4: Diversification with Stocks.

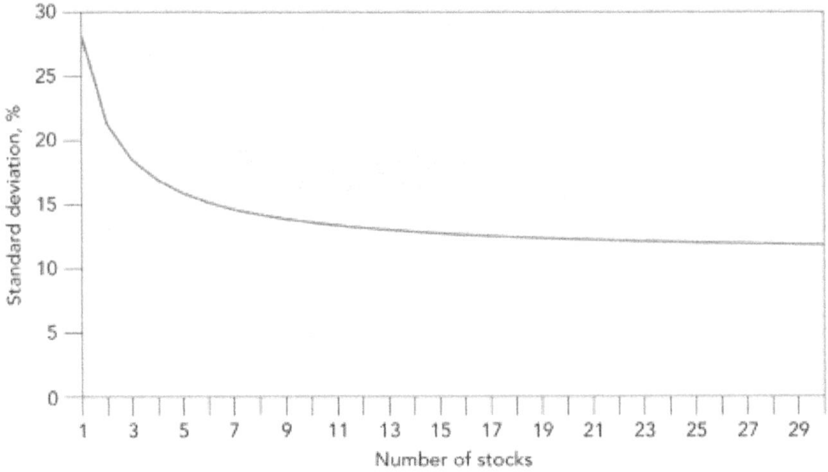

Figure 5: Portfolio Deviation.

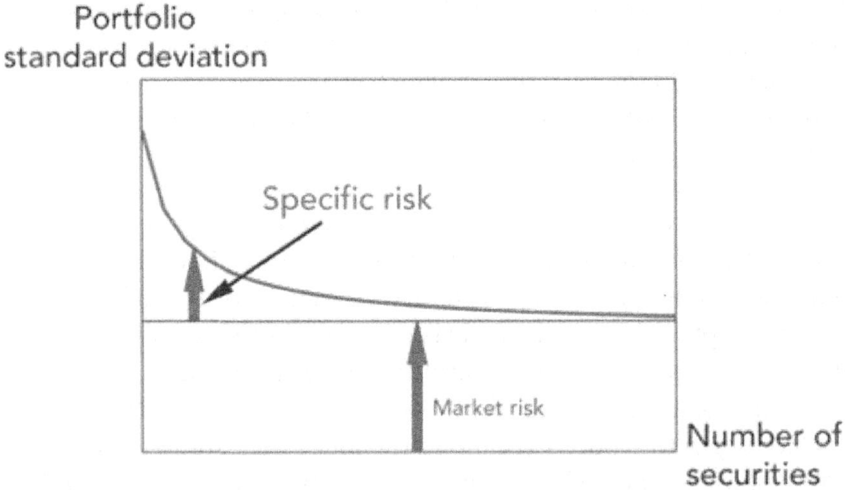

In both asset allocation and focus investing, the investor is able to limit his or her exposure to risk via diversification, and each accomplishes this in a different way. The asset allocation investor chooses to limit their risk by selecting a combination of investments that work together to achieve a diversified portfolio while expecting a return that is the weighted average return of the assets. The focus investor seeks a higher return than the asset allocation investor by accepting the risks of a concentrated portfolio.

TWO PRIMARY TYPES OF INVESTMENT ANALYSIS:

The two types are fundamental analysis, and technical analysis. Fundamental analysis studies the company's management, its financial statements, its assets, liabilities, revenue, earnings, and growth, and other fundamental factors. Technical analysis, on the other side of the coin, studies trends, momentum, relative strength, volume, price resistance and support channels, moving averages, stochastic processes, Bollinger Bands, etc.

Both types of analysis have value and are meaningful in determining whether an investment should be included in your portfolio. Synergy Asset Management employs both analysis types, using many of the top institutional investment research firm's data platforms and world class investment tools and techniques to acquire the most relevant and accurate data necessary to make precise and timely decisions when necessary.

Figure 6: Fundamental vs. Technical Analysis.

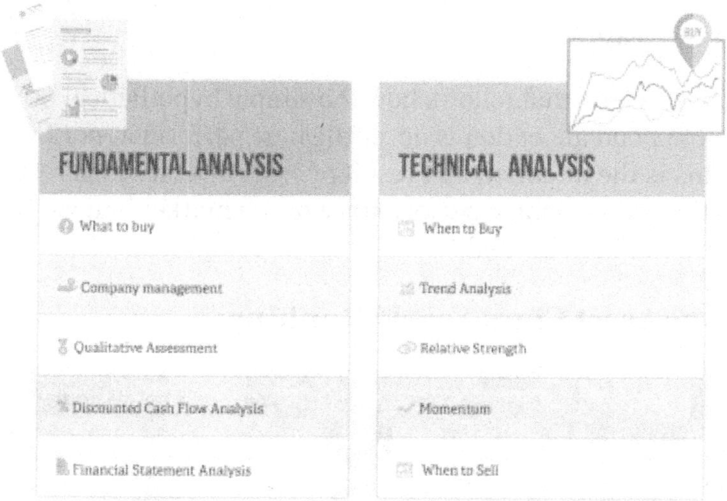

YOUR INVESTMENT GOALS:

More is usually accomplished when goals are set. The more precise your goals, the more likely you will achieve them. It's assumed you have already created your financial goals for the short term, midterm, and long-term horizons, and it's also assumed you have created your Investment Policy Statement which guides your philosophy of investment and investment decisions. If this is not something you've yet done, your advisor can explain how to do this, and will help you with the process so you can be comfortable knowing how and when your goals will be achieved.

STRATEGIC INVESTMENT VERSUS TACTICAL INVESTMENT:

A necessary decision before you invest is determining your portfolio design, which is described in your Investment Policy Statement. If you prefer a strategic long-term approach to investment that carefully considers your risk tolerance, time horizon and the estimated returns for the different asset classes, you may prefer asset allocation. Or you may be a-buy-and-hold investor who is willing to ride up and down with the fluctuations of the market, accepting returns and losses through the years.

Notice in the chart that follows how the simple hypothetical 60% equity, 40% bond allocation is never the best performer, nor the worst. This is the intention and result of asset allocation...a result that mirrors the proportionate performance of the market indices. Risk and return are both limited.

Figure 7: Asset Class Yearly Ranking.

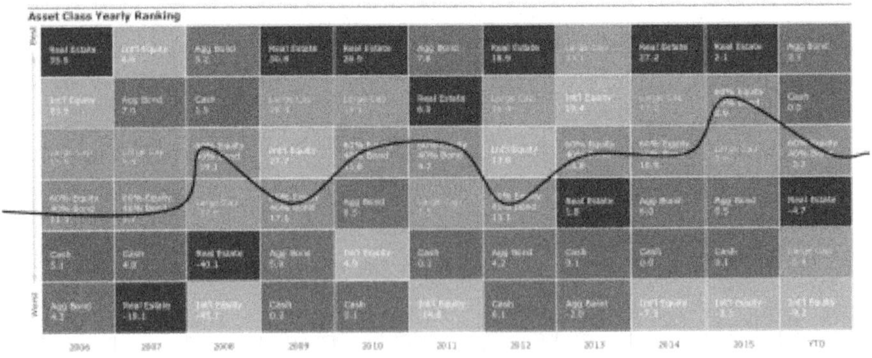

By contrast, a tactical investor tends to be more opportunistic, taking advantage of changing market conditions by investing a greater percentage in the asset classes that are currently outperforming relative to other asset classes, or that are currently reducing risk.

Figure 8:
Tactical Investing Relies on Technical Data and Charts.

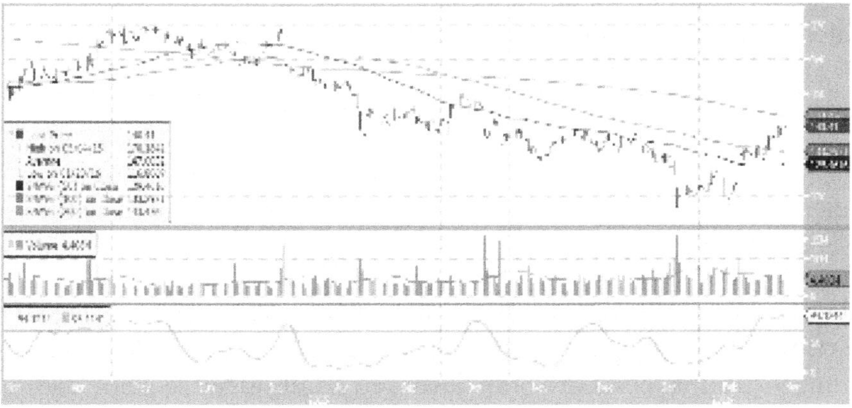

The chart above is an example of the types of technical charts used by tactical investors.

Synergy Asset Management has developed a collection of unique and effective investment portfolios that protect investments from unnecessary risk while aspiring to deliver above-average risk-adjusted returns. These will be presented later, in Chapter 15, after a discussion on the nature, value and insightful employment of several significant investment concepts, such as the one which now follows:

PASSIVE PORTFOLIO MANAGEMENT VERSUS ACTIVE PORTFOLIO MANAGEMENT:

• A passively managed portfolio attempts to match the performance of a benchmark index, and in the process, minimize expenses that can reduce an investor's net return.

• With an actively managed portfolio, a manager tries to exceed the performance of a benchmark index by using his or her judgment in selecting securities and deciding when to buy and sell them. In doing so, the manager can deploy both bottom-up fundamental analysis and/or technical analysis.

Passive Investing: Advocates of unmanaged passive investing, sometimes referred to as indexing, argue that the best way to capture overall market returns is to use low-cost market-tracking index investments. This approach is based on the concept of the efficient market, which states that because all investors have access to all the necessary information about a company and its securities, it's difficult if not impossible to gain an advantage over any other investor. As new information becomes available, market prices adjust to reflect a security's true value. That market efficiency, proponents say, means that reducing investment costs is the key to improving net returns.

Indexing actually does create certain cost efficiencies. Because the investment simply reflects an index, no research is required.

Also, because trading is relatively infrequent, as passively managed portfolios typically buy or sell securities only when the index itself changes, trading costs are often lower. In addition, infrequent trading typically generates fewer capital gains distributions, which means relative tax efficiency.

Adding value with active investing: However, it's just as important to increase wealth as it is to protect wealth. Proponents of active management believe that by picking the right investments, taking advantage of market trends, and managing risk, a skilled investment manager can more completely protect investment funds from risk and unnecessary losses in down markets, as well as increase returns in up markets.

When an investment loses money (negative compounding), it can take a long time, or require higher rates of return, to be restored to its original value. As an example, a manager might reduce a portfolio's overall risk by increasing the percentage devoted to more conservative investments, such as cash alternatives. By actively protecting an investment portfolio, a manager can limit losses so when the market improves, the portfolio has retained more of its value so it can now effectively take advantage of the market's growth.

Figure 9: Negative Compounding Erodes Wealth and Time.

	Period One	Period Two
Beginning Value	$100,000	$90,000
Return	−10%	+10%
Ending Value	$90,000	$99,000

Break-Even 11.1%

When a portfolio loses 10% of its value, it must now earn 11.1% to return to its break-even point, not just 10%. This may take time that would otherwise have been positive investment time, not break-even investment time. Both wealth and time are lost...a double loss.

Figure 10: The Cost of Breaking Even.

Beginning Value $100K	Percentage Loss	Ending Value	Percent to Break-Even	Years to Break-Even (Assumes 7% Annual Return)
	−5%	$95,000	5.26%	0.76
	−10%	$90,000	11.11%	1.56
	−15%	$85,000	17.64%	2.40
	−20%	$80,000	25%	3.30
	−30%	$70,000	42.86%	5.27
	−40%	$60,000	66.67%	7.55
	−50%	$50,000	100%	10.24

If your portfolio lost 40%, such as happened to many investors in 2008, and you could earn a 7% return, it would take 7.55 years before your portfolio would recover its original value. That's a lot of lost money...and lost time!

Figure 11: Growth of a Dollar.

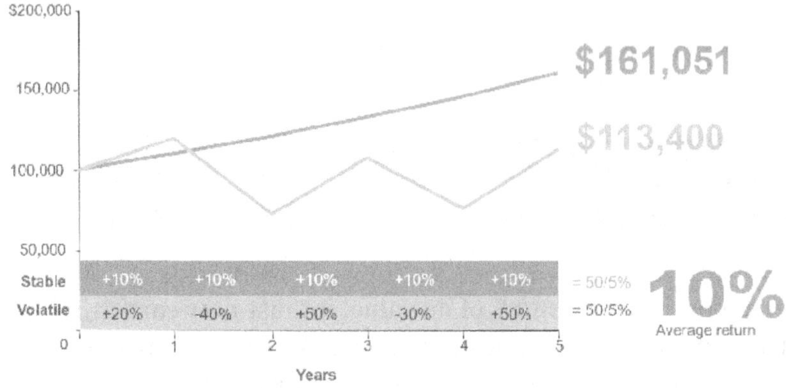

Based on an initial investment of $100,000 with earnings compounded annually. Assumes no taxes, fees or other costs of investing. This is a hypothetical example, not an investment in any mutual fund.

Both fictional investments in the chart above are averaging a 10% rate of growth over a 5-year period...but look at the difference! Based on an initial investment of $100,000 with earnings compounded annually, and assuming no taxes, fees or other costs of investing, you can see the significant difference in wealth over time with an investment that grows at a steady rate, and doesn't chase the gold at the end of rainbows. (This is a hypothetical example for illustrative purposes only, and does not represent an actual investment.)

Key takeaway: Two investments that average 10% are not equal. The one with less volatility is the one achieving greater wealth.

A skilled investment manager can also generate returns that outperform a benchmark index. For example, an active manager whose benchmark is the Standard & Poor's 500 Index (S&P 500) might attempt to earn better-than-market returns by overweighting certain industries or individual securities, allocating more than the index does.

An actively managed portfolio also permits its manager to consider and more effectively manage tax issues. For example, a managed account can harvest capital losses to offset any capital gains realized by its owner, or time a sale to minimize capital gains.

The Three Buckets

You will also be introduced to a concept we call the Three Bucket Investment Strategy. Very simply, this strategy divides an investment portfolio into three segments or "buckets" with different time horizons that are personalized to serve an investor's cash flow and wealth appreciation needs. The buckets differ in their purpose and investment strategies, and are aligned with the investor's goals and risk tolerance.

The short-term bucket is designed to serve the client over the subsequent 2-5 years; the mid-term bucket addresses financial needs from 5-10 years; and the long-term bucket is constructed to provide cash flow and security 10+ years and thereafter, for multiple decades.

Each of these bucket portfolios are specifically aligned with time horizons and objectives, different levels of risk appropriate to their duration, and customized according to individual circumstances. These buckets are regularly monitored and rebalanced so they achieve their planned objectives and satisfy our clients' fiscal requirements.

If this concept makes sense to you and you'd like to know more about how we manage our clients' portfolios, we'd like to introduce you to SAAM™, our Strategically Aligned Asset Manager program.

The SAAM™ Program

Thank you for considering Synergy Asset Management as your trusted partner in managing your portfolio. We understand that every investor is unique, and our mission is to provide you with an investment experience that aligns with your financial goals, risk tolerance, and time horizon. In this part of the introduction, we'll guide you through the process of working with Synergy Asset Management in our Strategically Aligned Asset Manager (SAAM™) program.

SAAM™ represents a revolutionary approach to enhancing the investment experience for our valued clients. Synergy Asset Management works with top-tier financial advisors nationwide. Our mission is to craft investment portfolios that prioritize reasonable returns, maintain a balanced risk profile, and achieve objectives over sensible timeframes.

Most significantly, this program integrates the investment management process with the financial planning process, offering our clients a holistic wealth management solution customized to their precise financial needs.

The SAAM™ program operates through two essential components. Your chosen financial advisor assumes the role of your Chief Wealth Officer, overseeing your comprehensive financial well-being. Simultaneously, Synergy Asset Management takes the role of Chief Investment Officer (CIO) and portfolio manager, orchestrating the design and management of your investment portfolio.

This dynamic synergy between financial advisor and asset manager harnesses substantial resources, resulting in a distinctive fiduciary-driven and comprehensive wealth management approach tailored exactly to your unique financial goals and aspirations.

Here's how we work with advisors in the SAAM™ program:

1. Advisor Selection and Alignment:

- Clients typically have their own independent fee-only financial advisors, or seek assistance finding one.

- Synergy Asset Management aligns clients with approved financial advisors who are a good fit for their financial goals, risk tolerance, and values. This alignment ensures that you receive personalized and tailored advice.

2. Chief Wealth Officer (Your Financial Advisor):

- Your advisor works closely with you to understand your financial situation, goals, objectives, and risk tolerance and then guides you through the financial planning process, developing a comprehensive financial plan that includes elements such as retirement planning, estate planning, and goal setting.

- Together, you, your advisor, and Synergy create an Investment Policy Statement (IPS) that outlines your investment objectives, risk parameters, and expectations.

3. Synergy Asset Management as Chief Investment Officer (CIO):

    - Synergy Asset Management designs and manages investment portfolios that align with your financial plan and IPS.

    - Our expertise lies in institutional investing, allowing us to create diversified portfolios that aim to achieve reasonable returns while managing risk effectively.

4. Investment Portfolio Construction:

    - Based on your financial plan, risk tolerance, and investment objectives, Synergy Asset Management constructs your personalized Lifestyle Protection Portfolio.

    - This portfolio is designed to provide you with a balance between risk and return by including a personally designed mix of asset classes, investment strategies, and securities aimed at achieving your financial goals.

5. Ongoing Collaboration:

    - Your financial advisor and Synergy Asset Management maintain continual communication to ensure your financial plan and investment portfolio remain aligned and adapt to changing market conditions or shifts to your adjusted financial goals.

The SAAM™ program leverages the strengths of both the financial advisor (Chief Wealth Officer) and Synergy Asset Management (Chief Investment Officer) to deliver a comprehensive and fiduciary-driven approach to managing clients' wealth. This integrated program aims to provide you with reasonable returns, risk management, and a tailored investment experience aligned with your financial objectives.

Getting started with Synergy Asset Management is a simple process:

1. We match you with an approved financial advisor who aligns with your financial goals and values.

2. Your financial advisor works with you to develop your Lifestyle Return Benchmark, Investment Policy Statement (IPS), and financial plan.

3. Once your financial plan is in place, Synergy Asset Management will build your Lifestyle Protection Portfolio, tailored to your unique needs, risk tolerance, and investment objectives.

4. Your financial advisor and Synergy Asset Management will work closely to monitor your portfolio's performance, make necessary adjustments, and ensure that your wealth management strategy evolves with your changing needs.

We are excited to embark on this wealth management journey with you. Our commitment to reasonable returns, managing risk, and aligning your investments with your financial plan is the core of what we do.

Thank you for considering Synergy Asset Management as your trusted partner in achieving your financial objectives, enhancing your confidence, and securing your lifestyle.

Your Choice

It's now possible to protect your investment funds from risk and unnecessary losses while benefiting from risk-adjusted returns that allow you to build your wealth prudently. Your decision is whether to subscribe to passive management, active portfolio management, or a combination of both.

If you prefer the compelling benefits offered by active management, you should be prepared to personally dedicate the lengthy time necessary for conducting extensive research, and possess sufficient experience as a master technician with proven strategies for securing wise and timely trades...or have someone with more experience handle the process for you by investing in actively managed portfolios through the professional services of a Chartered Financial Analyst (CFA), the industry's gold standard in investment management.

Synergy Asset Management provides this value and service with its active portfolio management program.

Synergy Asset Management has developed a unique, thoroughly tested method of portfolio construction that combines the advantages of both the strategic and tactical investment process by employing a mix of asset allocation principles with focus investing principles. The benefit of this proprietary application of combined principles with fundamental and technical analysis results in achieving both diversification and wealth building, which minimizes your risk while maximizing your returns.

The Core and Satellite Portfolio Concept

A compromise between the asset allocation method and the focus investing method is the core-and-satellite approach. An investor places a portion of their portfolio, based on the investor's strategic goals, in a core investment such as a strategic or tactical asset allocation strategy.

In addition, the investor establishes a smaller percentage of the portfolio in a focused strategy. The focused strategy could be a tactical asset allocation portfolio, a focused stock strategy, a focused bond strategy, or a focused portfolio build on whatever asset class the investor wants to highlight.

Figure 12: Core Investments with Satellite Investments.

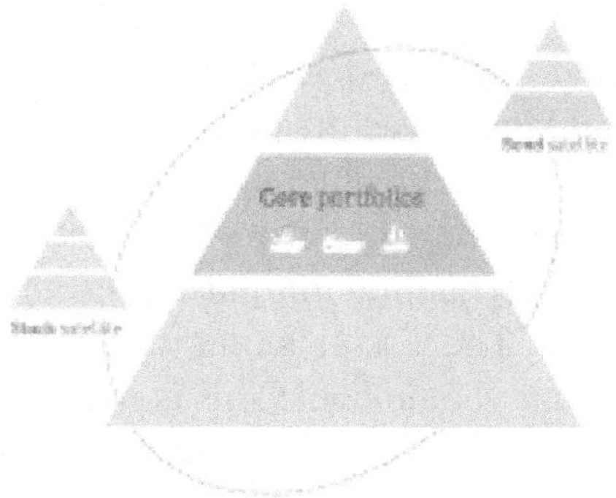

While the core investment funds are carefully secured by holding securities designed to meet the essential goals of the investment portfolio, the satellite investment funds are designed instead to either advance the value of the portfolio through concentrated investments, or protect the portfolio with risk-averse investments.

The key is having an active manager with the proven experience and skills to consistently monitor the fluctuating markets, prepared to make decisions that benefit your entire portfolio when the market signals the potential for increased gains, or signals the need to withdraw into safer investments.

As an example of how to take advantage of the market tactically, the investor could shift some of the tactical funds of the portfolio into small cap stocks if the indicators suggested that small cap stocks were poised to do well. The investor could then move out of small cap stocks if the signal proves incorrect, runs its course, or another type of investment presents a better opportunity.

Portfolios Offered by Synergy Asset Management

Our goal is to provide our clients with adaptive portfolios built for all market conditions. We accomplish this through a sophisticated blend of advanced focused tactical asset allocation mathematics, bottom-up fundamental analysis, and professional technical analysis.

Portfolios are updated as the facts change. We are reluctant to make these changes unless we have strong convictions. Mindful of the cost of trading expenses, we always base our decisions on the effect to the different Synergy portfolios. Our primary obligation is the preservation and expansion of our clients' wealth.

Our process also provides a sell-discipline that is as clearly defined as the buy-discipline. Most investors don't have a problem deciding on which securities to buy...but when it comes to knowing when to sell, it's a different story. Many investors learn that losing positions can become a serious detriment, eliminating the gains that were so enthusiastically earned. The lesson is that what you don't own is every bit as important as what you do own. This is why Synergy portfolios are so carefully monitored; we work to preserve your wealth as much as we work to increase it.

Investors can entrust their wealth to any one of Synergy's portfolios because our methodology is based on duplicable, systematic, and logical management systems that accelerate success.

Portfolio Categories: We have created several portfolios built for all risk and return temperaments. One of these portfolios or combination of portfolios (core-satellite approach) is the right one for you. These portfolios are discussed in Chapter 15, The Core Satellite Solution. We call them our Tugboat, Speed Boat, and Sailboat portfolios, and we also have focused stock portfolios, and focused bond portfolios.

Whichever style you prefer, we have an investment portfolio that will serve your financial needs. Rigorous monitoring and tactical rebalancing provide the increased probability of your success and reaching your main goal: financial independence.

Now let's get started with Chapter 1 and dig a little deeper into the core concepts of the two investment strategies by analyzing the value of either diversifying wealth among the asset classes, or focusing exclusively on investments that exhibit the strong potential for high performance...or...even better...exploring a unique and compelling method for combining the best features and best results of both!

Joseph M. Maas

Founder, Synergy Asset Management, LLC

13231 SE 36th Street, Suite 215

Bellevue, WA 98006

Phone: 206-386-5455

www.synergy-am.com

Chapter 1

Risk and Return: Twins of Investment

When you have finished reading this chapter, you will:

- Possess introductory knowledge that diversification is more than simply investing in a variety of asset classes
- Know the most important element of being diversified
- Understand how devastating risk can be to investments. Recognize the effect of negative compounding on a portfolio
- Clearly realize that return alone is insubstantial when assessing the value of a portfolio's performance
- Be able to explain the difference between compounding, and negative compounding

Introduction

This is a book about investing for profit. You can go to a bookstore and see shelves of books on this topic, but not a single one of them is like the book you are about to read.

Investing is a very old subject, and there are many great theorists and practitioners who have written their highly worthwhile thoughts, philosophies, and practices in the books you'll find on those shelves. Over time, because of the adjustments the markets make, because of new investment products that are brought to market, because of new trends, new fads, and even new discoveries of correlations that show the potential for increased upside and limited downside, new theories come to the fore, are analyzed and either adopted or discarded.

Making money with money has been a passion for mankind from the beginning of history, and the current theories and practices in vogue in the marketplace today have substantial value for investors because they have been tested repeatedly through time.

Important:

This book is unique because it will show you how to look at the diversification (...or not!) of the assets in your portfolio in a very different way than you do now.

Of course, these theories are only as valid as the ability of the investors for following them...with patience, fortitude in changing circumstances, confidence in planned decision-making protocols, and a reliance more on the dictates of the mind than the passions of the emotions.

All of this you probably know.

What you don't know is how this book is different.

This book is unique because it will show you how to look at the diversification of the assets in your portfolio in a very different way than you do now. This book will not only help you see diversification from a new perspective but will also teach you how to structure your investment portfolio so your assets are diversified for an increased potential of more growth and less risk.

More growth, less risk.

I bet you like the sound of that. Most investors do! But most investors have succumbed to the same old investment and diversification philosophies in vogue when the United States landed on the moon... which is to say a long time ago!

And yet, here is another reason why this book is unique. This book is not only about diversification and asset allocation, as these represent only one side of the proverbial coin. You'll remember that the title of this book is "To Allocate or Concentrate", and that's because this book presents an alternative to traditional asset allocation that you may find even more compelling than merely following today's predominantly popular and premier investment theory.

Of course, this is a choice you can only make once you possess a more developed understanding of diversification and can determine its benefits and detriments as applied to your particular personal and financial circumstances. Asset allocation is absolutely the best choice...for some investors...and absolutely the worst...for others. We'll explore the details that will ultimately lead you to a place of determination from which you can make the decision of whether you are best suited as an asset allocator...or focused investor. Or a combination of both! This is a decision you must absolutely make if you are going to elevate your role from an investment hobbyist to a serious investor.

As with any topic you study, there are layers upon layers of information, theories, protocols and tools, and a depth of understanding that's necessary if you are to become more competent in the subject you're studying. You know that lawyers don't think like doctors, and doctors don't think like teachers, and teachers don't think like generals, and none of these professionals think like financial planners. Every profession has its own perspective, its own viewpoint of how the world works...so when it comes to investing, a superficial level of knowledge will probably only get you in trouble.

If you're going to do your own investing, and there is certainly nothing wrong with this if you know what you're doing, you must become a serious student or you will be either lucky or unlucky, and though eventually you will probably wind up making some money...it won't be the amount of money your investments could have earned with less risk in the limited time you had to earn it. Not taking investing seriously means you are choosing haphazard success. You are choosing minimal results. You are choosing to squander your resources of money and time. You are throwing the dice on your future.

Obviously, because you are reading this book, you believe you have more to learn. It's quite fortunate that you chose this book because there are some surprises ahead that many investors...hundreds of thousands or millions of investors...don't know, and this information may be so valuable to you that it may place you in the class of highly successful investors, a special class of investors who enjoy the most efficient returns for the limited risk they choose to accept.

That's a mouthful. The most efficient returns? The limited risk they choose to accept? Yes, when you know what you're doing, it is mathematically possible to earn the highest and most efficient returns for the risk you are willing to take. This information will be presented to you later in the book, and your questions will be answered then. However, this is only one of the many important concepts presented which can change your financial life for the better.

Another key concept that's important to mention at the outset is you will be reading about two opposing investment theories. The first is diversification through asset allocation; a healthy portion of this book explains what you need to know on this topic. The second is focus investing, which is the other side of the coin; it's a theory and practice that is less popular than asset allocation, but it is also potentially more powerful. In effect, this book's discussion about focus investing can help you see how to "crack the code" so you might increase your investment return while keeping your risk exposure within the limits you choose to set.

What?

Yes, read that last sentence again, please.

Most investors have read a few articles or a few books, attended a workshop, maybe, and then have tried their hand at picking investment winners. This is not a formula for success, of course. These people have no business investing because they may either wind up losing a lot of money or they may earn modest returns over the 10, 20, 30 years they are in the market. How much better it is to have an informed respect for the market, and take action based on reasoned decisions that are deduced from an awareness of the market's mechanics, while knowing one's own strengths and foibles. Having some degree of rational certainty that a profitable return is likely, with decreased risk, is a confidence that must be celebrated!

Long story short, the point remains that you are about to become an investor with an informed perspective to asset allocation and its competing theory, focus investing. But the possibility does not stop here. Perhaps the most astonishing information that will be revealed is there may be a way to both protect and increase your wealth simultaneously with the application of a distinct strategy and corollary but divergent tactics.

Well, yes, the mystery will be revealed, but not here, not now. You will have to do your due diligence and work your way pleasantly through the intervening chapters so that the secret, when revealed, makes absolute sense and stirs you with the impulse to shriek "Eureka!"

I'm being funny, of course, but also truthful. When you get to the reveal later in this book, if there was a light bulb switched on over your head it would probably be an 18,000 lumen spotlight. In essence, we are hoping to teach you how to accelerate your returns while maintaining a safe degree of risk, which is priceless information because it can mean the difference between a lifetime of average returns doled out by the Dow in yearly disbursements of profit and loss...as compared to using a strategy with precisely sculpted tactics that control your risk while accelerating your returns.

No, this is not easy, but yes, it is not hard. You will have a thorough insight to the process and the opportunity by the time you reach the back cover, but in the meantime it is important to start from the beginning and proceed sequentially through the logical steps that increase your comprehension of how to perform this wealth-building activity yourself.

The first part of the book emphasizes several key issues that impact all investors, offers instruction on the basics of an investment plan, challenges you to know your predilections and inhibitions as an investor, and leads you through the steps of determining how you want to engage with the market. Then you will subsequently be exposed more deeply to the two theories which represent the two sides of the coin; after this is when your path becomes even more exciting.

Chapter 10 focuses on asset allocation and diversification; Chapter 11 is centered on the philosophy, risks, and benefits of focus investing. Then the debate of asset allocation or focus investing is described for your consideration, along with a complete revelation of the promised solution, at which point the 18,000 lumen spotlight should automatically come on with blinding inspiration. Now, however, it is time to begin your odyssey.

Watch Out for the Last Step... It's a Doozy!

Using asset allocation as an example, most investors feel generally content when they have apportioned their assets in a mix of stocks and bonds investments. Understanding the wisdom of spreading their assets among a mix of large cap, mid-cap and small cap stocks, short term, mid-term, and long term bonds, international stocks, technology stocks, REITs, and the variety of other investments the market generously makes available, careful investors have considered how to make the best allocation of their investment resources based on their personal circumstances.

These same investors have reflected on their tolerance for risk, their investment horizon, their financial goals, their expectations for life in retirement, and their hopes for the quality of their estate when it's time for its distribution to their heirs. The predominant theories and practices are well and good and are probably observed by millions of investors... but they may fall short.

They fall short because most investors innocently fail to complete the next and most important step.

Faced with an avalanche of investment choices, careful investors must take the time to become sufficiently familiar with each potential investment before taking the risk of placing their hard-earned funds in jeopardy for the potential reward of a good return. Then, as if this wasn't intimidating enough, investors must decide on the percentage allocations of their resources among the variety of investment temptations. This is too frequently an arbitrary or subjective decision, or is guided by a mythical and widely advertised generic formula of insubstantial assumptions based on their current age or investment horizon.

This might be the basis for a good comedy...if the results weren't so unerringly tragic.

Key:

The important next step: Every investment in your portfolio must perform well in tandem with every other investment in your portfolio.

When the curtains are pulled and the study begins, it soon becomes evident that commonly accepted practices only go so far and that at a critical point in the investment process, the failure to follow through to the next level of investment wisdom with more astute analysis and planning can leave investors at the gaming table with loaded dice favoring the house.

The important next step that most investors fail to take, and the key message of this book, is that the practice of creating more modest diversification is not simply a matter of making thoughtful choices about allocating your funds in a carefully prescribed distribution of investments, but, in addition, it is essential to precisely calculate the synergy and interaction of your selected investments so your returns from the combination of these assets result in maximum growth with minimum risk.

Said in a different way: every investment in your portfolio must perform well in tandem with every other investment in your portfolio. It is the synergy of all the investments working together as a single efficient unit that magnifies your potential for significant growth and maximizes your potential for limited risk.

Every individual investment represents specific qualities of risk and return, of course, but it is the combined effect of the individual quality of each of your investments, blended with the effects of the other selected investments, that provides the best potential for creating a cohesive and effective portfolio that magnifies your reward and minimizes your risk.

Understanding how to make these careful and cogent selections is not a task for the faint of heart! It requires rigorous consideration with a strong academic and experiential background in financial planning.

It is not the purpose of this book to teach you how to analyze the correlations between a pair of investments, let alone a portfolio with a dozen or more. However, it IS the intent of this book to demonstrate a new way of thinking about asset allocation...or not...so your portfolio can benefit from a better performance with effective upside capture and downside protection.

By the end of this book you will know the answers to the following questions, and you will also know the best course to take so you can achieve your financial freedom.

- Are you inclined to be a passive or active investor?
- Are you willing to be an investor who values average risk for average return?
- Are you eager to commit yourself to work for higher than average returns?
- Are you open to considering controlled risk combined with the potential for accelerated return?
- Are you proficient enough to calculate the required rate of return (RRR) that mathematically defines your financial goals?
- Are you truly capable of analyzing investment securities and creating a portfolio that sits on the efficient frontier of the risk you are comfortable taking for the return you are desirous of having?

And so we begin!

Two Sides of a Coin

The following concept may seem elementary, yet it is the basis for the conversation that happens afterward. Everyone who has ever considered a bet, an opportunity, a choice, an investment has had to consider how the coin would land. Will it be heads or tails? Will I win or lose? Will I be happy or discontent? Though there is a world of gray gradations in our daily lives, some results are truly black or white. In the following case, the coin never lands on its edge.

Figure 13: Heads? Tails?

Upside Capture

Upside capture is the measurement in percentages of the gains achieved. This is preferred over downside capture, which is the measurement in percentages of the losses incurred. Upside capture is likely to be one of the reasons you are investing. Unless you are deliberately trying to lose some of your investment's value, upside capture is normally a cause for party; you are that much closer to achieving your financial goals!

Downside Protection

Perhaps not as celebrated, though it certainly should be, is protecting your investment from loss. Losses sustained by an investment portfolio can be crippling, not just in the loss of monetary value, but also in the loss of investment time. Each of us have a timeline of when we'd like to enjoy the sums we've worked so hard and so long to gain, and when the portfolio loses 5% or 10% of its value, or more, precious time will be consumed in returning to the break-even point that instead could have been dedicated to further portfolio growth and a more advantageous use of the time that instead was allocated to catching up.

As you will see in the following section, negative compounding can have an outrageous effect on your investments, and severely limit your financial health.

Compounding vs. Negative Compounding

Here is another coin with two sides; most of us are familiar with its head, but not so much, if at all, with its tail. Even so, when described, it will probably be familiar to you. It's important that we look at this coin so we can clearly define the effect, both good and bad, on an investment portfolio's value and potential for growth.

Compounding

Everyone knows the joy of compounding money, usually introduced to us at a very young age. The miracle of compounding money is a welcome delight. Money which stays in an account that's earning interest will continue to increase as the initial principal and its accumulating interest together earn even more interest.

At 6% a year, the original principal will double in 12 years, and after 24 years the principal will be four times larger than its original amount. Compounding money can add up, as you well know. It's mentioned here to introduce its companion, negative compounding.

Definition:

Compounding is the continual growth of money based on an ever-expanding sum consisting of the initial principal and the ongoing accumulation of interest.

Negative Compounding

Just as money compounds in a positive way, it can also compound in a negative way. After reading this section, you may have a new perspective on the importance of preventing investment losses. The consequence of losses in your investment portfolio is harmful not only to your bottom line, but also sabotages your effective use of time, limiting the growth of your portfolio.

Understanding the effect of negative compounding may result in changing the way you think about investing, accepting risk, planning your investment strategy, your expectations of results, and ultimately the quality of life you can achieve with more diligent reflection and decision-making.

Negative compounding is not a familiar term to most people, and even if they have heard of it, the chances are they have not given it much thought. Thinking about one's portfolio losses is not a happy pastime!

As noted, compounding is the continual growth of money based on an ever-expanding sum consisting of the initial principal and the ongoing accumulation of interest. However, negative compounding is present when you have suffered an investment loss; you can only return to your break-even point by consuming additional time at the market's rate of return, or increasing your risk by investing at a higher rate of return. Negative compounding is detrimental because you will either sacrifice valuable investment time or increase your risk and potential investment injury. Financial loss is a hardship for a number of reasons: lost resources, lost investment time to add new growth, and the potential for increased risk if investing at a higher rate of return to catch-up with the lost time and money.

Key:

Negative compounding causes you to sacrifice valuable investment time, or increase your investment risk, or both, just to return to your break-even point.

Though you may be thinking you kind-of knew this already, seeing the numbers may be startling and bring you to a new level of informed discomfort.

Here's an example: if you have $100,000 and you lose 10%, your account is reduced to $90,000. Most people think that if they earn

10% the next year, they're back to where they started. However, that's not the case. 10% of $90,000 is $9,000; that would bring your account to $99,000 which is $1,000 less than where you started. Therefore, to break-even, you require not a 10% return, but an 11.1% return...and remember, you've also lost a year of investment time...just to break-even.

Figure 14: Portfolio Break-Even.

	Period One	Period Two
Beginning Value	$100,000	$90,000
Return	−10%	+10%
Ending Value	$90,000	$99,000

Break-Even 11.1%

Another analogy is a 4.0 student. If you are a 4.0 student and you receive a B in one class, mathematically you can never be a 4.0 student again. You might be a 3.9 student or something like that, but you'll never again be a 4.0 student.

The lesson is that one of the most important elements of making money is preventing losses.

The preceeding chart shows the losses of an account with a beginning value of $100,000. The percentage losses in the second column result in the ending value in the third column. The fourth column shows the percentage needed to break-even, and the last column shows how many years it would take to break-even based on the different percentage losses this account suffered, assuming a 7% annual return. This is just to break-even.

Figure 15: Example of Percentage Gains Required to Recover Losses

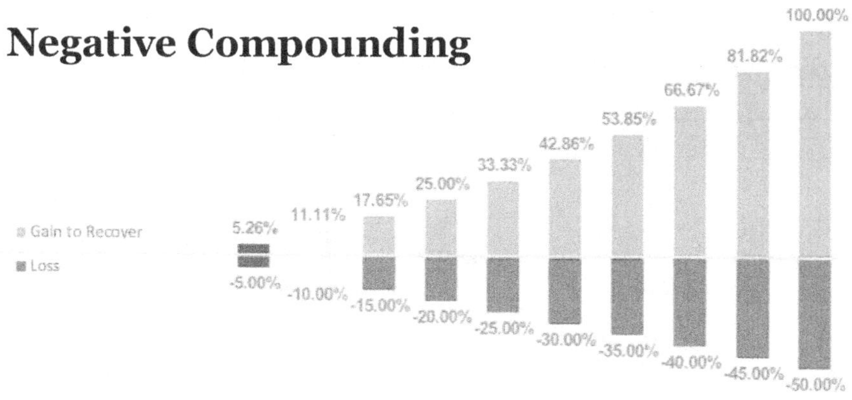

Using the table above, if your account lost 50% of $100,000, your account is $50,000. You would need a 100% annual return to break-even in one year. Instead, if you could earn a 7% return on your remaining $50,000 it would take you 10.24 years to once again have your original sum of $100,000.

The other columns tell their own terrifying stories.

The effect of portfolio loss is painful not only because of the lost funds, but also because of the lost investment time. Losses cost time to rectify, and time is one of the most important factors for achieving financial freedom.

Note:

When the S&P 500 was down approximately 40% in 2008, anyone who was caught in that downturn needed 66.67% to break-even, and at 7% return it would take them 7.55 years...JUST to break-even.

Considering the effect of losses is an unpleasant task, but while we're in it, there's even more valuable information to be learned here. Looking at the next chart, "Growth of a Dollar", you'll observe the investment history of two investors. Both investors start with the same amount of money, but one investor, whom we label the "stable" investor, has a portfolio valued 30% higher than the volatile investor.

Figure 16: Growth of a Dollar.

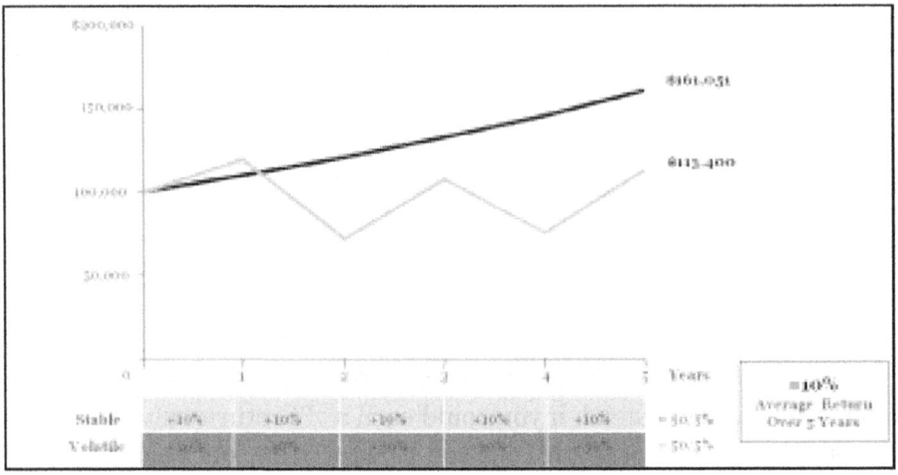

What's going on here?

The graph lines show two portfolios, both managed by the same advisor. One portfolio is stable and its growth for each of the five years is 10% +10% +10% +10% +10%. Its five-year average return is 10%.

The other portfolio is volatile, and its growth is 10% +10% +10% +10% +10%; its five-year average return is also 10%, even though it's up 20%, down 40%, up 50%, down 30%, and up 50%.

Both portfolios have averaged 10% over a five-year period.

When your advisor asks if you would like either the portfolio with the 10% average return, or the portfolio with the 10% average return, you might say, "It doesn't matter to me. They both averaged 10%...", and yet negative compounding has clearly had an immensely negative impact on the performance of the volatile portfolio.

The stable portfolio has almost $48,000 more than the volatile portfolio... $161,000 versus $113,000...about a 30% difference...even though both averaged a 10% return during the same five-year period.

Key:

An essential purpose of this book is to show you how to limit negative compounding.

The lesson is evident. The path of least volatility is the more lucrative because the portfolio consistently had more funds contributing to its annual return. Mathematically, 10% of a higher amount of money will generate a higher quantity of dollars than 10% of a lower quantity of dollars. It seems simple, but when you do the math you can clearly see that protecting your portfolio from loss is a vital priority.

This example illustrates another lesson about investing: one of the most significant factors for achieving positive portfolio performance is avoiding losses.

An essential purpose of this book is to show you how you can diversify your assets so you can limit negative compounding and retain as much of your principal as possible to benefit from the positive effect of compounding.

You may remember when you were younger, and a sage financial advisor recommended that you could take an aggressive attitude toward portfolio risk because of your youthful age and the long time horizon that lay before you until retirement. "You're 25? How lucky! Your retirement is 40 years from now. With all that time, you can afford to invest aggressively!"

Consider how much further along that young investor would be with a more professional hand guiding those investments for four decades, an authority who recommended steady growth that limited losses with a less aggressive (risky) philosophy.

Note:

Manage the downside; do not chase the upside.

Volatility is exceptionally destructive. The real key to long term growth and your happy financial future is selecting investments with strong upside potential, limited risk, and the synergy of your investment instruments working together, providing a strong foundation for solid growth and limited loss.

Remember your purpose as an investor. Your goal is to have the highest amount of money at retirement, not achieve the highest annual return.

To emphasize the point, there is no wisdom in chasing returns because the volatility can rob you of time and money. Taking a step forward, two steps back, a half step forward, one step back...plus all the unnecessary anxiety... it's not as strong or sensible as the investment strategy this book will show you.

As an investor, you always want to be moving forward, and keep moving forward.

To do so, it's imperative to manage the downside and not chase the upside. Your best choice is to find an advisor who is expert at managing volatility; when you follow this mathematically proven strategy, you can actually earn more money with a lower return and less risk!

This idea is counterintuitive. It takes some reflection to absorb. We've been taught to chase a ball since we were kids! Now, however, we can play a different game with a different ball, one that has more potential for scoring points than the hopes for a homer or a grand slam.

You now have the opportunity for learning a unique financial concept that can improve your investment strategy and results. This is a Gold Nugget.

Note:

Your purpose as an investor is to have the highest amount of money at retirement, not achieve the highest annual return.

By the way, there is only one situation in which this diversification strategy is ineffective, and that's when the market only goes up. If straight up is the only direction and there is no volatility, the highest return will win.

But if there is volatility, and there is always volatility in the existing market system, return is not the most important factor. A good investor and a good financial advisor study the dynamic relationship between risk and return, between upside capture and downside protection, and make their investment choices based on the potential performance of the whole.

Every selection in your investment portfolio must be evaluated and measured not only on its individual merits, but also on its capacity for harmonizing with all the other investment instruments into a symphony of financial success.

Summary

Diversification of assets in a portfolio is a larger task than is popularly conceived. The notion that assets should be varied is the first step in a process of several, and an investor who does not look more deeply into this subject is a candidate for limited portfolio growth and potentially severe investment loss. The example in this chapter about the harmful effects of negative compounding should sufficiently alarm investors to seriously regard their investment's vulnerability, and create an eagerness for learning how to protect their financial future from unnecessary risk. Not only will the value of the investment suffer, but the time sacrificed in making a full recovery to the breakeven point can rob the investor of lost opportunities for further gain.

Chapter 1 Review Questions

1. Every investment in your portfolio must perform well in tandem with every other investment in your portfolio. True or false?

   A. True

   B. False

2. Portfolio diversification is best accomplished by:

   A. Carefully selecting a variety of asset classes so risk is distributed.

   B. Investing with a formula of stocks and bonds based on your age.

   C. Selecting investments that have been precisely calculated to work together to increase return while protecting against risk.

   D. Investing with a formula of stocks and bonds based on your proclivity to accept risk.

3. Negative compounding is harmful to a portfolio's growth because:

   A. Wealth is lost.

   B. Investment time to make new gains is lost.

   C. It could take years to return to the breakeven point.

   D. All of the above.

4. One of the most important elements of making money through investment is:

   A. Preventing losses.

   B. Achieving the highest annual return.

   C. Having enough time to make-up losses.

   D. Always select aggressive stocks.

Chapter 1 Review Answers

1. Every investment in your portfolio must perform well in tandem with every other investment in your portfolio. True or false?

   A. True

   B. False

   Answer: A. True. All your investments must work together so there is no duplication and your risk-return components are maximized.

2. Portfolio diversification is best accomplished by:

   A. Carefully selecting a variety of asset classes so risk is distributed.

   B. Investing with a formula of stocks and bonds based on your age.

   C. Selecting investments that have been precisely calculated to work together to increase return while protecting against risk.

   D. Investing with a formula of stocks and bonds based on your proclivity to accept risk.

   Answer: C. The selection of investments must be mathematically calculated to offer the most return for the risk you are willing to accept.

3. Negative compounding is harmful to a portfolio's growth because:

   A. Wealth is lost.

   B. Investment time to make new gains is lost.

   C. It could take years to return to the breakeven point.

   D. All of the above.

   Answer: D. All of the above. Losing investment funds is painful for all these reasons.

4. One of the most important elements of making money through investment is:

   A. Preventing losses.
   B. Achieving the highest annual return.
   C. Having enough time to make-up losses.
   D. Always select aggressive stocks.

   Answer: A. Preventing losses. Protecting your portfolio from losses and retaining as much wealth as possible saves time and money which can then be used to further expand your wealth.

Chapter 2
Challenges to Success

When you have finished reading this chapter, you will:

- Have a clearer understanding of the personal challenges investors must overcome
- Know eight investor biases that can interfere with making good decisions
- Recognize an investment bias that you may be susceptible to having
- Be able to identify most private investors' greatest mistake
- Realize the effect of the two most powerful emotions at work in the market and their possible effect on your choices

Introduction

As an investor, you want to always see your portfolio's value increasing. Erratic growth with a volatile portfolio is likely to average less growth over time than a stable portfolio. This is why it's best to build a portfolio that is structured for continued and steady growth as well as limited downside risk.

Chasing returns may leave you financially disappointed. Remember that one of the key advantages in your favor is the amount of time you have in your investment horizon. When this advantage is squandered with enticements that result in either a negative compounding situation or even merely a breakeven, there is still the financial loss of your investment time.

Education and Experience

If you were building a house, you would work from a set of blueprints that was developed before you started building. You would know the square footage and how many floors, bedrooms and bathrooms there will be. You would also know what the finished house will look like... the types of windows, variety of doors, carpeting, and deck. You may even have a contractor in mind.

You can see the folly of building a house any other way. Yes, people do, but they also may have limited success and probably lots of visits from concerned building department agents.

Obviously, the same is true when building your investment portfolio. In fairness, most private investors have probably read a number of books about portfolio construction, may subscribe to a few online newsletters, and might also have attended a local investment workshop offered by a financial planning firm in their town.

Key:

Current practices in the market are not wholly understood by private investors, leading to assumptions that result in mismanagement and loss.

While these activities seem sensible, they may also be only an extension of the larger problem that is prevalent among investors today. There is a preponderance of either generic information that is good for everybody but not good for anyone, or information that's biased in favor of a philosophy that's out of context, or, what's even more likely, information based on the current popular practices in the market today and which are not wholly understood by private investors.

This is one of the major reasons why most investors have underperforming portfolios...a lack of investment education. Only in the rarest of occasions does financial wealth come easily, even for well-trained and strongly experienced financial investment advisors. For most, it takes years of training followed by years of daily experience observing and participating in the marketplace, plus having the rare long-range experience of witnessing and being a part of decade-long markets that are going up, going down, and going sideways.

The average private investor simply cannot dedicate sufficient time to the academic and experiential education necessary for prolonged success in the markets. In the great bull market of the 1990s, it was very hard to shoot at the side of the barn and miss. The rising tide floated all boats, and everybody won a chicken dinner.

The market is now in a different cycle and careful investment selections are the wise word of the day. Because the financial climate has changed, a critically educated and experienced hand is now needed when selecting the investments that will bring your portfolio to success in the limited time you have left, whether that's 10 years or 30 years from now.

The greatest mistake most private investors make is assuming they know what they're doing. Most investors are unaware of how to read market cycles or know the best investment strategy to employ in those different cycles. Calculating the different effect and value of a long-term Treasury bond versus a TIPS (Treasury Inflation Protected Security) is not a task most private investors are equipped to handle, to their detriment. The proper time to invest in commodity stocks remains a mystery, as does knowing how to shift their portfolio when the economy is down, and inflation is low...compared to when the economy is up and inflation is high.

How is it possible that the average private investor with a day job, a family, and limited free time will be able to read enough financial investment theory and investigate the thousands of stocks, bonds, and other investment opportunities that are available?

The short answer is that the numbers of private investors who are likely to do well are equal to the number of Powerball winners in the last 10 years. There is simply too much to know unless portfolio investment becomes a full-time job and sufficient time is dedicated to earning first-hand experience.

Undisciplined Emotions

Not only is a lack of investment education and experience an affliction of the private investor, but so also is the investor's degree of investment discipline. It is no secret that the two predominant emotions in the market are fear and greed.

Fear of loss is a frequent cause of investors selling too soon, and greed for more wealth often causes investors to hold on to their investments too long.

Key:

Savvy investors have a plan, and they work their plan. What's your plan?

Steady confidence can be achieved with practice, experience, a disciplined investment strategy, and a commitment to obeying the self-imposed rules of that strategy.

When you think of the mind-set of most individual investors, it becomes clear why fear and greed are so influential. Money is dear, and the idea of losing hard-earned cash is frightening. Conversely, the idea of rapidly accumulating unexpected wealth can become a mania. The markets have seen both emotions at play frequently; perhaps you have witnessed some of these extreme patterns in the market, or in your own investment behavior.

Disciplined investors do not try to catch every dollar in an up-market, nor do they panic in a downturn. Savvy investors make a rules-based plan, and then they work their plan. Their plan gives them insight about when to get into a market for an investment, when to hold, and when to sell. We'll discuss buying, holding, and selling rules later in this book. Remember, these rules should live in your investment policy statement (IPS).

To achieve the rewards of powerful portfolio performance, it is imperative that you accede to following the rules of your own plan. You probably won't catch every dollar, but you also won't have to fear excessive losses. Over the long term, disciplined obedience to the protocols set within your plan is the most likely avenue for achieving your financial goals in the tumult and commotion of today's modern market.

Say Goodbye to Your Biases

It's only human to fall into a comfortable pattern. Most of us resist change, and we love the Comfort Zone. Of course, the danger is that the Comfort Zone becomes uncomfortable as we struggle to stay put rather than make necessary changes.

Living in our Comfort Zone, we are susceptible to a variety of thought patterns that keep us quiescent. These biases can sabotage our progress, inhibiting the performance that would result in our best good.

Here are a few behavioral biases a disciplined investor must overcome.

THE CONFIRMATION BIAS:

In psychology, the confirmation bias, also known as myside bias, is the inclination, whether consciously or unconsciously, to identify information and data that confirms what you want to see, excluding all the information and data that does not support, or confirm, your belief. Wise investors can spot this tendency in themselves and protect against its dominance in their decision-making.

THE OVERCONFIDENCE BIAS:

This particular blindside comes from a person's belief in the extreme merit of their judgments, and is based on illusory subjective opinion, not objective rationale. You may remember the proverb, "Pride goeth before a fall". Anyone who has ever had an unjustified moment of overconfidence, which is most of us, will identify with the pain that follows.

THE LOSS AVERSION BIAS:

No one likes to suffer loss, so if this behavior is in an investor's decision-making psychology, hesitation to act when the plan's signals are given can result in lost money or a lost opportunity, or both. A disciplined investor is impassionate and does not allow his or her emotions, such as fear or greed, to come into play. Successful investors know that following their plan's protocols will result in more gain than loss over time, so they can afford to be disassociated from their emotions. This does not mean they are overconfident in their plan, because as we shall see, a disciplined investor's plan is founded on solid investment principles.

THE HERDING BIAS:

We might like to think of ourselves as individuals, but how do you explain that we tend to like the same restaurants, the same movies, the same fashions, and the same best-selling books? Once again, here is our old friend, the bell curve. Most of our population likes and dislikes the same things. This is the crowd mentality appearing in the decision-making process. The herding instinct is evident in the financial markets when a bubble is generated, such as the dot-com bubble of 2000 and the housing bubble of 2008. Following the herd is seldom a good idea because the herd will turn, and a stampede often follows.

THE FAMILIARITY BIAS:

This goes back to our Comfort Zone. As creatures of habit, we love the familiar. Many investors have a bias for what they know. Over the course of time, a satisfying relationship has been built with a set of investments, and the investor knows, likes, and trusts these investments. This bias might cause an investor to restrict investments to his or her own country, or to a particular sector of investments. While it may make sense to invest in what you know, this type of bias could result in the over-allocation of assets in this category.

THE STATUS QUO BIAS:

Another version of the Comfort Zone, this bias is a preference for the current situation. This can be a dangerous attitude to have because the markets are fluctuating and changing all the time. Intelligent investors recognize that because change predominates in the markets, maintaining the status quo is more likely to result in loss than profit.

Investors need to guard themselves against this assortment of mental-emotional traps. By making yourself neutral to the influence of these biases, your decision-making will become more clear, and you will more capably respond to the signals your investment plan is communicating to you. Mental-emotional baggage has no place in your investment psychology; the more conscious you are of your tendencies for bias, the more likely you will dispel them as they appear. There is enough going on in the markets to distract and confuse you; being unaware of what are normally subconscious influences will be one less factor interfering with your investment success.

Too Much Noise

As for distraction and confusion, the stock market's constant flow of data and never-ending changes can be quite raucous with price and volume fluctuations that may impede an investor's understanding of market direction. Some examples of noise are program trading and dividend payments; these may not reflect market sentiment and can distract investors from meaningful market movement, or, worse yet, lead unsuspecting investors to make decisions based on the illusory noise they are seeing. Having experience with the effects of market noise, a well-trained investor would know what to look for and could weed out unnecessary data.

Time is Fleeting

Even though everybody has 24 hours a day and seven days a week, time is like rust...it never sleeps. Time is one of your most important commodities because of the value it brings your portfolio. Whatever your investment horizon, whether five, 10, or 30 years, every year is a precious resource for advancing the achievement of your financial goals. "The years shall run like rabbits," wrote the poet W.H. Auden, and you have only so much time to build your portfolio and attain your financial freedom. Having a solid investment plan and following your plan over time is the surest way to make your financial dreams come true.

SLOW TO GET YOUR GAME ON:

Another hazard to avoid is not saving enough money during the early years. If you've been unable to save sufficiently, for whatever reason, when you had a multitude of years before you, you will be forced to increase your risk when you're older when you have less tolerance for risk. Starting a savings and investment program with limited resources early in your adult life is more effective than taking excessive risks later in an attempt to catch up.

Summary

Private investors can face a series of tough challenges in their desire for financial success. There's a reason why there are millions of investors, and, while some are making money...some aren't.

An investor must master the two key emotions of fear and greed, known objectively as risk and return. It's easy to be an armchair investor without any skin in the game, but once you have several thousand dollars in the market, emotions quickly surface as the market starts siphoning off your cash like a boat with a gaping hole below the waterline, or conversely starts dropping buckets of money in your account like its monsoon season.

Then, too, we all have the human tendency to be influenced by our biases, which can blindside us and lead us in wrong directions. Being an investor, a serious investor, means staying alert to all of the many distractions that can dull our perceptions of what's really happening in the market. When your money is the measuring rod of your clarity, an investor needs to be completely present. If you intend to make money in the market, you have to be as attentive, informed, organized, proactive, prescient, and dedicated to your goals as you are in your day job. If you're ready to do this, then let's talk about the underlying reasons behind your desire to become wealthy.

Chapter 2 Review Questions

1. Being a successful investor requires which of the following traits?

   A. Years of critically educated training.
   B. Years of daily market experience.
   C. Experienced familiarity with a wide variety of investment categories and hundreds of investment products.
   D. All of the above.

2. The greatest mistake most private investors make is:

   A. Investing as a contrarian.
   B. Assuming they know what they're doing.
   C. Over-diversifying their portfolio.
   D. Under-diversifying their portfolio.

3. The two most prominent emotions in the market are:

   A. Fear and greed.
   B. Jealousy and anger.
   C. Indecision and confidence.
   D. Misery and joy.

4. Steady confidence can be achieved with which of the following?

   A. Practice.
   B. Experience.
   C. A disciplined investment strategy.
   D. A commitment to obeying the strategy's rules.
   E. All of the above.

Chapter 2 Review Answers

1. Being a successful investor requires which of the following traits?

   A. Years of critically educated training.
   B. Years of daily market experience.
   C. Experienced familiarity with a wide variety of investment categories and hundreds of investment products.
   D. All of the above.

   Answer: D. All of the above. Non-professional investors have very little chance of being successful unless they dedicate years to regular and active participation in the markets.

2. The greatest mistake most private investors make is:

   A. Investing as a contrarian.
   B. Assuming they know what they're doing.
   C. Over-diversifying their portfolio.
   D. Under-diversifying their portfolio.

   Answer: B. Assuming they know what they're doing. Most non-professional investors are not sufficiently educated or trained to make wise investment decisions. Often, decision-making is based on having read only a few books or attending only a few workshops.

3. The two most prominent emotions in the market are:

   A. Fear and greed.
   B. Jealousy and anger.
   C. Indecision and confidence.
   D. Misery and joy.

   Answer: A. Fear and greed. Investors are driven by fear of loss and greed for quick wealth.

4. Steady confidence can be achieved with which of the following?

   A. Practice.

   B. Experience.

   C. A disciplined investment strategy.

   D. A commitment to obeying the strategy's rules.

   E. All of the above.

   Answer: E. All of the above. The only way to achieve investment confidence is by having a plan, possessing the discipline to obey the plan when under pressure, and having the practice and experience that provides informed awareness.

Chapter 3
Rules for Your Investment Road

When you have finished reading this chapter, you will:

- Know the four essential elements of the investment process
- Recognize the value of setting concrete financial goals
- Possess introductory knowledge about creating your financial investment plan
- Realize the importance of establishing your return objective
- Understand the difference between short term, mid-term, and long-term goals
- See the wisdom of establishing your personal financial pyramid
- Identify several constraints to your portfolio's progress
- Appreciate the importance of an investment policy statement
- Know the difference between fundamental and technical analysis
- Be familiar with the terms alpha strategy and beta strategy
- Have an initial understanding of the efficient frontier
- Be able to explain the difference between the active, passive, and conservative investment strategies
- Value the significance of monitoring your portfolio at prescribed regular intervals

Introduction to the Investment Process Overview

Every time the stock market jolts up or down, it is relaying information about expected risk and return. For many people, this jolting action sends a shiver down their spine, challenging them about who they are as an investor.

If this market turbulence frightens you, you may find Synergy Asset Management's (SAM) Lifestyle Protection Planning Process (LPPP) comforting. In short, the LPPP integrates investment management with financial planning.

The LPPP process will help you better understand why you own risky investments in the first place. It will also help you find the right balance for you between investments that possess return characteristics, and investments that possess risk management characteristics.

You can think of these two approaches being like a coin, heads on one side and tails on the other. The investing coin has risk on one side and return on the other. You can also think stocks for risk-related investments and bonds for less risk-related investments.

Finding the ***right combination*** of these two types of assets, while monitoring and adjusting them on a continuous basis, is what leads to our success.

We are not recommending that you only invest in stocks or bonds. We recommend that you allow our process to integrate your appetite for risk and return with your lifestyle goals and aspirations. Hence, we present Synergy's Lifestyle Protection Planning Process (LPPP).

Here is how it works.

Investing, when done right, is never haphazard. As with everything, care must be taken to determine what you want and how to use what you have to gain your intended objectives. A thoughtful plan identifying the steps toward your ultimate achievement must be developed. The plan must be followed, with reasonable adjustments based on new evidence, as steady forward accomplishment through time is patiently and bravely achieved.

Similar to baking a cake, most chefs refer to their recipes. When planning a holiday, itinerary, reservations, packing, and funding are all important elements for a successful trip. Planning a dinner party, consulting your Christmas list, preparing to buy a car, or bringing home a puppy or kitten all entail thoughtful consideration. This is particularly true when investing your hard-earned money.

In this chapter we'll review the four essential elements of the investment process and provide insightful details designed to guide you toward becoming an informed and successful investor.

1. Understand Your Goals

The first and most important task is to decide on your financial goals. Like most people reading this book, you have realistic expectations for your financial future, and are not planning to own a villa with 15 Mercedes in the south of France. If you win the lottery, anything can happen, but until that glorious moment occurs, you are likely to have a realistic expectation for how your life will unfold. Neither do you want to hold back and restrict your dreams by aiming low and being willing to accept only a straw-thatched hut on the edge of an infested bayou. Fortunately, we live in a great country with a remarkable investment system that is structured toward financial reward... when you know how to intelligently interact with it.

Figure 17: Lifestyle Goals.

GOALS	FOUNDATION	SHORT TERM	MID TERM	LONG TERM
BUSINESS	• Valuate business • Review buy-sell agreement	• Establish or review 401(k) retirement plan • Reduce taxes	• Business expansion and rapid growth • Identify a successor	• Retire • Sell business
PERSONAL	• Prepare wills & trust • Evaluate insurance	• Evaluate investment portfolio • Reduce taxes	• Wealth accumulation • Pay for college	• Leave an estate • Income planning

Most people who look to their future envision a peaceful life with a loving partner, a home with enough property in a safe area, whether urban, suburban or rural, good and decent neighbors, healthy children who go to college and build a rewarding career, annual vacations that satisfy curiosity and wanderlust, an interesting hobby, the pleasures of family, friends, and a reasonably active social life, and strong resources for one's elder years so expenses are covered and there are no financial burdens for loved ones.

Key:

What are your precise financial goals? Exactly what do these goals represent in dollars? Have you taken inflation into account?

This is a reasonable and achievable American dream, and it can be yours through intelligent and careful investing. Since the first step toward achieving your goals is having some, let's analyze the goals in this vision in more detail... because the vision contains layers of goals built one upon another that must first be achieved before the ultimate vision depicted here can materialize.

Important:

Successful investors typically have foundational, short term, mid-term, and long-term goals because this structure provides a strong basis for building wealth. For those who own businesses, your business goals need to be integrated with your personal goals. Moreover, your personal financial planning needs to be coordinated with your business planning.

Imagine a pyramid with a solid base that satisfies daily needs and security, a middle section composed of investments for a range of short to middle to long term financial objectives, and a pinnacle reserved for accelerated portfolio growth.

SHORT TERM PERSONAL GOALS:

Short term financial goals are the base of your financial foundation. The first essential element is to live within your means. When you extend your credit unnecessarily, you are compromising your future and making money work against you, not for you. A second essential element is to conserve your spending so you can set aside funds every month that will help build your initial financial foundation. Having enough cash flow every month to take care of the bills and provide key commodities like food, gas for your car, etc., and being mindful of your other expenses can result in a conservative but comfortable lifestyle affording the opportunity for wealth building. It may not be necessary to have a daily $5 coffee or a daily $10 lunch. These expenses add up fast and may provide short term pleasure at your long-term expense.

Short Term Personal Goals. Short term goals are meant to satisfy your daily living expenses, provide a few thousand dollars as a set-aside for emergencies like an unexpected dental treatment or a broken water pump in your car. Having this cash on hand will provide peace of mind and also means you don't have to quickly sell an appreciating stock in an untimely manner to access the cash you suddenly need.

Another key function of short-term goals is to provide a reserve in case you lose your job. Things may be dicey enough without having to wonder how you're going to make ends meet until you find a new position. Having money in a rainy day fund gives you an umbrella in stormy weather.

Short term goals also protect you and your family from the variety of health and medical risks that can severely damage your financial progress and future. A variety of insurance programs should be thoughtfully selected to protect your financial well-being. No one knows if or when an unexpected medical disaster can occur. Most people see the value (and legal responsibility) of insuring their car, insuring their home and property, and purchasing or being a member of a medical and dental insurance plan.

This same careful consideration should also include life insurance in case of sudden death, long term care (LTC) insurance in case of a medical disaster that extends beyond a health insurance policy's protection, and disability insurance that provides a steady income in case you are rendered incapable of earning a living. The harm in unnecessarily spending monthly premiums if you have the good fortune not to be afflicted is dramatically less than the harm of not being covered if the unimaginable occurs. This, of course, is the premise of insurance. Hospitals and care centers are full of people needing assistance; how lucky do you plan to be?

While it may seem prudish to set aside funds for this variety of short-term purposes, it is prudent to accommodate these financial components. Preparing your financial house with these elementary steps will advance your potential to avoid loss and secure the opportunity to subsequently build wealth without eroding factors. Taking care of first things first assures more confident developments later.

The following diagram visually explains the personal financial pyramid:

Figure 18: Personal Financial Pyramid.

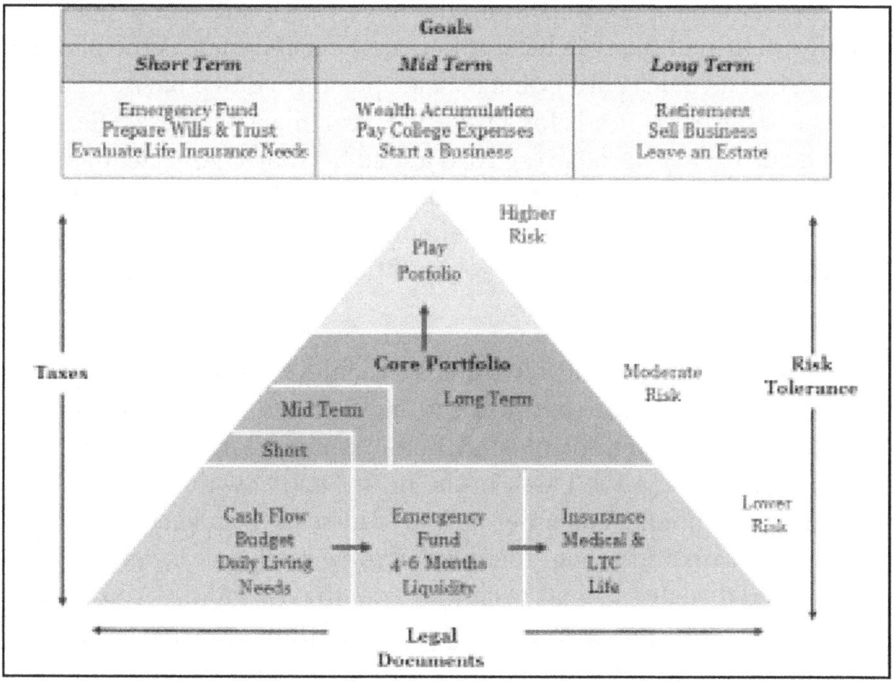

SHORT TERM BUSINESS GOALS:

Short term business goals are also necessary, because they assure a solid foundation for your business. Establishing or reviewing your company's 401(k) plan serves several purposes. First, it helps you reduce company taxes, an activity that must always be in the front of your mind. Second, it helps you invest funds for your retirement, another extremely important financial step. Third, a company 401(k) helps your employees save for their retirement, which is important for demonstrating the value you place in your employees, and which has the effect of assuring their loyalty and performance. This s a win-win-win!

In general, you are best advised to always look for ways to cut taxes because taxes are the largest predator your company faces. The less you pay in taxes, the more funds you have for all the important plans and activities you have in mind that can expand the profitability of your company.

MID-TERM PERSONAL AND BUSINESS GOALS:

Mid-term financial goals focus on the next 3 – 5 years. These goals are usually identified to serve life's anticipated events, such as the planned purchase of a vehicle, attending college, placing a down payment on a home, setting aside funds for a wedding, starting a business... Setting these goals is easy because the road ahead becomes more clear as time rolls along. An investor needs discipline to forego short term gratification in exchange for the enjoyment of mid-term fulfillment. Monthly budgeting and paying yourself first are good strategies for having delayed satisfaction.

In business, two good mid-term goals to achieve is creating or revising your strategic plan for expansion and rapid growth. Now that your company has survived the most difficult years of starting up and stabilizing, having a solid view of the future and how to get there becomes paramount. The other task is to identify your successor so you can train and groom that person to be ready in case of an unexpected disaster such as premature death or disability. You want your family's fortunes to be safe in case something horrible occurs, and you also want to prepare this individual to relieve you of your duties gradually, perhaps even becoming the future owner when you're ready to retire or sell.

LONG TERM PERSONAL AND BUSINESS GOALS:

Long term financial goals focus on a horizon of five years and more. These goals are typically more substantial, such as eliminating all debts, paying off the mortgage, securing a comfortable retirement, and creating an estate for heirs.

Achieving long term goals usually requires steady progress over decades, with careful planning that calculate the effect of inflation, taxes, and compounding interest for 20 or 30 years, and is based on a dedicated savings and investment strategy combined with genuine investment knowledge and experience. Doing this on your own may not be the wisest choice because most people don't know everything they should know about investing, and don't have the time to study effective strategies or research thousands of tempting companies in the market. A professional opinion, such as from a CFP®, a

Certified Financial Planner®, might make all the difference between a comfortable retirement and retirement resources that are found to be wanting when time has run out. Your long-term business goal is to sell your business as a going concern, and not let the business become shuttered. You'll have spent years, possibly decades building your business and the market is likely to be interested in buying a smoothly operated profit generating business like yours. Obviously you already have an exit plan in place (you do...don't you?) so you know that the years of dedicated planning, practice and production will reward you and your family when it's time to turn your eyes to other interests. Now is the time to plan for that day because it's not as far away as you used to think!

2. Create a Plan

An investment plan is a great blueprint for success. You've probably created a number of plans for a variety of purposes in your life, and those plans were likely to have started with a vision of what you intended to achieve, and all the developed details of how you were going to accomplish your goals. An investment plan is no different. Its purpose is to provide guidance along your path toward wealth accumulation, wealth protection, and wealth distribution through the variety of challenges you may face over the course of 10, 20, and 30 years or more.

Thus, investment planning is quite a serious matter! The results of your planning will determine the financial quality of your life. Being casual with the factors that compose your plan will increase the likelihood of limited financial prosperity, compared with taking an intelligent and circumspect attitude now by intentionally creating a future of financial abundance. You are setting the compass of your financial circumstances, and drawing the map so you can arrive at the destination of your personal financial freedom, and that of your loved ones. While a high degree of solemnity is unnecessary, knowing how to create an investment plan that serves you through the vicissitudes of market turmoil, or market stasis, is essential to your financial well-being many years in the future. Whether your portfolio will become a shipwreck or come into harbor with all flags flying will be determined to a great degree by the comprehensive investment plan you are now creating. An investment plan does not need to be complex, but it does need to be sufficient.

The Key Parts of an Investment Plan

The most essential element of your investment plan is your Investment Policy Statement (IPS). The Investment Policy Statement is the blueprint for your investment plan. The IPS clarifies your investment goals, identifies the ROI you need to achieve to reach your investment goals, expresses the risks involved so you can be prepared to make adjustments when warranted, and indicates the anticipated amount of time necessary to achieve your desired outcomes. Without this plan, you are sailing the high seas without a compass; with this plan, you can follow your stars with a fairly reasonable expectation of finding home port.

The Investment Policy Statement (IPS). There are a wide range of details that must be considered when developing your investment policy statement such as, and not limited to, your willingness and tolerance for risk, your thoughts about core and non-core investments, and your philosophy on diversification. When you deliberate about selecting your investments, you'll need to identify the qualities an investment must have to be considered for your portfolio. You will also need to decide how you'll select investments based on their costs, and on the taxes that may be generated.

Your IPS must clearly state how often you'll be monitoring your portfolio and how you'll know if each of your investments are meeting your expectations; you will also need to establish the criteria for eliminating assets that are underperforming. The IPS establishes the guidelines you intend to follow, guidelines that are without emotional influence so you can be protected from making subjective decisions when you feel the pressures of fear and greed.

The key elements of your IPS are your return and risk objectives, and the constraints that may limit the acquisition of your investment goals. Here is a brief overview of each.

Return Objective. Many people invest in the market without first determining the return they need to achieve their identified goals. Without a plan, it's hard to tell when you've achieved financial security. Investing money in the markets without knowing what you expect to achieve, how you expect to achieve it, and a projected and realistic pace of when you might achieve your financial goals can be highly risky. Just as you most likely wouldn't buy a house without first seeing it, investing your hard-earned dollars in the market without having a plan opens the potential for unfortunate results.

To have some reasonable chance of becoming financially secure, you must first determine the return objective for your portfolio. This means, given the financial goals you've established and taking into account the deleterious effect of taxes and inflation, that there is a specific dollar amount you are attempting to achieve over a set period of time which will result, with the miracle of compounding and the steady addition of savings and prudent investing, in the achievement of the financial future you envision.

Imagine! Your future lifestyle goals can be converted into an exact monetary sum which can then be calculated as an annual return objective! Over the course of 10, 20, or 30 years, assuming your return objective is met, the money you need will be waiting for you.

This is so much better than living on an endless treadmill trying to create an undetermined amount of wealth, chasing investment trends with the hope of increasing the value of your portfolio, creating needless anxiety and sleepless nights when the results are less than anticipated, and either becoming frantic or paralyzed as the market rises and falls, or does neither...as so many unqualified investors do.

Diversification is one of the keys to earning your return objective while also controlling your portfolio's risk because, as you will see, the synergy of all your investment assets working together can result in a whole that is much greater, stronger, safer, productive and more reliable than its parts.

Your Lifestyle Return Benchmark. Another critical element to your investment policy statement is designing your Lifestyle Return

Benchmark™ (LRB). The LRB is the amount of money your portfolio needs to earn so you can achieve your lifestyle goals and aspirations, making your dreams come true.

The LRB process will convert your lifestyle goals and aspirations into your personalized return objective. Additionally, it will act as your custom return benchmark which is much more relevant to you than a random benchmark like the S&P 500. The S&P 500 has nothing to do with your investment objectives, so it is a mistake to measure your investing success with it.

We establish your LRB through our proprietary required rate of return (RRR) process. Each year we will compare your LRB with the actual return on your portfolio to ensure you are moving in the right direction and gaining ground. If you are not on track, we will reevaluate your plan and make the necessary portfolio adjustments that are economically possible. Moreover, we will educate you on the other options you have so you stay on track.

Investing success hinges on the integration between the investor's unique circumstances and the prudent identification of long-term strategies that are positioned to achieve client goals with the highest probability of success.

At Synergy Asset Management, we take a different approach to constructing your portfolio by reverse-engineering your required rate of return (RRR) and using it as your Lifestyle Return Benchmark™.

Figure 19: The Required Rate of Return.

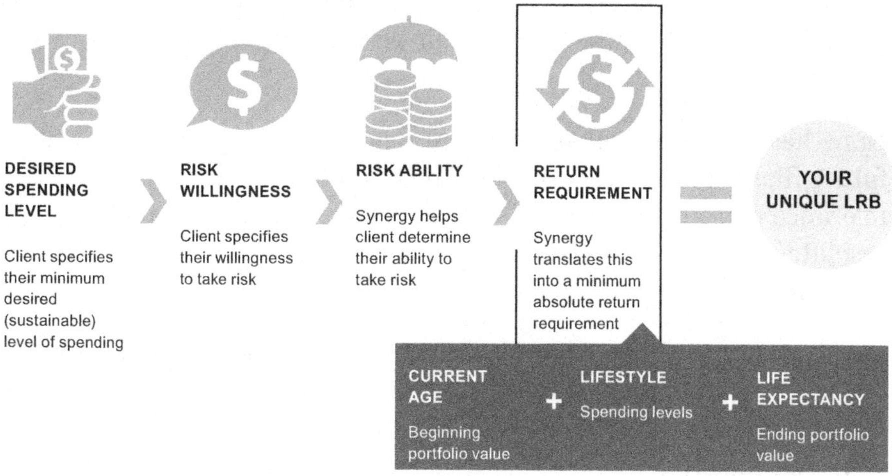

Okay, your lifestyle has been converted into a real number that actually means something to you. So now what? Now it is time to take your LRB and use it to build your portfolio. The goal is to build a portfolio that has a good chance of achieving your LRB with as little risk as possible.

Remember that there is a trade-off between expected return and risk. Some investors are strongly risk-averse while others possess a higher degree of risk tolerance. Therefore, it is very important that we build a portfolio that is respectful of your ability and willingness to take risk while also providing you with an above average chance of meeting your LRB objective.

Note:

The cost of your future goals can be converted into a precise monetary sum which can be translated into an annual return objective.

As mentioned, having the services of a Certified Financial Planner® can be a tremendous advantage in making and assuring the accuracy of these calculations and projections, especially with the complexities of tax law, the subtleties of inflation, and determining realistic portfolio growth as measured by your personal investment risk tolerance.

Nonetheless, sacre bleu! You can now determine the price tag of your future financial harmony and steadily build toward it within your risk tolerance margin, assuming a sufficient investment horizon and a resolute commitment to following your well-crafted plan. This is a gift from Heaven.

Of course, as you know, there is the other side of the coin and your IPS must alsoprepare you for the potential risks that may lie in your investment path. This is why your IPS should consider and include your risk objective.

Your Risk Objective. Your investment policy statement should describe your personal philosophy about investment risk and the degree of your willingness to tolerate it. Your IPS should also acknowledge that your portfolio assumes there will be risk and that your returns will be influenced both positively and negatively over time.

There are a host of risks to which your investments will be subject, such as liquidity, legal, political, regulatory, longevity, spousal, mortality, business and health risks. Granted, it is difficult to assess the influence any of these risk factors might have on your portfolio, but they need to be listed and described to the degree that permits you to recognize the generic vulnerabilities of your portfolio because it's important to consider not just the harm that could be caused, but also to guide your thinking on how you might overcome these sabotaging influences should they materialize. Be prepared!

When considering risk, there are two categories to analyze and assess. The first is your willingness to accept risks. Depending on your financial situation and the tempo of your emotional enthusiasm, you might be gung ho to take risk because you're ready to live the good life as soon as possible. The other category requiring your attention is your ability to take risk. Like a child in a candy store, your eyes might be as big as dinner plates, but your ability to take risks may not have as large an appetite, and the jeopardy in which you might place yourself and your loved ones could be completely unrealistic and dangerous.

Your tolerance for risk can be appraised through a careful and personal introspective that assesses your intellectual and emotional ability to accept and recover from potential losses. Questionnaires are available to help you make this determination, and not only about the degree of risk you can tolerate in your portfolio, but also guidance for reviewing your thinking and planning about maintaining your current standard of living, the value and cost of meeting your financial goals, and exploring the potential use of your wealth after you've achieved your desired level of accumulation. These exploratory ruminations can yield ideas that could further mature your thoughts about investment policies and procedures, such as employing stop-loss orders or refining your rebalancing methodology. Care and prudence should be healthy influences as you reflect on the best ways you can achieve financial independence.

Constraints. The other essential element of your investment plan must also identify and resolve how you will respond to the limitations that may potentially curtail your portfolio's growth.

A. One obvious constraint is your time horizon. If you have a long time for investing before you will need the funds, say, for retirement, time is on your side. Time is an amazing ally, or a deadly foe. With an extended time horizon, your portfolio can use time to grow your funds steadily with limited risk; with a limited time horizon, you may choose to make yourself vulnerable by accepting more risk than may be prudent, or you can also choose to not meet your original financial goals and live a different lifestyle because of the financial necessity of your situation.

B. Another constraint is taxes. Sooner or later, they must be paid, and it's the wise investor who tests the waters before jumping in. A careful analysis of how tax will affect the different investments in your portfolio may reveal the need for an interesting conversation with yourself, or with your fiduciary financial advisor or other qualified advisors. You should consider the returns on taxable vs. tax-free investments; the effect portfolio turnover has on accelerating your taxes; evaluating ordinary income tax rates and capital gains tax rates; and reviewing gift and estate tax effects if assets are intended for heirs. Your priority MUST be scheduling the disbursement of your financial assets so you have the most value in your portfolio after taxes have been paid.

Figure 20: Effect of Tax Rates on Return.

Tax Rate	10.00%	20.00%	25.00%	30.00%	40.00%
Gross Return	10.00%	10.00%	10.00%	10.00%	10.00%
Net Return	9.00%	8.00%	7.50%	7.00%	6.00%
Difference	**−1.00%**	**−2.00%**	**−2.50%**	**−3.00%**	**−4.00%**

Other constraints may need your attention as well.

C. Liquidity could be a concern if you need to convert assets to cash but the penalties are too severe, making it financially painful to access your money when you need to.

D. There may be legal and regulatory constraints that will have to be navigated; some assets may have prohibitive management or participation fees; you may decide to avoid certain markets or certain asset classes because of their high risk or your unfamiliarity with these investment vehicles. Other legal and regulatory issues might include the prohibition of buying particular asset classes; you might want to impose a restriction on the purchase of a country fund because of the country's political, military, or social activities, or your portfolio may have an investment restriction placed upon it because of the jurisdiction in which it is domiciled.

E. There is also a category for constraints that are considered "unique circumstances".

This is a general category for miscellaneous constraints such as a trust fund designed to provide support for a special needs child, or perhaps a portion of the investment is reserved for building a home for an elderly family member, or a specific sum of money is dedicated to the grandchildren's college education. You may also decide to impose your own unique constraints on investing in companies that make munitions, pollute the environment, create foods that cause ill health, or are socially unacceptable to you in some other ways.

All the constraints mentioned provide good cause for reflection when planning to invest, and they can be accommodated by inclusion in your investment policy statement. Ultimately, you want to create a plan that achieves your financial vision while also providing the flexibility you may need through the expanse of time remaining in your investment horizon.

Consulting with a fiduciary financial advisor could be a sensible and time-saving tactic. Most investors simply don't know everything they should know, and with good reason. With a busy career and an active family and social life, there isn't enough time to learn about the markets more than on a superficial level.

There are thousands of funds and companies to study, and reliable expertise comes with years of experience. It doesn't make sense, really, to trust your future to your own devices, engaging with the markets as a hobbyist when you would benefit most from a highly qualified investment professional.

It's your money! And that's the point.

3. Craft Your Portfolio

After you have established your Investment Policy Statement and resolved the variety of details involved with building a comprehensive and effective plan for achieving investment success, the next step is to implement the investment strategies set forth in the IPS.

Your portfolio manager will build your portfolio based on your financial goals, not on the continual jolts and convulsions of the market. Our primary objective for you is real wealth accumulation, preservation, and distribution through portfolio construction practices that are inherently sensible and thoroughly tested, resulting in market-like returns with a reasonable level of risk. If your lifestyle planning calls for a more conservative approach, we can achieve that, too. This tactic may result in a slightly lower rate of expected return, but will provide better protection in the event of a severe bear market. In the end, most investors prefer a plan that will ensure their standard of living against severe short-term loss while allowing them to maintain and improve their lifestyle over time. Remember, the goal is not to beat the S&P 500, it is to earn your Lifestyle Return Benchmark™ (LRB).

To accomplish your objectives, we use a mix of safe and conservative investment strategies, core investment strategies, alternative investment strategies and, if appropriate, a mix of real estate and small business assets. Annuities and insurance can also play an important role in a broadly diversified portfolio to buffer sudden shocks and unexpected perils.

Our mix of strategies will keep you sleeping tight at night regardless of what the stock and bond markets are doing. Based on your Lifestyle Protection Plan, we can adjust the size of your safe and secure investment so you can afford to withstand more risk elsewhere. Though there are thousands of investment choices, your plan is limiting you from considering them all, which will provide some small relief! Even so, there are still many hundreds of possibilities that await your review. In addition, there are hundreds of different ways to build an investment portfolio, though typically the following two investment approaches are the most widely employed today. They are regarded as the most sensible, largely because they are based on decades of proven performance.

Strategic Decisions. Strategic decisions focus on the broad factors of:

- An investor's time horizon;
- The degree to which the investor can take risks;
- The annual returns the investor must achieve to attain his or her goals;
- Cash flow requirements of the investor;

- The amount of assets available for investment, both now and in the future;
- The effect of the investor's tax bracket on earnings;
- Anticipated inflation rates;
- The projected average returns of the asset classes.

Figure 21: Strategic and Tactical Features.

Strategic

Accounts for investor specific factors in asset class assumptions

5. Time horizon
6. Risk profile
7. Required rate of return (RRR)
8. Taxes
9. Inflation

Tactical

Accounts for special knowledge or views on asset class returns

1. Accounts for trends
2. Stocks over bonds
3. International stocks over US stocks

Tactical Decisions. Tactical decisions are more narrowly focused on judging which asset classes will perform best in the coming quarters and years. Will stocks outperform bonds? Will real estate outperform commodities? Is the 10-year Treasury bond a more lucrative investment than tax-free municipal bonds?

Strategic and tactical decisions will ultimately generate a collection of mixed assets that are believed to accelerate the investor's return and limit the investor's risk. Choices become more complicated as asset classes are then subdivided and analyzed for portfolio inclusion by size, such as small cap, mid-cap, and large cap equities. Asset classes can also be subdivided by industry, such as energy, healthcare, technology, and industrials, to name a few. Location can also be another subdivision of asset classes, such as domestic equities and international equities. Of course, each of these segments can be even further categorized by even more subsets. Monitoring performance is critical, and these asset classes and their subdivisions can be compared with indexes of similar assets so that each individual element of a portfolio's performance can be measured.

When researching securities, investors analyze a security to determine whether or not it is mispriced. The obvious objective for every investor is to place his or her money in an asset that has the potential for growth, not the potential to remain the same or diminish in value. By finding a security that is mispriced, the investor has the reasoned belief that he or she can purchase the security at a good price, and is thus willing to accept a reasonable and calculated risk that the security will increase in value over a specific length of time. As you know, there are many ways for determining the potential value of a security, and all of these methods are the children of either one or two of these main systems: technical analysis, and fundamental analysis.

Technical analysis is a method for studying a security's potential monetary value by forecasting its future price through a study of its market data, particularly its history of price and volume.

Fundamental analysis is a method for studying a security's potential monetary value by examining the underlying influences (fundamentals) of the security, such as economic and political conditions, competitive advantage, sales revenue, financial reserves, experience of its management, etc.

Definition:

Technical analysis is the study of a security's prices and volume to predict its future value.

Fundamental analysis is the study of a security's cash flow to predict its future value.

In either case, once the value of the asset has been defined as closely as possible, the value is compared to its current market price. This informs the analyst if the asset is attractively valued or not. Assets that are priced higher than the analysis are considered overpriced and generally not a good choice for an investment. Assets that are priced lower than the analysis are regarded as underpriced and may be a favorable choice for investment. This is a simplistic view of the decision-making process for identifying good choices for a portfolio. Financial analysts thoroughly investigate asset candidates before recommending a decision on whether or not an investment will provide a good return. This is a matter of extreme professional diligence and another example of why an investor with limited experience and insufficient time should seriously consider hiring the services of a Chartered Financial Analyst (CFA).

Figure 22: Active and Passive Features.

HEADS **Active/Tactical**	TAILS **Passive/Indexing**
Tries to exceed the performance of a benchmark "ALPHA"	Attempts to match the performance of a benchmark "BETA"
May apply fundamental and or technical analysis	Minimize fees and trading costs
Can be used with asset allocation and or focused investing	Assumes markets are efficient
Assumes markets are not efficient	
Dynamic Management	
Rules based technical and quantitative procedures	

At Synergy Asset Management we use four investment strategies that are unique to our firm. We work closely with each of our clients and customize their portfolios for the best combination of growth with risk protection, as determined by the client's unique circumstances and personal financial needs.

1. THE ACTIVE STRATEGY:

Also known as the Alpha Strategy, or Stock Strategy, this investment strategy's purpose is to earn a return that is higher than the return earned by the general U. S. stock market. The return that exceeds the stock market is called the alpha. An investor who uses this strategy is willing to accept a higher degree of risk than an investor who chooses to earn the index averages.

Identifying alpha opportunities is a function of both fundamental analysis and technical analysis. Good investment prospects for the active strategy show strong historical performance with indications that the performance is sustainable based on the analysis of several key value drivers, such as cash flows, management expertise and stability, and return on invested capital, to name a few.

The active equity strategy might include stocks from a variety of sectors, or it may concentrate on specific sectors, depending on the influences in the current market and the carefully refined analysis of potential market direction.

Risk control is also a significant feature in the calculations and is managed by the thoughtful allocation of limited positions, as well as the placement of stop loss orders that would be executed if the equity's price declined to a premeditated level.

Equities are purchased for a long-term position, so transaction costs and taxes are minimized, contributing to increased growth and value. Because the market is a dynamic and ever-changing environment, this investment strategy has a degree of flexibility built-in so an alpha return can be achieved. Taxable and nontaxable assets may be treated differently because of their inherent nature; selling a selected equity within 12 months might be a wise investment decision in some cases.

Selling an equity requires having a disciplined exit strategy founded on legitimate objective factors. Among the reasons for exiting a position:

- The fundamentals are no longer strong
- The equity's intrinsic value is well below its current market price
- The allocated funds would be better served in another investment
- A significant percentage drop below the original position has occurred
- An error in the original selection is identified

The active strategy is a good strategy for investors who seek a more rapid appreciation of their portfolio's value, and are willing and able to accommodate a higher risk tolerance for loss.

2. THE SEMI-PASSIVE STRATEGY:

This investment strategy is also referred to as the Beta Strategy, and as the Asset Allocation Model. The focus of this strategy is to diversify investment funds among the different types of asset classes so return-rate volatility and risk are reduced.

The task of your financial planner is to place your investment funds in a mix of equity, debt, and cash investments in carefully measured allocations, so your return is optimized and your risk reduced.

As you are probably aware, equities can be grouped into subcategories such as small cap stocks, mid-cap stocks, and large cap stocks. Equities can also be grouped according to whether they are defined as growth equities or value equities, and these can be further subdivided among industry-specific sectors such as technology, energy, healthcare, etc. International equities may also be an attractive addition to your portfolio, and can be subdivided into a variety of investment groupings such as European, Asian, and assorted combinations of emerging markets.

Fixed income investments, which are company or government debt instruments, can also be grouped in subcategories. Among the many choices are investments in government bonds, mortgage-backed bonds, and corporate bonds. These can be even further sub-grouped based on the duration of the debt instrument, specifically short term, intermediate term, and long term.

While there are only a few basic asset classes, the variety of subdivision within the asset classes increases the population of investment choices quite substantially, and optimizing your return while being cautious with the degree of acceptable risk can consume an intense amount of reflection and calculation to arrive at a properly customized assortment specific to each individual's financial goals.

The performance of a Beta Strategy portfolio is measured against a sector-weighted index or collection of indices that reflects the combination of investments in the portfolio.

The next figure demonstrates an example of asset allocation for the semi-passive strategy.

Figure 23: Traditional Allocation.

STOCKS (EQUITIES) 60%	
Large Cap Growth	10%
Small Cap Growth	10%
Mid Cap Growth	10%
International	10%
Mid Cap Value	30%
Total	100%

BONDS (FIXED/DEBT) 25%	
Mortgage-Backed	25%
U.S Govt.	25%
Corporate	25%
Municipal	25%
Total	100%

CASH 15%

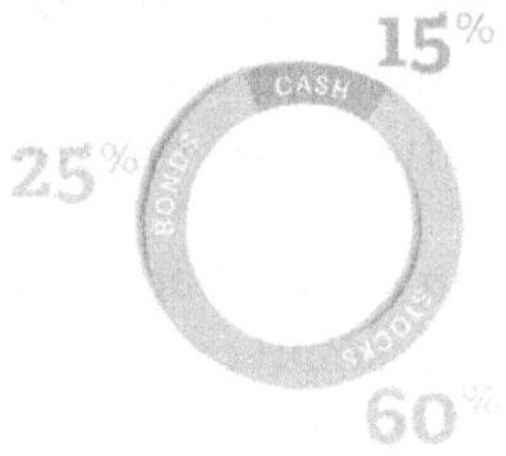

Figure 24: Asset Allocation Example.

Asset Allocation the New Way

STOCKS (EQUITIES) 60%	
Large Cap Growth	20%
Small Cap Growth	20%
Mid Cap Growth	15%
International	15%
Mid Cap Value	30%
Total	100%

BONDS (FIXED/DEBT) 15%	
Mortgage-Backed	25%
U.S Govt.	25%
Corporate	25%
Municipal	25%
Total	100%

ANNUITY 20%	
Growth Annuity	50%
Income Annuity	50%
Total	100%

CASH 5%

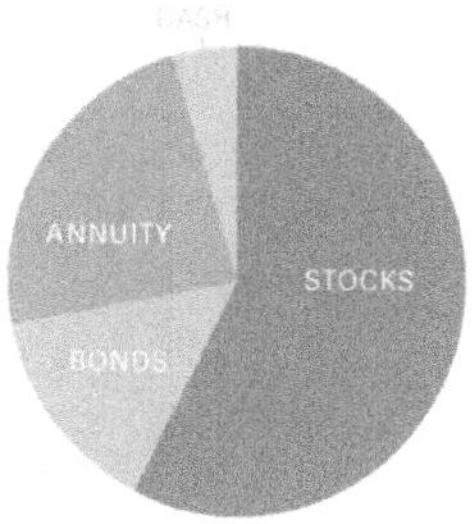

Traditional asset allocation seeks to achieve the 'efficient frontier', which is the deliberate and carefully calculated selection of investments whose combined return is as high as possible while also keeping within the acceptable range of the individual investor's tolerance for risk.

The following chart is an example of an efficient and inefficient portfolio. The chart is for illustrative purposes only and the expected return and standard deviation are hypothetical.

Figure 25: Efficient and Inefficient Portfolio Example.

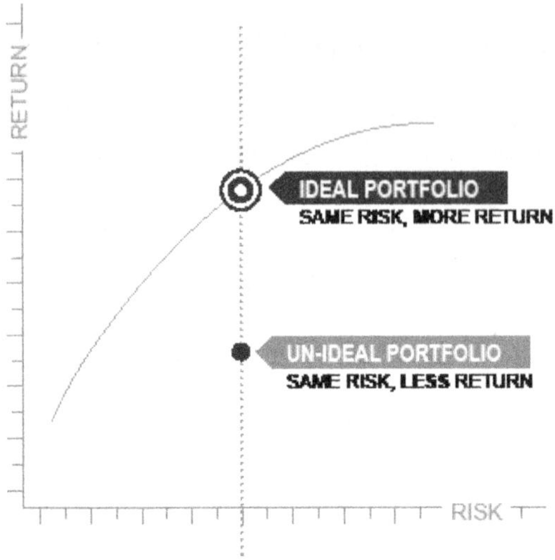

Your financial planner, seeking to obtain the benefit of diversification, selects investments from asset classes that are fundamentally different from each other. The underlying investment concept of the semi-passive strategy relies on the supposition that one asset class rises in value to offset the losses of another asset class diminishing in value...limiting potential losses and simultaneously increasing the overall portfolio's value. Simply stated, since the selected asset classes are so different from each other, should one asset class lose value, the portfolio's other asset classes are likely to offset the loss by increasing their value.

A subsequent step in the process of developing a portfolio with the semi-passive strategy is applying a mathematical analysis, developed in Modern Portfolio Theory, which identifies a range of portfolios that are appropriately diversified for your financial goals. Your financial planner will construct these portfolio choices for you for your review, discussion, and decision.

The next figure demonstrates an example of a portfolio that's been constructed using the tenets of the semi-passive strategy.

Figure 26: Example of a Semi-Passive Portfolio.

Semi-Passive Portfolio

Asset Class	Current Target	Minimum Holding	Maximum Holding
US Large Cap	10.00%	9.00%	19.00%
US Mid Cap	7.00%	5.00%	9.00%
US Small Cap	5.00%	3.00%	7.00%
Non-US Developed Stock	7.00%	4.00%	1.00%
Non-US Emerging Market Stock	8.00%	6.00%	10.00%
Global Bonds	2.00%	1.00%	3.00%
US Taxable Intermediate Bonds	10.00%	8.00%	12.00%
US Taxable Short Term Bonds	7.00%	5.00%	9.00%
US Inflation Protected Bonds	8.00%	6.00%	10.00%
US Tax-Mortgage	2.00%	0.00%	4.00%
US High Yield Bonds	5.00%	3.00%	9.00%
Non-US Developed Bonds	7.00%	5.00%	9.00%
Non-US Emerging Market Bonds	8.00%	6.00%	10.00%
Real Estate	7.00%	5.00%	9.00%
Commodities	3.50%	2.60%	4.40%
Cash	0.00%	0.00%	100%

For illustrative purposes only.
The above numbers are hypothetical.

The figure above illustrates a variety of asset classes and subcategories, and also demonstrates that a portfolio can allow a minimum and maximum range of holdings as provided by the portfolio's Investment Policy Statement (IPS).

The semi-passive strategy is not as aggressive as the alpha strategy because it seeks average or slightly above average returns, favoring the avoidance of risk in exchange for the potential assurance of index-based returns. This, of course, keeps gains, and losses, close to the average gains or losses of the selected index.

3. THE CONSERVATIVE STRATEGY:

This strategy is also commonly known as the Bond Strategy, the Fixed Income Strategy, or simply the Fixed Strategy. The conservative strategy is best suited for investors who desire, most of all, to retain the value of their portfolio, eliminate risk almost completely, and achieve only modest pre-calculated returns. Typical investments that are part of the conservative strategy include cash equivalents, certificates of deposit, money market investments, Treasury bills, government-issued fixed income instruments, and fixed annuities. These investment instruments are regarded as ultra-safe, and while the returns are quite limited, an investor who values portfolio security above all else will be especially pleased with this strategy.

When using the conservative strategy, considerations of investment duration must be considered. Strategies using short term, intermediate term, and long-term periods can be employed to meet a client's goals. A number of strategies can be executed to increase return and further limit risk:

- Bullet strategies
- Barbell strategies
- Immunization strategies
- Cash flow matching strategies
- Combination strategies
- Laddering strategies
- Asset and liability matching strategies

Making a cogent selection from among these investment instruments and strategies depends on the careful estimation of the current and projected economy, and analysis of trends in the fixed income markets, and the analysis of yield curves, the credit market, futures and options spreads, risk-adjusted returns, total return projections, etc. This wide variety of factors will be calculated to determine the best combination of benefits suited to the individual investor's unique set of circumstances.

While the conservative strategy focuses significantly on risk avoidance, as with everything to do with investment, there is still a degree of exposure to risk. The portfolio might experience the loss of principal or value for any of the following reasons:

- Market fluctuations
- Termination of the investment before maturity
- Reinvestment at a lower current rate
- Unexpected increase in inflation
- Inappropriate diversification of assets

The conservative strategy is often a good choice for investors who are either close to retirement or already in retirement, and for whom the preservation of principal is paramount.

4. ALTERNATIVE INVESTMENT STRATEGIES:

Your portfolio might benefit from investment alternatives that provide the opportunity to augment your return and decrease your risk. Though not for everybody, these alternative investment strategies might include hedge funds, real estate, and private equity securities, and private equity debt. Using real estate in your portfolio may be particularly alluring because of the variety of possibilities available for acquisition. Synergy Asset Management can provide attractive strategies if real estate is an appropriate investment vehicle for your customized portfolio.

These four distinct investment strategies, active, semi-passive, conservative, and alternative, are the generic choices available to all investors. Within these strategies are other strategies of asset class selection and asset weighting which will be discussed later.

4. Selecting, Monitoring, and Staying on Course

SELECTING:

When you and your financial planner have decided which investment strategy is most appropriate for your unique circumstances, the asset classes which are most appropriate for your portfolio, and the percentage of asset allocation within each of these asset classes, the next step is the selection of the individual equity or debt investments.

To guide your thinking, here is a list of criteria you and your financial advisor should apply to your review and discussion of the hundreds or thousands of investments available to you:

1. How does past performance compare with the past performance of other investments with the same objective? Consider its performance ranking over different time frames, and the consistency of its performance in those periods.

2. How high are the costs when compared with the costs of other funds with similar objectives and investment styles?

3. What is the size of the fund? Is the fund a market leader, or a smaller company that can be more agile?

4. How long has the fund existed? If it is a somewhat new fund, it may not have had enough time to build a sufficient performance track record.

5. How long has the fund been under the direction of its current manager? A new manager may adjust the fund's organization and personnel which could affect the fund's performance in the near term.

6. What is the fund's history of volatility, or price risk?

7. How effectively will the proposed investment complement the performance of the other investments in the portfolio?

8. How will the proposed investment perform in the current economic environment, and how will it perform as the environment changes?

9. Is the fund likely to have sustained success, compared with other investment opportunities?

10. What are the criteria for removing the investment from your portfolio?

The foregoing are just a few of the initial questions that should be asked, and they will spark the scrutiny and discussion that ultimately guides your selection and investment commitments.

MONITORING:

Once your investment plan has become operational, you will now need to monitor your investments over a reasonable period of time to confirm they are performing, singly and together, as you intended. A period of three to six months should provide enough data to tell you your portfolio has either been properly constructed, or that some of its elements need to be exchanged for more appropriately performing assets.

Once you have the proper mix of assets working synergetically, you should conduct a review of your portfolio every six months.

STAYING ON COURSE:

During your periodic review, you'll need to decide if it's time to sell underperforming assets or keep a steady hand as the variety of asset classes move through their individual cycles. You may find that market conditions have changed since you first established your portfolio, and one or more of your selected investments are performing less than expected. Perhaps an entire asset class has experienced a shift and now has diminished returns, though you may also be pleased to find that another asset class has excelled.

A further consideration is the potential for your portfolio to need rebalancing; as an asset class either increases or decreases in value, it may distort the percentage allocations required by your Investment Policy Statement (IPS). Your IPS is the roadmap to your success, so adjusting your portfolio to realign with your investment strategy will require your attentive reflection. Should you adjust your IPS...or obey it? This is a worthy exercise, and the six-month review protocol is a good time for an analysis of this question.

Important:

The different assets in your portfolio are likely to keep shifting in their dollar value and in their representative percentage. Monitoring these changes is a critically important task, perhaps requiring periodic adjustment.

REPORTING:

If you are working with a financial planner, you should expect regular reports that detail how your portfolio is performing. Here is a suggestion for two reports you should request:

1. A monthly report listing all the assets in your account, their individual value, and all the transactions that occurred during the month.

2. A quarterly report that shows:

   - The performance of your portfolio over the quarter and since inception

   - The performance of each individual investment for the quarter

   - The performance results of comparative indices for the quarter

   - The asset allocation percentages for the asset classes in your portfolio

   - A comparison of the asset allocation percentages with the requirements of your Investment Policy Statement (IPS)

   - Recommendations for adjustments

Your financial planner should meet with you at least once annually, and preferable once per quarter to review your portfolio's performance. After all, this is your money and your financial future, and regular review at reasonable interludes will keep you continually informed and actively engaged with your progress. You may go to the movies once or twice a month; it certainly makes good common sense to stay on top of your financial well-being at least quarterly!

Here is a list of the different types of investments that might be included in your portfolio:

MUTUAL FUND:

A fund created by an investment management company that invests pooled investor money for a particular performance goal.

STOCK:

A security representing ownership in a company, entitling the owner of the stock to a portion of the company's assets and earnings.

BOND:

A note that promises repayment of a debt with interest; bonds are usually issued in $1,000 multiples.

ANNUITY:

An investment that provides payments at prescribed intervals; annuities are typically issued by insurance companies.

REAL ESTATE:

Land and permanent fixtures such as buildings; natural resources are included.

CERTIFICATE OF DEPOSITS (CDS):

These are time-deposit savings instruments that provide interest on the specified maturity date; premature withdrawal creates penalties.

MONEY MARKET FUNDS:

Money market funds are mutual funds that earn interest by investing in short term debt such as Treasury bills.

DERIVATIVES:

Securities that derive, or receive, value from another asset. Futures and options are examples of derivatives.

ALTERNATIVE INVESTMENTS:

a. **Hedge Funds:** Hedge funds are portfolios of funds that are managed using advanced investment strategies to generate high returns. Hedge funds are illiquid because investors are usually required to stay invested for at least one year. Having hedge funds in your portfolio can reduce your portfolio's overall risk because they may offset some of the other risk in your portfolio with their market position.

b. **Private Equity:** This is an asset class composed of securities and debt instruments from companies that are not publicly traded on a stock exchange.

Summary

It is essential to have clear financial goals, and knowing what you want and the dollar value of that goal at a determined date in the future is the crucial first step. While it might be fun to walk up to an airline counter and ask for a ticket to anywhere, most travelers have a strong idea of where they want to go, and so must you as an investor. When you know where you're going and how much it costs, you can set a plan for getting there. Otherwise you will just be will o' the wisp and float among the nebulous clouds at the whim of the breezes. This is not a good idea for your financial future!

Your concrete goals should be fashioned into short term, mid-term, and long-term goals as illustrated by the personal financial pyramid so the value of time can be determined and a plan put into action to achieve your goals based on a specific investment return. Your investment policy statement (IPS) is the rule book that instructs you on how to invest your money for the returns you need, and guides you on making decisions when the twin-headed monster of fear and greed appears.

When crafting your portfolio, you must consider the level of your willingness to accept risk, and also your capacity to accept risk. A determination must be made on whether you will favor an active, semi-passive, or conservative strategy based on your ability to accept risk in relation to the goals you desire. Ultimately you will have an investment portfolio that will need regular monitoring and occasional adjustment...because investing in the market requires an active presence.

The market is a dynamic environment and if you are doing your own investment management, there truly is no safe way to "set and forget"; there are different types of investors and traders, however, and in the next chapter you may find a style that best suits your personality and needs.

Chapter 3 Review Questions

1. The four essential elements of the investment process are:

   A. Understand your goals.
   B. Create an investment plan.
   C. Build your portfolio.
   D. Monitor investments and stay on course.
   E. All of the above.

2. The purpose of short-term financial goals is:

   A. To start an investment program.
   B. To set aside funds for college, or to start a new business.
   C. To satisfy your daily living expenses.
   D. To build enough savings to buy a house.

3. Mid-term financial goals focus on the next:

   A. 3-5 years.
   B. 3-10 years.
   C. 5-10 years.
   D. 8-15 years.

4. The Investment Policy Statement (IPS) is the blueprint for your investment plan. True or false?

   A. True.
   B. False.

5. Fundamental analysis is a method for studying a security's potential monetary value by forecasting its future price through a study of its market data, particularly its history of price and volume. True or false?

   A. True.
   B. False.

6. The efficient frontier is:

   A. The nexus point of highest return for a stated amount of risk.
   B. The nexus point of highest risk for a stated return.
   C. The nexus point of stated return for the most amount of risk.
   D. The nexus point of the least amount of risk for the least return.

Chapter 3 Review Answers

1. The four essential elements of the investment process are:

   A. Understand your goals.
   B. Create an investment plan.
   C. Build your portfolio.
   D. Monitor investments and stay on course.
   E. All of the above.

   Answer: E. All of the above. The process is clear: know where you want to go, make a plan to get there, follow the plan, observe your progress, and make adjustments as necessary.

2. The purpose of short-term financial goals is:

   A. To start an investment program.
   B. To set aside funds for college, or to start a new business.
   C. To satisfy your daily living expenses.
   D. To build enough savings to buy a house.

   Answer: C. To satisfy your daily living expenses. Short term goals build the foundation for a strong financial base, taking care of your immediate needs, with a little extra for emergencies.

3. Mid-term financial goals focus on the next:

   A. 3-5 years.
   B. 3-10 years.
   C. 5-10 years.
   D. 8-15 years.

   Answer: A. 3-5 years. Mid-term financial goals are intended to serve life's anticipated events, such as buying a vehicle, attending college, placing a down payment on a home, funding a wedding, or starting a business.

4. The Investment Policy Statement (IPS) is the blueprint for your investment plan. True or false?

   A. True.

B. False.

Answer: A. True. The Investment Policy Statement provides all the details about your tolerance for risk, your thoughts about core and non-core investments, and your philosophy on diversification...or not. The IPS also clearly states how you select investments, the features you want in investments, the impact you are willing to accept from taxes and investment fees, and your intentions for exiting an investment, among other details.

5. Fundamental analysis is a method for studying a security's potential monetary value by forecasting its future price through a study of its market data, particularly its history of price and volume. True or false?

   A. True.
   B. False.

   Answer: B. False. The question identifies technical analysis, not fundamental analysis. Fundamental analysis is a method for studying a security's potential monetary value by examining the underlying influences (fundamentals) of the security, such as economic and political conditions, competitive advantage, sales revenue, financial reserves, experience of its management, etc.

6. The efficient frontier is:

   A. The nexus point of highest return for a stated amount of risk.
   B. The nexus point of highest risk for a stated return.
   C. The nexus point of stated return for the most amount of risk.
   D. The nexus point of the least amount of risk for the least return.

   Answer: A. The nexus point of highest return for a stated amount of risk. The brilliance of the efficient frontier is that an investor can choose an acceptable level of risk for a portfolio, and then select assets with a potential for the most return at the chosen risk level.

Chapter 4
Are You an Investor or a Trader?

When you have finished reading this chapter, you will:

- Know the difference between an investor and a trader
- Be able to explain the difference between various types of investors and traders
- Realize the importance of having an investment philosophy
- Be familiar with the characteristics of a conservative investment
- Possess an introductory knowledge about the 11 different investment and trading styles
- Be able to explain the difference between a value investor and a growth investor
- Recognize if you are better suited as an investor or trader

Introduction

There are two types of people in the market today, investors and traders. Each one has a very distinct philosophy about creating wealth in the markets. Both methods generate profits and suffer losses depending on the acumen of the individual. Neither method is better than the other, though each has benefits and disadvantages. In this chapter we'll look at the different types of investors and traders so you can better determine which category and subcategory best suits your temperament for generating financial gain.

What is Your Investment Philosophy?

The best way to be successful as either an investor or a trader is to know yourself well. Some people only have a temperament for buying an asset based on a careful and scrupulous review of data, assuring themselves with a carefully considered choice. On the opposite side of this range, others have a temperament for rapidly buying and selling assets, holding positions for limited terms as long as a month or a week, or as slight as a day or an hour. You know just by reading this statement whether you are an investor or a trader, and everybody makes their own choice based on how comfortable they feel with buying and selling assets for profit.

As you read and learn about how the markets operate, you can begin to draw conclusions about how people make investment decisions and how those decisions influence the market and provide opportunities to your advantage. Volume, stochastics, trends, Elliott waves...these are all data interpretations of human behavior. By studying these indicators you can refine your view about how the markets behave. As you gain experience and confidence, you can devise strategies based on your perceptions, and eventually your strategies may result in profits.

Information:

A simple distinction between the two is that an investor typically holds an investment position while a trader typically buys and sells positions with frequency.

Of course, not having an investment philosophy can have a cost you are unwilling to pay. Without a set of beliefs about how the market works, you can be easily victimized by the lure of ephemeral strategies with little chance of success, or you could jump from strategy to strategy and pay unnecessary transaction fees and taxes.

Having an investment philosophy protects you from assuming too much risk, or engaging in markets that are unfamiliar. A philosophy can keep you mindful of your short term, mid-term, and long-term goals, and focused on the limitations of your time horizon. A philosophy helps guard against unsound asset diversification, chasing fads and trends, responding emotionally with fear and greed, and regretting decisions based on subjective decisions and overconfidence.

An investment philosophy is as important to your financial health as eating well and exercising is important to your physical health.

Emotional Decisions

People make decisions with their emotions or their mind, or a combination of both. It's very easy as an investor or a trader to allow your emotions to make decisions when you become caught in the fear and greed prevalent in the market. In those instances, your emotional instinct is to either sell as rapidly as you can to avoid painful losses, or buy as rapidly as you can to increase easy wealth. Decisions made with an emotional bias may sabotage your plans and cause substantial losses of money and time.

There are several different emotional states which can undermine your financial plan, which you'll recall, was made without duress and with the calm reflective capacities of your intellect, not during the excesses of your emotions! Here are some common emotions investors and traders are likely to experience when engaged in making decisions about their money:

EUPHORIA:

The state of intense excitement and happiness accompanying sudden and rapid wealth accumulation can feed an investor's or trader's sense of overconfidence and contribute to the "bubble" psychology of the market.

OVERCONFIDENCE:

When an investor or trader continues to do well over a sustained period of time, continuing success can create a false sense of one's spectacular abilities...even though the financial increases are more a result of a rising market than genetic sagacity. An investor or trader afflicted with overconfidence often does not see warning signs, or chooses to ignore them.

GREED:

Every investor and trader is laboring toward the achievement of a single ultimate goal: increasing the amount of money in their account. When that magical moment happens, and an investor or trader is profiting from the decision, the inclination is to add to the position and gather even more wealth more rapidly. Based on market conditions, that could be a good thing to do, as long as the decision is not based on emotions. The investor's or trader's intellect should remind them that the desire for more return also includes the possibility of increased risk.

FEAR:

After a difficult week or month, watching a portfolio's value steadily erode, investors and traders can lose their confidence and want to cash out their holdings in an effort to save something against the onslaught of downward prices. A decision to exit the position could result in both a lost opportunity as the market recovers, and lock in unnecessary losses.

DENIAL:

An unwanted situation is sometimes inappropriately ignored. The owner of an asset may become reluctant to recognize the need to take action and accept a loss, which means admitting failure.

Cognitive Decisions

Becoming aware of how your emotions feature in your investing or trading decisions is the first step toward eliminating this potentially harmful practice. Developing discipline is the second step. A well-designed plan, such as your Investment Policy Statement (IPS), can guide you through market turmoil, rewarding you with cognitive and rational decision-making at a time when your emotional composure is being shredded.

YOUR LONG-TERM INVESTMENT PLAN:

Having a written plan you can consult during market-induced emotional quandaries will provide the guidelines for financially sound cognitive, not emotional, behavior. Details such as when to sell and when to buy, developed during a time of relative tranquility, will provide you with a steady mind for making important decisions, releasing you from making haphazard choices during periods of emotional crisis.

REVIEW YOUR PROGRESS ON A REGULAR SCHEDULE:

Although the industry standard for performance reporting is quarterly, an annual portfolio review is regarded as a good pattern for checking your assets and determining if they are performing as originally expected. As the markets rise and fall, the value of your assets will also experience price adjustments, and this is expected. If you observe an alarming change in an asset's value, this is a good time to study the circumstances more closely. Is it time to sell? Is it time to add to your position? What does your Investment Policy Statement (IPS) confirm as your correct response? Did you write an exit strategy for each asset, and what was your determination when circumstances were calmer?

Key:

It is an excellent idea to review your portfolio annually; an annual review is a long enough time period to know if you should consider making changes to your asset selection... and to your IPS. Another excellent idea is to let your active manager do their job and manage the portfolio. Excessive portfolio review can lead to poor decisions resulting from ad-hoc portfolio decisions based on emotion.

Reviewing your portfolio every twelve months allows you to get the Big Picture. You won't be engaged with the daily turbulence of the markets or get caught up with pennies when you need to stay focused on dollars. This is also a good time to reflect on your Investment Policy Statement (IPS) and consider whether the value of its guidelines is continuing to serve you, or if you have a different set of interests that would be better served with adjustments. Spending periodic quality time with your IPS and your portfolio is the best way to maintain familiarity with the financial information so vital to your future. "Set and forget" might be good for a slow cooker...not for your investment accounts!

MAINTAIN YOUR ASSET ALLOCATION PLAN:

During your annual review, you'll want to check your asset allocations to confirm they are still within the percentage allotments required by your Investment Policy Statement (IPS). This is a topic that will be explored more thoroughly in this book, but for now and in general, you want to assure that your assets are allocated as you originally planned. This is because your investment plan was deliberately structured with certain weightings, so you have the best opportunity for growth with limited risk.

If the allocations deteriorate, your portfolio may or may not bring you the results you desire. A quarterly review will help you determine whether or not you are still on course with your original plan. If not, you should realign your portfolio with your plan's asset allocations or consider an adjustment to your plan if a cognitive review, not an emotional one, suggests the need for an improved strategy.

WHEN IN DOUBT, VISIT YOUR FINANCIAL PLANNER:

One of the best pieces of advice you'll read in this book is the recommendation to keep a periodic appointment with a qualified fiduciary advisor...a trained professional such as a Registered Investment Advisor (RIA) whose primary responsibility, as a fiduciary, is to put your needs first. To sing an old refrain, unless you have years of professional experience and are spending many hours a week studying and actively engaging with the markets, you are a minnow among sharks. This may not be what you want to hear because everyone is a Superman in front of their mirror, but the truth is you're playing with fire. Yes, you might be successful up to a point, but without the experiential knowledge and training that takes years to acquire, sooner or later you're going to fly off a cliff.

Definition:

Qualified fiduciary advisor, such as a Registered Investment Advisor (RIA).

A qualified fiduciary advisor, such as a Registered Investment Advisor (RIA), is a trained professional who provides financial information about all aspects of financial planning and makes recommendations in the best interests of his or her client.

It's worth paying for a professional consultation to make sure you are not on a one-way track to oblivion. This is your money! Why would you risk the loss of financial resources (remember negative compounding) and lost investment time...which you can never get back...on the grand assumption that you know everything you need to know? If you've ever made an investment mistake, you understand the value of meeting with a professional advisor from time to time, or even the wisdom of having a professional financial expert manage your funds for you.

Figure 27: Know or No?

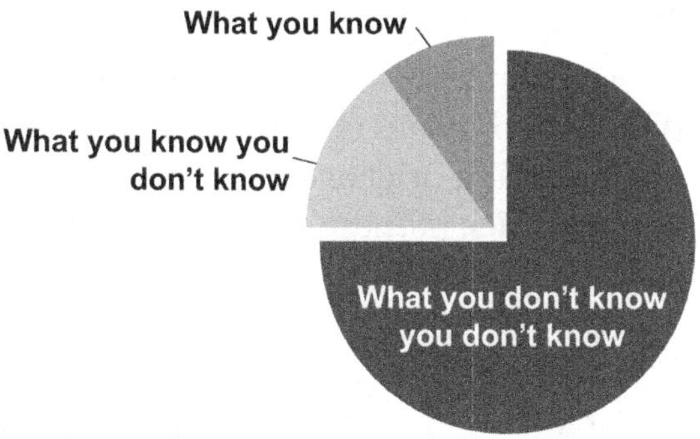

LEARN PATIENCE:

Building wealth prudently often takes time, so steer your expectations toward steady growth. There will be times when a sudden windfall will come your way, and that will be cause for celebration. However, the gradual accumulation of wealth, while taking proper care for avoiding undue risk, is the best way to reach your financial goals. Patient progress is more likely to achieve your eventual success than creating and suffering with the anxiety caused by impulsiveness.

Quite simply, money can be a very emotional subject for people. The desire to have a safer car, a nicer house, a welcome vacation, a paid college education for the children or a life of ease in retirement...these are a few of the wonderful things that money provides. The lack of sufficient money can manifest the dread of being inadequate to meet one's needs and responsibilities, and living with disappointment or worse.

There can be no doubt that passion has a part to play with the accumulation of wealth because passion creates the drive to stay disciplined and keep focused on the goals which may take decades to achieve...but it's the sensible planning and the curbing of emotions, the dedication to the intellect as the arbiter of decisions that provide the results for which investors and traders are striving.

Be ruled by your plan and by your mind. When investing or trading, these are the tools that will bring your harvest home.

Investor vs. Trader

The market needs both investors and traders. Each serves a function that supports market activity and provides either stability or fluidity through their separate roles. Here is a brief overview of their functions and their differences. Consider which of these market participants most suits your own style of profiting from the activity of the market.

INVESTOR:

The distinguishing factor that identifies an investor is that the investor chooses to build wealth by purchasing and holding investment instruments over a reasonably lengthy period of time, usually years and sometimes decades. An investor's profits may increase through the benefits of compounding, by reinvesting dividends through the purchase of additional stock, and through stock splits. These advantages are available to the investor because of the function of time.

When a downtrend depresses the price of their assets, an investor usually expects prices to recover because an investor's focus is on market fundamentals such as a stock's price-earnings ratio and other significant details such as good products, loyal customers and solid management. An investor takes the long-term view and wants to own shares in a company that is making money now and will continue to make money in the future.

TRADER:

On the other hand, a trader is only interested in the short-term view, choosing to engage in more frequent buying and selling. The goal of the trader is to generate rapid profits; while an investor might be delighted with a 10% annual return, traders might seek a return of that size every month. Instead of using fundamental analysis, which is the hallmark of investors, traders often prefer to use technical analysis such as volume and moving averages to identify market situations that will give them a high probability of substantial profit.

Note:

There are four general categories of traders:

Scalp Trader: A position is held for only a few seconds or a few minutes.
Day Trader: A position is held for the day only, and not overnight.
Swing Trader: A position is held for a few days or weeks.
Position Trader: A position is held for a few months or years.

Both investors and traders offer advantages to the market. Investors are good for companies because their buy-and-hold investment provides funds the company can rely upon for long term growth, while traders provide liquidity with their steady buying and selling, allowing the efficient exchange of assets between people wanting to enter or exit their positions.

Would you profit more as an investor or a trader? It's up to you to decide which one best suits your personality. If you like fast action, staying focused on market timing, and making money quickly with the risks entailed, being a trader could be the best choice for you. If you prefer long term investing and steady growth without the anxiety of quick decisions, being an investor is probably better.

Conservative

Being a conservative investor does not mean having low-risk, low-return expectations. While it is true that a conservative investor invests in stocks that are most likely to preserve the original capital and generate profits with the least potential for risk, a conservative investor also understands the characteristics of an asset that is properly considered a conservative investment.

What are the characteristics of a conservative investment?

Safety. A conservative investment must be able to resist the pressures of a downward-trending market better than other investments. One of the ways a business can do this is by having a low cost of production; for example, if the cost of resources increases, this company should still be able to generate a profit or suffer a smaller loss. In addition, a company of this type needs to have a strong research department so new products can keep the company in front of its competitors. A strong marketing department is also essential.

Management and Employees. The management team should have astute financial skills to help the company cut waste and improve efficiencies, etc. the company also needs a solid organization that creates a culture of employee loyalty and strong work ethic.

The Company and its Industry Sector. A conservative investor should also consider both the advantages and disadvantages that face the company presently and in the future. The inquiry should focus on whether or not the company can continue to sustain growth and generate more profits, or if such factors as competition or regulation might curtail optimistic conjecture.

Therefore, when a conservative investor is interested in making a conservative investment, and investigative process should be followed to assure the investor that not only is his or her money relatively safe, but also has the potential for a significantly worthy profit.

Moderate-Balanced

The moderate investor seeks a balance between risk and return. Normally a balanced portfolio has a fairly equal collection of equities and fixed-income securities. A balanced investment strategy is for investors with an investment horizon of over five years who are willing to tolerate a higher degree of risk than the conservative investor. A moderate portfolio, also known as a balanced portfolio, may have a fairly precise 50/50 split between stocks and bonds, or it might favor stocks with a 60/40 split. Stock assets can be from large companies, small companies, international stocks, etc., and the bond component could include government bonds, corporate bonds, foreign bonds, etc.

With a 50/50 or 60/40 mix, the moderate investor has a healthy exposure to the rewards and risks of the stock market without the potential excesses of a portfolio with 100% stocks. The bonds provide a stabilizing effect to the stock market's gyrations and may also contribute some income as well.

There is always a risk with investments, and in this case the risk is two-fold. First, a balanced portfolio can lose value if the stock market drops and stays depressed for a length of time, or the bond holdings are compromised by climbing interest rates. Second, the efficient use of time is always a resource worth protecting, and a balanced portfolio may not be capable of earning the returns necessary in the time available to the investor. A moderate-balanced investment strategy might be right for certain investors, but not for others.

Aggressive

The aggressive investor is willing to accept a high degree of risk for a high return. The primary investment objective is the rapid appreciation of capital, which means a high allocation of stocks and other high-risk classes such as commodities. There are varying degrees of aggressive portfolios; a portfolio with 80% stocks and 20% fixed income is less aggressive than a portfolio with 90%/10%. Also, a portfolio with a high degree of blue chip stocks is probably less aggressive than a portfolio with small cap stocks...so the composition of the portfolio must be individually considered to determine the degree of its aggressiveness.

A portfolio with an aggressive strategy requires more dedicated attention than a conservative or balanced portfolio because changes to its value are likely to be more rapid and more extreme...either for good or ill. The aggressive investor will also probably need to make more allocation adjustments because the portfolio's asset classes are subject to disproportionate distribution as the subclasses expand or contract.

Speculator

A speculator is a person who trades equities, bonds, currencies or commodities with a higher than normal risk for a higher than normal return, sometimes through the futures or options markets. The speculator is not basing the decision to speculate on the underlying fundamentals of the asset but on indicators such as volume, chart anomalies, moving averages, and annual highs and lows where there may be an opportunity for a large, quick profit. The risk is high, but so also may be the return. While there are people who succeed as speculators, this is a situation where you must really know what you're doing and be willing to lose the entire stake.

A stock speculator looks for short-term advantages in the price of stocks, and buys or sells stocks frequently. This type of trader is not interested in the company's products, or their management, or anything about the company except the price per share. Stock traders believe the price per share is incorrect and will soon be adjusted in their favor.

Asset Allocator

An investor who subscribes to an asset allocation model supports the philosophy of balancing reward and risk by apportioning his or her portfolio's resources in a distribution tailored to their investment goals with the degree of risk tolerance particular to their circumstances and according to the time available for achieving the financial success they have planned. An investor using this strategy carefully assigns different investment amounts to the three main asset classes of equities, fixed income, and cash, and specifically to the subclasses within each, mindful that the risk and return among the subclasses is varied and will yield different results.

Focus Investor

A focus investor concentrates their portfolio on stocks which they believe will perform extremely well; they then purchase a large position on the expectation that their selection will result in a large profit. A focus investor believes it is more sensible and profitable to add to an existing successful position rather than take a chance by investing in an untried asset. Investments are infrequent and occur only when there is a high degree of confidence in the asset's strong performance.

Being a focus investor requires intelligent portfolio management. A focus investor must carefully consider how many stocks the portfolio should hold, how big a position should be, the diversification of the portfolio, when to expand the position, and when to sell part or all of the holding.

Focus investing is a good strategy for acquiring high long term returns, once the investor has determined how to identify stocks that meet the criteria, the acceptable range of their portfolio's diversification, how much risk can be tolerated, and acquired some experience with trades of this type to more completely comprehend the subtleties of buying and selling large positions.

Stock Trader

When it comes to buying and selling stocks, there are typically two types of stock traders, those who purchase a company's stock because of its unrecognized value, and those who purchase a company's stock because of its potential for growth. Here is a more detailed explanation:

Value

A value investor looks for companies whose share price undervalues the company's intrinsic worth. By purchasing shares that are undervalued, a value investor believes that the value of the company will eventually be realized by the market and the share price will rise accordingly, providing a healthy profit.

By seeking companies of this type, a value investor has a built-in margin of safety that reduces the risk of losing money. An astute value investor does his or her due diligence by analyzing the company's value, concluding that the value of the company is more than is currently reflected in its share price, thus indicating that further reduction is unlikely to be steep or costly. A value investor's expectation is that the market has misjudged the value of the company, and that over a period of time the market will realize its error and re-value the share price at a higher amount.

While the margin of safety is a positive feature of value investing, this strategy requires the value investor do a high degree of analysis before purchasing the company's stock. This strategy also requires a high degree of confidence in the value investor's abilities to analyze company data. Furthermore, a value investor must have a well-developed sense of patience because it is unlikely that there will be an indication of when the company's share price will appreciate.

Value investors typically invest in companies in which they possess a developed degree of competence, affording them the ability to more completely recognize a company that is undervalued. This allows them to identify companies with the potential for a long-lasting competitive advantage.

Note:

Another desirable feature for value investors is when the company is owned by insiders, indicating that the management has confidence in its products and mission.

Successful value investors never follow the herd or chase a hot tip because they are often in the role of contrarian, and regard fads and tips with a high degree of suspicion. A value investor will always take the time to carefully analyze a company's fundamentals before making a decision to purchase.

Some of the reasons why a company's share price may be undervalued are:

1. Some companies go unnoticed because they are not yet well known and have not received widespread notice. Value investors look for companies like this because their fundamental criteria could be exceptional while their value and share price are still unrecognized.

2. There are times during the year when a company's share price may ebb because the company is in a cyclical industry, or due to the effects of the economy. These natural influences may not have any bearing on the company's intrinsic worth, making a company like this an attractive purchase for value investors.

3. Many investors are irrational, investing their money for emotional reasons, not analytical reasons. Investors may regret they didn't sell their stock sooner, and this herd mentality could drive down the share price of all the stocks in a particular industry sector. When this happens, value investors carefully filter the availability of good companies available for bargain prices.

4. Market analysts sometimes have a strong influence on the way investors think about a company and its stock. Analysts are not always capable of seeing the future, but because of their influence, a company's share price could drop. A value investor could take a closer look at the analyst's commentary yet make a completely different determination. Sometimes analysts are like movie critics; they get so involved in the characters and the plot

that they don't see the movie's potential for a pleasant evening out.

5. Companies that are not sexy may be undervalued because they blend into the proverbial wallpaper. A hot technology stock is likely to get a lot more press coverage and attention than a company making health foods for infants and young children. Value investors are like the people you see going to antique stores and garage sales; they don't mind picking through a stack of bituminous coal for a hidden diamond.

6. A company might have a division that is underperforming, though the rest of the company is quite solid. The market might view this situation in a negative light, causing the price share to diminish. However, a value investor will consider investing in a company with this circumstance if there is some indication that the division will be improved or terminated. Information from the management team about the prospects of this underachieving division could yield some profitable clues.

7. No one likes bad news, and this goes double for investors. Sometimes a company is the harbinger of an unfortunate circumstance. An unprofitable quarter, the loss of a founder, a product recall, litigation, or perhaps a government regulation requirement can all be the sponsor of a share price reduction. The mass hysteria that could occur will likely drive down the price of the company's shares. However, these are the kinds of events that attract the attention of value investors because while the herd turns and runs away, the value investor could take the contrary position that an opportunity for a discounted purchase may be at hand.

The contrary investment life of a value investor requires the ability to carefully scrutinize companies to determine whether or not the share price is a true indication of a company's actual worth. While this work may be time-consuming, the benefits could be rewarding.

Growth

An investor who is interested in the growth potential of a company is focused on finding companies whose earnings are likely to grow more rapidly than the average rate of its industry or the market as a whole. Growth investing is also known as "capital growth" because the investor's goal is to maximize capital gains.

Morningstar, the independent investment research company, classifies all stocks as being either a growth, value, or a blended growth and value investment.

Growth investing means that an investor is looking for companies with the most growth potential, as opposed to a value investor who is looking for companies with unrecognized intrinsic value.

Note:

Several categories of growth stocks are known to historically have the greatest growth potential: Small cap, technology, healthcare, and speculative stocks.

Small Cap Stocks. A small cap company is usually defined as a company that has a capitalization between $300 million and $2 billion. Because small cap companies are often in the initial growth phase of development, their potential for rapid growth and share price appreciation can be substantial.

Technology and Healthcare Stocks. Because of advances in technology and healthcare, companies in this category are often poised for meteoric growth if their products are innovative and become popular.

Speculative Stocks. Some investors look for high-risk growth in such companies as precious metals companies, oil and gas drilling companies, real estate development, and other aggressive ventures.

Growth investors study certain key factors to determine if a company will sustain sufficient capital growth. Return on Equity (ROE) informs a potential investor about the amount of profit the company makes with the equity provided by shareholders. Earnings Per Share (EPS) is another indicator of how well a company is doing; investors look for companies whose EPS continues to increase over time. A third key indicator is projected earnings that also trend upward. These are just a few examples of the key factors that may attract growth investors.

While some investors maintain that value investing and growth investing are different investment strategies, Warren Buffett disagreed, stating in his annual letter to Berkshire Hathaway shareholders in 2000, "Market commentators and investment managers who glibly refer to 'growth' and 'value' styles as contrasting approaches to investment are displaying their ignorance, not their sophistication." Mr. Buffett's point is that growth is an important part of analyzing a company's value, not a distinct investment style.

The intrinsic value of a company is the commodity that investors purchase when they buy shares. A good investor always wants a good value for a good price. Unless your analysis reveals differently, there is no point purchasing shares in a company that is not performing well or whose potential is unknown or diminishing. Your analysis as an investor is critically important...you are investing your money with the intention of making more money. The last thing you want to do is invest your money in a company where you're going to lose it!

Your ability to analyze the prospects of the company and accept a reasonable risk for the profit you estimate you will receive is the essential issue of your success as an investor. For this reason, studying everything you can about stock analysis, and acquiring the experience of buying, holding, and selling stocks is the single most essential element of your venture as an investor. If you are unable to dedicate the time to become an expert analyst, then you should seek the services of a fiduciary advisor who can do this critically important work for you.

Important:

Studying everything you can about stock analysis, and acquiring the experience of buying, holding, and selling stocks is the single most essential element of your venture as an investor.

In summary, a value investor looks for companies that are performing at a lower than average rate; the assumption is that the company's share price has been misjudged and undervalued by the market, and when the market realizes its error, the share price will rise. The risk for the value investor is that the market may not have made a mistake in its analysis of the company's intrinsic value, and the share price will never increase. The growth investor seeks companies that have an above average growth rate that indicate a continuance of capital growth and share price. The risk for the growth investor is that the growth may not continue and share price will diminish, creating an investment loss. Mr. Buffett has added to this discussion by stating that value investing and growth investing are not distinctly different investment styles, but rather both play an important role when analyzing a company as a good investment.

Momentum Trend Following

This is an investment or trading strategy in which an investor or trader identifies a trend, either rising or falling. Once the trend has been identified and meets the requirements for purchase, the investor or trader rides the trend until a predetermined exit point. The intention is to ride the trend and "let profits run". Sometimes investors or traders choose to enter and exit a position multiple times, depending on their analysis of the trend's potential, or as their analysis adjusts with new data. Sometimes a position can last for weeks or months, or can be as short as a few days, hours or even minutes.

Dividend Capture

There is also a dividend capture strategy in which an investor purchases a company's stock in anticipation of the issuance of stock dividends, holding the stock just long enough to receive the dividend, and then selling the stock as soon as possible after the dividend has been paid. Investors are advised to carefully study this strategy because there are a number of details that could result in a negative outcome, such as incorrect timing, transaction costs, taxes, and the potential of the stock to suffer a decreased share price during the transaction period. However, if the investor is sufficiently prepared, the dividend capture strategy could return a healthy profit.

Options Trader

An options trader purchases the option to buy or sell a stock or commodity at a certain price within a certain time period; the price and the time period are specified by the options trader when the option is purchased.

The options trader buys a call if he or she thinks the price of the underlying stock or commodity will rise during the specified time, or a put if he or she thinks the price will decline within the timeframe indicated. The value of the option depends on how high the price rises with a call option, or how low the price decreases with a put option, and this determines the profit or loss the options trader will enjoy or suffer by the expiration date of the call or the put. If the call or the put is sold before the expiration date, the call or put may have a price value which the options trader then receives.

A key advantage with trading options is that the purchase of the call and put options cost less than buying the investment itself. This allows the options trader to leverage their buying power, and if they are successful with their options trading, they may receive a larger profit with a smaller investment of capital. It's also true that an options trader can quickly see the value of their options erode, and may have to vacate their position to save what remains of their purchase.

An options trader has a variety of different strategies available for turning a profit whether the market goes up, down, or sideways. Combinations of calls and puts on the same stock or commodity will yield different results that may add to profits or safeguard against losses. Risk can be limited with stop-loss orders, while a trending position can be supplemented with more option purchases. Options are a worthwhile investment tool, providing the options trader has spent sufficient time learning the strategies and gained practical experience.

Summary

This chapter began by asking the question, "Are you an investor or a trader?" There are many types of both, so it remains for you to consider which of this variety is best suited to your temperament for making profits and taking risks.

The first question to resolve is how much risk you are willing to take, realizing that what you perceive now as the level of your willingness may turn out to be quite different in actual practice. People are sometimes braver on paper than they are in real situations where greed and fear come into play.

The next question is a determination of how much money you want to make through investing or trading. The answer to this question is based on your financial goals, which should identify an exact dollar number; you know this number because you've calculated it by pricing out the dollar value of the goals you've set. Too often, investors and traders have ambiguous financial goals, and this leads to a strong sense of insecurity. Without knowing what you want or need, you can never have enough.

The final question is knowing how long you plan to invest your money. With an investment time horizon, you can better decide which investments and which style of investment is the best choice for you. If you only have a limited time to achieve your goals, knowing that you can guarantee your goals will become a determining factor in the investments and investment style you choose. If you have a longer-term investment, you might decide to tolerate more risk.

Whether you are an investor or a trader, knowing the answer to these three questions are essential to your financial success.

Chapter 4 Review Questions

1. The advantage of having an investment philosophy is:

    A. You can afford to take risky chances.
    B. You can limit your fear of being too greedy.
    C. You always know the best way to increase your wealth.
    D. You have a set of well-defined beliefs that guide your decisions.

2. The difference between an investor and a trader is that the investor:

    A. Purchases and holds investments over time.
    B. Often reinvests dividends in the holding.
    C. Wants to own shares in a company that will continue to make money.
    D. All of the above.

3. Which of the following is not true for a focus investor?

    A. A focus investor concentrates their portfolio on stocks which they believe will perform extremely well.
    B. A focus investor looks for short term advantages in the price of stocks, and buys or sells stocks frequently.
    C. A focus investor believes it is more sensible and profitable to add to an existing successful position rather than take a chance by investing in an untried asset.
    D. A focus investor must carefully consider the diversification of the portfolio, when to expand the position, and when to sell part or all of the holding.

4. Which of the following statements is true?

    A. A value investor looks for companies that are performing at a lower than average rate.
    B. The growth investor seeks companies that have an above average growth rate that indicate a continuance of capital growth and share price.
    C. Both statements are true.

D. Both statements are false.

Chapter 4 Review Answers

1. The advantage of having an investment philosophy is:

   A. You can afford to take risky chances.
   B. You can limit your fear of being too greedy.
   C. You always know the best way to increase your wealth.
   D. You have a set of well-defined beliefs that guide your decisions.

   Answer: D. You have a set of well-defined beliefs that guide your decisions. A philosophy is an understanding of how a system functions, from which you can create your Investment Policy Statement (IPS) that guides your decisions.

2. The difference between an investor and a trader is that the investor:

   A. Purchases and holds investments over time.
   B. Often reinvests dividends in the holding.
   C. Wants to own shares in a company that will continue to make money.
   D. All of the above.

   Answer: D. All of the above. An investor takes a long-term view; the trader is only interested in short term profits.

3. Which of the following is not true for a focus investor?

   A. A focus investor concentrates their portfolio on stocks which they believe will perform extremely well.
   B. A focus investor looks for short term advantages in the price of stocks, and buys or sells stocks frequently.
   C. A focus investor believes it is more sensible and profitable to add to an existing successful position rather than take a chance by investing in an untried asset.
   D. A focus investor must carefully consider the diversification of the portfolio, when to expand the position, and when to sell part or all of the holding.

Answer: B. A stock speculator, not a focus investor, looks for short term advantages in the price of stocks, and buys or sells stocks frequently.

4. Which of the following statements is true?

   A. A value investor looks for companies that are performing at a lower than average rate.
   B. The growth investor seeks companies that have an above average growth rate that indicate a continuance of capital growth and share price.
   C. Both statements are true.
   D. Both statements are false.

   Answer: C. Both statements are true. Value investors look for companies that are undervalued; growth investors seek companies that show signs of continuing rapid growth.

Chapter 5
Genie in the Bottle

When you have finished reading this chapter, you will:

- Know the five steps to financial freedom
- Understand the three investment stages of a person's life
- Be able to explain the six different ways to generate income from your investments
- Be familiar with several ideas for generating income in retirement

Introduction

The title of this chapter may be a bit creative, but it certainly makes its point. Making money with money is magical, but not everyone is a good sorcerer. It takes a lot of training and experience to know how to invest safely and wisely so you receive a healthy return for limited risk. The word "healthy" is important because safe and wise investment is not about earning the highest return. This was explained in Chapter 1 when we discussed negative compounding. A healthy return is one in which you achieve your annual investment goals, and only by taking a reasonable risk.

Everyone has a genie in the bottle, but not everyone knows how to make a wish that secures their financial stability and future well-being. As we've said before, both in this book and our others (*Exit Insight: Getting to "Sold!"* and *401(k) Insight: Getting to "Retired!"*), you can be successful only when you know your goals. Most investors, and there are millions and millions of investors, don't really know how to set concrete financial goals for their investments. Instead of knowing exactly what they want to achieve, most investors think in nebulous terms, and because of this, their results are usually less rewarding than they could otherwise be.

Some investors know they want to have a comfortable life in retirement, but they have not measured the actual price for it. Does retirement mean living in a home on a beach in Florida, or a condominium in Arizona? Does a comfortable life in retirement mean having an international vacation once a year, or visiting the grandchildren four times a year? What are the annual living costs 10, 20, 30 years in the future? How does inflation impact living expenses that far ahead? What monetary resources will you have in retirement, such as Social Security, a company pension, a company 401(k) account, rental income from properties you own, etc.? How will taxes affect your income stream? Do you wish to leave an estate for your heirs?

THE FIVE STEPS TO FINANCIAL FREEDOM:

All these details can be evaluated with the help of a financial advisor. Frankly, it's a serious mistake not to clarify your goals from today forward to your eventual demise. The first step is knowing what you want, and the second step is finding out exactly what it costs. The third step is carefully creating a plan that will guide you with achieving the financial goals you desire. The fourth step is following your plan. The fifth step is monitoring your results and making adjustments to stay aligned with your plan.

It may seem strange that you can actually determine the exact amount of dollars you need to live the life you wish, for ALL your goals, including short-term goals, intermediate goals, and long-term goals, but it's so. This figure can be calculated by a fiduciary advisor; this professional can also help create all the tools you need so you can step onto your path and travel through the years with steady success toward your goals. Remember, if you don't know where you're going, you might never arrive, and if you do arrive, you may not know you're there!

Most investors, and this is a casual observation not based on statistics, know they have to have a lot of money to enjoy the bounty that life offers...but because they don't know exactly the amount they need to achieve their dreams, they believe they never have enough. This usually leads to a life of financial anxiety because they're never sure of their goal and don't have a sensible plan to acquire it. They choose to live on an endless hamster wheel, discontented with their successes and afraid of a future they have not defined. They can never leave the treadmill because there is always a nagging need to acquire more. If you don't know what you need, how do you ever know if you have enough?

Now imagine instead an investor who has taken the time to look into the crystal ball of their future and visualized what a satisfactory life looks like. Few people dream of having 12 Mercedes, a few billion in the bank, and a home-of-the-month in a dozen international cities. Sure, win the mega-millions lottery and you could buy a condo on the moon, but most people are realistic in their desire to enjoy life, own their home, help the kids with college, eat well, have a few vacations now and again, and enjoy a fulfilling hobby while sharing their life with their special loved one.

Note:

If you don't know where you're going, you might never arrive, and if you do arrive, you may not know you're there!

The good news is two-fold: It is possible to calculate the amount of money you'll need in the future to enjoy the lifestyle you envision, and it is also possible to carefully invest over a period of time to acquire the funds you need to live that lifestyle. There is, of course, an assumption.

The assumption is that you have enough time to invest your money so you can earn the sum you need without undue risk. Time is your best friend. If you don't have sufficient time, then you either have to tolerate increased risk with the threat of loss, or consider an alternate lifestyle. However, if you do have enough time, and the amount of time you need is variable depending upon your financial goals, you should regard yourself as one of the most fortunate beings on Earth. That's because you have a veritable genie in the bottle.

The genie is the tools you need and the resources you have available, and the bottle is the ever-fluid market with thousands of investment choices, all of them either moving up, down, or sideways, with the possibility of your investments earning a regular return that eventually will bring you to your financial destination. "May the odds be ever in your favor" is an expression that applies to you because you truly have everything you need at your disposal, if you choose to wisely apply the tools and the knowledge offered to you in this book.

Important:

Tools and resources to help you become financially independent:

Tools:

1. The Investment Policy Statement (IPS)
2. Your investment goals
3. Your Required Rate of Return (RRR) ...
   to be discussed...

Resources:

1. Professional fiduciary investment advice
2. Time
3. The information in this book

In the next section, we're going to take a close look at the three different investment stages that every person will face. This is one of those facts about life that no one can avoid because it is organic to the human condition. It's easy to understand because it's so obvious and simple, and yet, as with most simple ideas, it can also be deeply profound.

Investment Stages

We like to call this concept the Lifestyle Protection Plan because it explains the dynamics of a person's three stages of financial life. Please take a look at Figure 30, Lifestyle Protection Planning. You'll notice that there are three sections: the wealth accumulation phase, the wealth spending phase, and the wealth distribution phase.

Figure 28: Lifestyle Protection Planning.

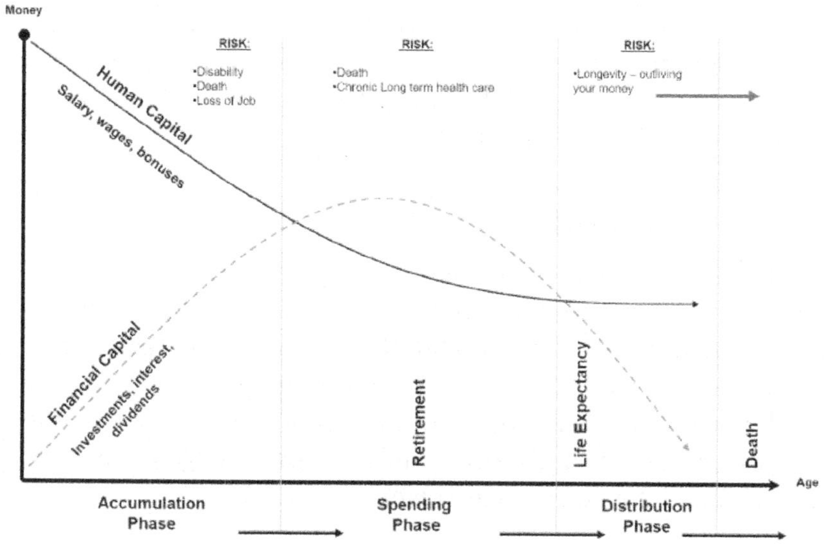

Wealth Accumulation

In the first phase, when people are young, they possess a lot of human capital, which means they generally have good health, a strong body, a lot of energy, and a desire to work hard to enjoy a good life over the course of their remaining 60 or 70 years.

Something they typically lack is financial capital, because most people start out needing to find a job, develop good work skills, and improve their abilities so they can increase their salary as their experience and value to the company increases or, if self-employed, develop their business into a position of substance.

This is the time of life when people usually get married, have children, consider buying a house, and want to enjoy the perks of young adulthood. Because they are at the early stages of wealth accumulation, there normally isn't a lot of extra cash for extended pleasures and experiences. There may be college loan debt, credit card debt, a mortgage that may be a little bit too big, children's dental bills, etc.

There are also several risks that need to be accommodated: disability insurance is necessary to protect the many years of human capital that lie ahead; life insurance is a wise choice in case of premature death and the resulting financial burden of the survivors; and a savings account containing at least nine months of salary could also provide a needed resource in case of job loss. As the years roll by, human capital diminishes as financial capital increases.

Wealth Spending

In this phase, people begin thinking more seriously about their approaching retirement, or have entered retirement. While they are still accumulating financial capital, they are also recognizing the need to preserve their gains for use during the length of their Golden Years. Their home may be nearly paid off, their debt is under control, they are enjoying their grandchildren, and can now indulge themselves with personal interests such as travel.

The risks they face are now mostly related to their health. Because their human capital is nearly spent, medical issues may become more significant. The need for long term health care must now be recognized and steps taken to prepare for this potential situation. Death is also an increasingly proximate outcome, so steps should be taken to preserve their estate so their survivors may benefit.

Wealth Distribution

The third stage encompasses the final years of life when human capital dissipates completely and financial capital must now be used to sustain the individual in the final years of life, and to plan for passing on their wealth to the next generation. This could be a period of as much as 20 – 30 years; with medical and technological advances extending the general population's life span, more and more people may find themselves living too long, which is to say, longer than their available funds.

In summary, most people's lives have changing needs and expectations as they move through these three phases. This is why it is so important to make good use of your resources and the miracle of time to establish the foundation of your financial security as soon as possible.

Income

There are multiple reasons why a person chooses to become an investor. Some investors are focused on their long term goal of having a comfortable retirement, while other investors are more interested in a combination of investing for the future and also receiving a steady stream of income to either pay bills or augment their current lifestyle by having more cash available for personal interests.

Generating Current Income

Of course, as usual, there are the three basic caveats when selecting investments for their cash-generating ability: your time horizon, your risk tolerance, and diversifying sufficiently to achieve the best rate of return with limited risk.

INCOME PRODUCING ASSETS:

Here are six different types of income producing assets.

1. **Bonds.** Bonds are a traditional vehicle for providing income, and there is a wide variety of bonds and bond funds from which to choose. A bond portfolio might include municipal bonds offered by a local or regional government raising funds for a new library or building a new road. Corporate bonds are debt issued by companies to raise funds for purposes generally related to a company's growth. U.S. Treasury securities are debt issued by the United States government; there are also agency bonds and mortgage-related securities. Bond mutual funds provide investors with professional management, while bond index funds can help bond investors earn benchmark averages.

Within the category of bonds are a wide variety of interest rates, maturity rates, and bond strategies an investor can use for structuring the amount and frequency of desired income. Because the variety extends across a broad range of choices, it is recommended that you seek the advice of a professional such as a fiduciary advisor. It just makes good sense to protect your investments and make your money work as efficiently and effectively as possible so you benefit as completely as circumstances offer. Always remember that you may not know all the possibilities available to you, and there is no point missing out on an arrangement that may help you reach your financial goals faster and safer.

2. REITs and Real Estate. A REIT, or real estate investment trust, is an entity that buys and sells real estate for the investors in its professionally managed portfolio. A REIT may also develop and manage real estate. Some of the investment properties included in a REIT may be housing developments, shopping malls, office buildings, skyscrapers, or apartment buildings. You can find REITs trading on the stock exchange, while others are privately held. REITs can be a good source for income. Of course, you can also invest in properties independently to receive rental income, but you should be prepared for the responsibilities of being a landlord.

3. Annuities. Annuities may be another good source of income. Usually purchased through an insurance company, an annuity can guarantee scheduled payouts of income, assuming the issuer is solvent. Payouts can be monthly, quarterly or yearly and the funds you elect to receive can be fixed or variable. You can also choose to receive your funds over a set period of time, or over the course of your lifetime, or over the course of a survivor's lifetime. You can also choose to make draws against your annuity at your own discretion. Annuities can be complicated, and you should read the prospectus with care to understand the investment objectives, risks, fees and expenses before signing the annuity contract.

4. Distribution Funds. Distribution funds are mutual funds specializing in stocks or bonds that pay income. These funds are structured so they pay a certain amount of income over a specified amount of time, but because of market fluctuations, there is no guarantee that the investment will consistently provide the advertised return. Still, in the right market environment, these funds might be a good choice.

5. Dividend-Paying Stock. Dividends from companies that share their profits with stockholders might be a good source of income for you. Be aware, however, that there are a number of restrictions that may preclude the value of this type of investment. For example, dividends from common stock are not ordinarily guaranteed as the shareholders of preferred stock are paid first; also, the board of directors could vote to limit the size of the dividend or even cancel them altogether. In addition, there are other details that warrant careful review, such as taxes and conditions on how long the stock must be held before dividends are paid. Even so, this may still be a worthy investment for you; several mutual funds offer dividend-paying stock. They may be called equity-income funds, growth and income funds, or simply income funds.

6. Certificates of Deposit (CDs). CDs pay a fixed amount of interest over a defined period of time. CDs are usually offered in three-month, six-month, and annual multiples of time, with varying degrees of interest depending on both the length of the investment term and the amount of funds invested. Interest is not paid until the CD matures, and if the CD is cashed-in before its maturity date, a penalty will be charged. If you are seeking a steady flow of income from CDs, you would have to structure your purchases so you receive your interest-earned income on a schedule that most benefits you. CDs are insured by the FDIC, but only up to $250,000 per depositor per bank, so if you are investing large sums of money in CDs, you will need to diversify your CDs among several banks. Also note there are brokered CDs which have different features, so find out before you buy.

TAXABLE? TAX-FREE?

When considering income from your investments, it is not enough to only consider the amount of money you wish to receive, the schedule of payouts, the inherent risks of the investment, and its related costs. Before making a decision, a wise investor also carefully considers the net revenue of a taxable investment compared with a tax-free investment. Even though taxes reduce earned income, it may not be true that a tax-free security will produce more income, as there are other factors at play such as the investor's personal tax bracket. To know whether taxable or tax-free investments are best for you, you'll have to compare after-tax yields. Because taxes play an important part in determining the income you are planning to receive, the effect of taxes should always be considered before your decision to purchase.

REMINDER...

You now have some ideas about how you might generate income for your monthly finances or to fiscally enhance your lifestyle. Each of the types of investments mentioned have complexities beyond the scope of this book and are brought to your attention as an introduction only, so it is imperative that you consult with a professional to determine which of these investments would be best for your unique circumstances.

Income for Retirement

Once you are in retirement, investment income is likely to be a primary source of revenue for paying monthly bills and augmenting your retirement lifestyle. Most people, when they are in retirement, have an absolute aversion to risk because time has become precious and financial risk is a threat to the funds they have accumulated during the course of their life.

Safe investments generally become preferred, and while their returns may not be earth-shattering, neither are they expected to be at this late stage. A conservative strategy, or a collection of conservative strategies, may now be the best choice for your investment portfolio.

A fixed income strategy can include a variety of investment vehicles such as:

- Cash equivalents
- CDs
- Money market instruments

- T-bills
- Government and credit fixed income instruments
- Fixed annuities

There are also a variety of strategies that can be devised over short term, intermediate term and long-term time periods to meet your goals and objectives. The following are a few of the strategies that may be employed:

- Bullet strategies
- Barbell strategies
- Immunization strategies
- Cash flow matching strategies
- Combination strategies
- Laddering strategies
- Asset and liability matching strategies

The use of each of these investment instruments and strategies can be analyzed for their suitability with your unique set of circumstances through a variety of factors, including:

- Economic analysis
- General trends in fixed income and equity markets
- Yield curve analysis
- Credit analysis
- Spread analysis
- Risk adjusted returns
- Quality analysis
- Sector analysis
- Total return projections

These financial factors will be considered along with your personal circumstances and your portfolio objectives and constraints.

Based on your current and projected ability and willingness to accept risk, a conservative strategy(s) can be the anchor of your portfolio.

Even with a conservative strategy, your portfolio may experience loss of principal due to market fluctuations or the termination of the strategy prior to maturity. Also, due to the mechanics of marking to the market, return performance reporting may show a current period loss or gain that may be different from the total return perspective or the actual return earned at time of maturity. Reinvestment risk, which is the risk that coupons or interest earned are reinvested at a lower current rate, also should be considered as part of your portfolio's economic and yield curve analysis.

DEALING WITH A SHORTFALL GAP:

Some people will find themselves facing a shortfall between what they need for retirement and what they've set aside. There may be some solutions to this situation, depending on the severity of the shortfall.

Women, unfortunately, may experience a retirement income gap because of the significant role genders play in contemporary society. Women typically earn less than men and sometimes withdraw from the workforce to care for children or aging parents, which affects Social Security benefits and retirement plan accounts. In addition, women tend to invest more conservatively and usually save less than men, and because women often live longer than men, assets reserved for retirement need to be larger so they will last longer.

People who are confronted with a shortfall should consider the following tactics:

Spend Less, Save More. If possible, take full advantage of IRAs; depending on your age, you may be legally allowed to set aside more funds with "catch-up" contribution rules if you're over the age of 50. This is also true if you have access to a 401(k) plan. If you are unable to set aside discretionary funds, look for ways in your current budget to reduce your spending so the money you have freed up may now be used for retirement plan investments.

Put Retirement on Hold. By staying in the workforce longer, you may be able to continue supporting herself with her salary, leaving your retirement savings untouched, thus extending their use in time.

You may also be able to add to your retirement plan by apportioning part of your salary during these extra work years.

Increase Your Portfolio by Investing More Aggressively. Perhaps you have been investing too conservatively, and if you still have 10-15 years before retirement, you should consider taking a more aggressive stance. It's important that you do this under the direction of a financial professional because that person's guidance may help you keep unnecessary risk in check. Remember that not only do you need funds for daily expenses, but you'll also need to account for the impact of inflation and the cost of taxation. A financial advisor can help you construct a more aggressive portfolio that will narrow the gap or even eliminate it, and, perhaps, provide the annual return you need with risk that's limited by careful diversification.

Consider Using Your Home. Your home may be able to help you save more money. The equity in your home may be used to consolidate your debt and reduce your interest payments. You might also consider refinancing your home to reduce your monthly mortgage and long-term interest payments. If you qualify, you might also consider a reverse mortgage as an opportunity to eliminate your mortgage and create access to cash you could use for any purpose, including income investments. Of course, you may be able to sell your home and live in a smaller residence, saving money on home expenses while also reinvesting the funds you receive from the sale.

Adjust Your Expectations. You may need to reconsider the lifestyle you can afford in your retirement years. Take stock of the things you need and adjust your expectations accordingly. While this is not your first choice, you may still have many options for a decent and comfortable life. Look for alternatives so you can acquire good housing in a decent community, good food, and interests that occupy you in healthy ways. One of the best ways to live a happy life is by volunteering to help others who are confronted by extremely difficult circumstances. By giving your time and yourself to a worthy cause or to people in severe need, one's own circumstances become ever more attractive.

Summary

As an investor, you have the miraculous opportunity to employ your financial resources in a variety of different ways, and with the strong likelihood that you will increase your assets when you adopt strategies suitable for your circumstances while carefully managing your portfolio.

Accumulating wealth is typically the initial activity for most people, followed by wealth preservation in the middle and later years. Ultimately, wealth is distributed during retirement to cover living costs, and given to heirs when there is a remainder.

Most people invest their money to generate income so they can either improve their current lifestyle or prepare for the income they'll need during retirement. This chapter reviewed a number of income-generating investments that could provide a solution for the income you desire. These investments have different risk-return characteristics which should be analyzed for their value to you with your unique circumstances. If you think you are facing a shortfall with the financing of your retirement, there are several tactics available to you, especially if you still have 10 or more years before you retire.

Chapter 5 Review Questions

1. True or false? Are these the five steps to financial freedom? Knowing what you want, finding out exactly what it costs, carefully creating a plan that will guide you with achieving the financial goals you desire, following your plan, and monitoring your results and making adjustments to stay aligned with your plan.

   A. True.

   B. False.

2. The three stages of a person's financial life are the wealth consumption phase, the wealth collecting phase, and the wealth combining phase. True or false?

   A. True.

   B. False.

3. A big fear of most people is:

   A. Not having enough money to travel in retirement.

   B. Outliving their accumulated wealth.

   C. Being uncertain of selling their home or getting a reverse mortgage.

   D. Drawing on their 401(k) account.

4. If you are facing a retirement funds shortfall, you should:

   A. Give up.

   B. Live with your children and consume their financial resources.

   C. Consider alternate strategies like retiring later.

   D. Invest in risky stocks and pray you hit the Big One.

Chapter 5 Review Answers

1. True or false? Are these the five steps to financial freedom? Knowing what you want, finding out exactly what it costs, carefully creating a plan that will guide you with achieving the financial goals you desire, following your plan, and monitoring your results and making adjustments to stay aligned with your plan.

   A. True.

   B. False.

   Answer: A. True.

2. The three stages of a person's financial life are the wealth consumption phase, the wealth collecting phase, and the wealth combining phase. True or false?

   A. True.

   B. False.

   Answer: B. False. The three stages of a person's financial life are the wealth accumulation phase, the wealth preservation phase, and the wealth distribution phase.

3. A big fear of most people is:

   A. Not having enough money to travel in retirement.

   B. Outliving their accumulated wealth.

   C. Being uncertain of selling their home or getting a reverse mortgage.

   D. Drawing on their 401(k) account.

   Answer: B. Outliving their accumulated wealth. Most people value their independence and do not want to consume the financial resources of their family.

4. If you are facing a retirement funds shortfall, you should:

   A. Give up.

   B. Live with your children and consume their financial resources.

C. Consider alternate strategies like retiring later.
D. Invest in risky stocks and pray you hit the Big One.

Answer: C. Consider alternate strategies like retiring later. You can also spend less and save more, invest more aggressively under the guidance of a financial planner, consider using the equity in your home or acquire a reverse mortgage, and adjust your expectations.

Chapter 6
Designing Your Portfolio's Risk and Return

When you have finished reading this chapter, you will:

- Have a broader view of diversification to guide you when building your portfolio
- Understand the importance of creating a portfolio focused on the dynamic between risk and return
- Be able to explain five different investment risks
- Know the three steps of portfolio optimization
- Begin a discussion with yourself on how you may want to design your portfolio

Introduction

With thousands of investments to choose from, your portfolio can assume a variety of different forms. It's important to give some thought, some substantial thought, to what you want your portfolio to look like. Because you get to create the portfolio you want, hopefully under the direction of your financial advisor, your portfolio will probably reflect your philosophy of life, as well as your philosophy of building wealth.

Your portfolio may reflect your attitudes toward a green lifestyle, in which you only invest in companies that support a minimal energy footprint, for example. Or perhaps your green portfolio will favor companies engaged in recycling, or cleansing the land, air, and water, or developing alternative energy.

On the other hand, you may choose to invest in your country and community by purchasing bonds that support the construction of a new library or schools; you can purchase stocks in construction companies with strong employee relations; you might choose to invest in companies that specialize in food production or urban renewal.

Maybe someone close to you has benefited from medical advances and because of this you decide to invest in companies exploring new technologies, or universities with strong medical programs. Your interest might be drawn to companies that promote exercise, or balanced nutrition, or elder care.

Of course, it doesn't mean that your entire portfolio should focus on a theme. You can choose to have any combination of companies represented in your portfolio...although you can clearly vote with your dollars as you wish.

While a theme might be interesting to contemplate and can certainly be accommodated, achieving your investment objectives must be a primary factor. This chapter will ask you to consider different objectives for your portfolio so you will be in a better position to make the investment choices that are most suitable for your unique set of circumstances.

Even though there are millions of investors in the market, no two zebras are completely alike...every person's situation, their desires and fears, their ability to take risk, their eagerness for a specific return or specific sum of money, their investment horizon, obligations, needs, dreams...are as different as they are numerous. When designing your portfolio, it must fit you precisely because no one else is in the same position as you. Please consider the following styles of portfolio content.

Minimize Risk

Risk is everywhere. When you drive to work, you protect your risk with vehicle insurance. When you get to work and spend your day working with the people on your team, you protect against the risk of losing your job by doing your work professionally. When you put your children in school, you protect the risk of their receiving a poor education by meeting frequently with the teacher during the year and assessing your child's quality of progress. Property insurance, liability insurance, life insurance...these are common ways people protect themselves against the risks that are part of daily life.

Every investment carries a risk. Some risk is extremely high, while some risk is extremely low...but there is risk in everything. The risk is, of course, loss against your expectations for a specific outcome.

You can also protect against the inherent risks in your investment portfolio. The typical way investors protect themselves is by diversifying their portfolio, but diversifying means different things to different people. Many investment advisors will tell you your portfolio should be diversified by spreading your investment resources among a variety of different types of investments such as cash instruments, bonds, mutual funds, stocks, and perhaps real estate.

Investment advisors may also recommend you select different types of securities such as blue-chip stocks, income stocks, cyclical stocks, defensive stocks, value and growth stocks, technology stocks, and maybe speculative stocks. Their advice might include a mixture of large cap, mid-cap, and small cap stocks, and in a variety of different industries such as health care, energy, consumer staples, telecommunications, industrials, etc. You may also receive professional advice to select investments that have different rates of return so when some investments do not perform well, which is likely to happen eventually, other investments that are performing well will protect you against loss. As the market rises, falls, or trends sideways, different asset classes respond in different ways to market movements. Protecting your assets from loss with a variety of investments is the rationale behind diversification.

Key:

People assign different meanings to the concept of diversification. What does diversification mean to you?

Please note we are referring to portfolio analysis, not security analysis. Portfolio analysis analyzes the effectiveness of the entire portfolio, while security analysis focuses only on individual securities. It's important to study the risk-return of your individual securities, of course; it is equally necessary to focus on the risk-return of your entire portfolio and how the individual investments work together to maximize your return while minimizing your risk.

A portfolio that is most diversified has securities with low correlations. This means that the value of the assets within the portfolio do not increase or decrease in synchronicity, but rather experience increases or decreases independently and with varying degrees so the portfolio's value grows efficiently while it also reduces the effect of those assets that are declining in value.

Because of the nature of economics, markets, industries and companies, correlations change regularly, so it is critically important to monitor developments in your portfolio continuously as necessary so you can make adjustments based on the changing investment environment. If you don't make these adjustments, your portfolio's growth may diminish or its risk may increase; both of these conditions limit the efficiency of your portfolio and slow your progress toward your investment goals.

Every investment carries a risk, and knowing what the risks are is the first step to understanding your portfolio's vulnerability and how you can protect your investments. The best way to restrict investment risk is by learning what these risks are. Here are five types of risk you should know and monitor.

1. **Market Risk.** This is the risk that your investments will mirror the direction of the market. If the market is going up, your investments also go up; if the market goes down, your investments do so as well. Obviously, there isn't much complaint if the value of your investments is increasing. You might have no concern if you have a somewhat conservative portfolio that was created intentionally to mirror the broad indexes of stocks in the asset classes you purchased. But then, how pleased will you be when the indexes decrease and your portfolio mirrors their decline? Or, considering another possibility,

do you want to create your portfolio to be free of market risk, so no matter what the market is doing, your investments are progressing independently? Deciding on the degree of market risk in your portfolio is worth a discussion with your financial advisor. Market risk is often call beta, or systematic, risk.

2. Interest-Rate Risk. Interest-rate risk is usually related to fixed-income investments such as bonds. Because the interest is fixed for a set period of time, if the interest rate increases during the term of the bond, the additional increase these funds might otherwise have earned will be lost. Some bonds are five year or 10-year bonds, and having your funds locked-in for a period this lengthy could work for you if interest rates drop, or work against you if interest rates rise. Of course, there is a penalty if you withdraw the funds before the maturity date.

3. Inflation Risk. While time is one of the best allies of an investor, time also has a nemesis called inflation. Prices continue to rise every year, sometimes in minor increments, and sometimes in large percentages. The effect of inflation over time is actually quite stunning. The average rate of inflation in the United States over the last 100 years is about 3%, depending on which source you accept. 3% may not sound too bad until you consider that at 3%, with compounding, prices double every 20 years. The danger is clear: your investments must not only increase so you have the capital to achieve your goals, but you must also have even more growth to counteract the ever-expanding effect of inflation. If your portfolio is too conservative, the risk you face is that you may not be growing your portfolio fast enough to outpace inflation, and may actually be losing the purchasing power of your resources in the future...which is inexorably growing closer.

4. Credit Risk. Credit risk refers to the risk of a company or a government agency to repay its debt and interest to its investors. Bonds are rated by rating service companies such as Moody's and Standard & Poor's. The higher the rating, the lower the investor's risk. As the rating decreases, the credit risk becomes more amplified; investors choosing to invest in risky securities will expect a higher yield in compensation for the increased risk they are accepting. If an investment is international, there is also a currency risk when the bond matures and is paid out; in addition, bonds and debt instruments issued by foreign countries could be subject to political and economic disruption that could eliminate all expectation of payment.

5. Investing Too Conservatively or Too Aggressively. If you are excessively conservative, the possibility that you may not achieve your financial goals is a real threat. If you invest too aggressively, the surfeit of risk may overwhelm you. Because everyone's circumstances are different, you have to find the right balance of risk-return for your temperament as an investor, and for your time horizon. Remember that your goal is not to amass as large a fortune as you possibly can, but rather to achieve the realistic financial goals that serve your future lifestyle given the time remaining before you need your funds. This means that your annual rate of return may not have to be either penny-pinching or shoot-the-moon; once you know your goals, you and your financial advisor can reverse engineer the calculations that will indicate the annual return you need. This can take the anxiety away because the unknown becomes known.

Optimize Return

You may want to maximize your portfolio's return; it may not surprise you that many investors don't know this is possible and instead purchase investments for a variety of unrelated reasons, winding up with a hodgepodge portfolio that is especially inefficient and risky.

When your portfolio has an optimized return, it means the individual investments selected for your portfolio are working synergistically to provide you with the highest return for the least risk. This relationship, which unifies the different components of your portfolio, is known as the efficient frontier. It's called the efficient frontier because your portfolio is on the balanced edge ("frontier") between the best return and the least risk, and performing at its optimal level ("efficient") on that balanced edge.

Achieving this degree of efficiency is not a simple task and requires some advanced mathematics to calculate the correlations between the

10 or 12 (or more) investments in your portfolio. It might be best to meet with a Registered Investment Advisor (RIA) who can help you determine the annual rate of return needed to achieve your financial goals by reverse engineering the calculations, and selecting the investments which will optimize your portfolio.

Figure 29: Asset Allocation Process.

The process of portfolio optimization is usually done in three steps. The first step is knowing the annual rate of return necessary to achieve your financial goals and knowing the level of risk you are willing to accept to achieve that annual rate of return. The second step is determining the optimal weight of the different asset classes that should be represented within your portfolio. An example would be the proportion between equities and bonds. The third step is calculating the optimal weight between assets within each asset class, such as identifying the right proportion between large cap, mid-cap, and small cap equities. Each element of your portfolio must serve a distinct purpose within the combination of the whole.

A continuing issue with portfolio optimization is ensuring the validity of the optimization. As noted previously, markets and companies change over time, and this will create a fluctuation in your portfolio's optimization that will need to be corrected periodically so your portfolio's performance stays on course. While this may create an ongoing labor of love, it will also cost you some cash because you will incur transaction costs for the sale of those assets you must divest. Though your individual securities will deviate from your expectations over time, which is a normal occurrence of business behavior, you must make an additional effort to select those investment instruments that will not require frequent purchase and sale. No one has a crystal ball, but if an effort is made to reduce transactions, you may have a higher degree of carefully selected investments, saving money and making your portfolio that much more efficient.

Reduce Taxes

Everyone has to pay taxes...but some portfolios can be constructed in such a way that taxes are reduced. There are funds available that offer tax-free, tax-deferred, and tax -reduced investments, and these instruments can be very helpful with reducing the effect of taxes within the portfolio.

Maximize Income

You may want your portfolio to generate the maximum amount of income possible so you can enhance your current lifestyle, as discussed in the previous chapter. There are a number of investments available to support this outcome.

Hedge Inflation

Because inflation is so destructive to a portfolio's growth, there are investments you can purchase that will counteract its effect. Aside from not including U.S. Treasury bonds in your portfolio, you could purchase a fund that buys puts against the U.S. Treasury. Another tactic is buying Treasury Inflation-Protected Securities (TIPS) designed to protect investors from inflation. Gold has always been purchased as a hedging tactic, and your portfolio could hold gold ETFs. These are just a few of the ideas you could incorporate in your portfolio if you wanted to outpace inflation.

Retirement

Perhaps your goal is to only build a retirement nest egg, and all your resources are dedicated to the growth of capital. Depending on your age, time horizon, and tolerance for risk, you may choose either a moderately aggressive portfolio, or an aggressive portfolio:

The Moderately Aggressive Investor. This investor has a relatively high tolerance for risk and a long-time horizon. With little need for current income, the investor seeks above-average growth from their investment assets. The main objective of this range is capital appreciation, and the investor should be able to tolerate moderate fluctuations.

The Aggressive Investor. This investor has both a high tolerance for risk and a long investment time horizon. The main objective of this model is to provide high growth without current income. Portfolios in this range may have substantial fluctuations in value from year to year, making this category unsuitable for those who do not have an extended time horizon.

College

You might be more interested in a mid-term goal of putting your children through college. Again, depending on your time horizon and your tolerance for risk, a portfolio that focuses on growth could be the right solution for your need. There are several different ways your portfolio could be constructed to help you achieve this financial goal.

Living Longer than Your Resources

When it comes to finances, one of the biggest fears, if not the biggest fear, of most investors is outliving their money. No one wants to be dependent on the good graces of their family, or the bureaucratic whims of the government. This is why it is so important that you take the initiative now and manifest the discipline to regularly save and invest as much money as you can. With inflation doubling the cost of products and services every 20 years, the technological advances in medicine that allow people to have a much longer life span, the depletion of some of Earth's resources that increases the price of commodities, and the geopolitical tensions and social threats that are ever-prevalent emphatically suggest the wisdom of disciplined and intelligent investing for the future.

Summary

Your portfolio can take different forms depending on your investment goals. Because there are such an amazing variety of investment choices, you can choose to design your portfolio so it can efficiently build toward the outcomes you desire. The key, of course, is knowing what you want and being willing to dedicate your resources to that end. You can always change your goals to suit the changing circumstances of your life, but knowing what you want is always the first step toward acquiring it.

The first underlying theme of this book is to remind you to get started right away if you haven't, or to commit more completely if you're not. The second underlying theme of this book is to encourage you to seek professional advice; investing in the markets may appear simple on the surface because all it takes is a phone call or a postage stamp...but it is anything but simple once you look below the epidermis.

We're talking about your money. If you're taking better care of your car than your investments, you may be headed for a crash. Do the smart thing. Make an appointment to see a fiduciary advisor so you can benefit from the expertise of a professional. You don't know what you don't know. We all laugh at the ostrich with her head in the sand. Find a fee-based financial advisor, pay a few hundred dollars to get set on the right path, and then begin the journey that will bring you home.

Chapter 6 Review Questions

1. A portfolio that is most diversified has securities with:

   A. The greatest negative correlation.
   B. The greatest positive correlation.
   C. The least positive correlation.
   D. The least negative correlation.

2. A diversified portfolio should be monitored at least twice annually because:

   A. The proportions of your assets may change, causing an imbalance.
   B. Your risks increase when your portfolio's proportions change.
   C. Your portfolio's expected rate of return might drift, making its performance less productive.
   D. All of the above.

3. The danger of investing too conservatively is:

   A. Market risk has your portfolio performing at the benchmark indices.
   B. Your portfolio may not outpace inflation.
   C. The credit risk with BBB-rated bonds is too risky.
   D. Interest rate risk can slow your portfolio's return.

4. A portfolio with an "optimized return" means the portfolio:

   A. Is optimized to capture the highest returns in the market.
   B. Has investments working synergistically for the highest return for the least risk.
   C. Is correlated to index benchmarks for limited risk.
   D. Has the ability to adjust its return based on shifting market trends.

Chapter 6 Review Answers

1. A portfolio that is most diversified has securities with:

   A. The greatest negative correlation.
   B. The greatest positive correlation.
   C. The least positive correlation.
   D. The least negative correlation.

   Answer: A. The greatest negative correlation. The less the securities correlate, the more likely they will protect the portfolio's value. When one security suffers losses, another security may increase in value. If the securities were too similar and have a positive correlation, they are likely to all move in tandem...which is good when the market moves in your favor, but disaster when it doesn't!

2. A diversified portfolio should be monitored at least twice annually because:

   A. The proportions of your assets may change, causing an imbalance.
   B. Your risks increase when your portfolio's proportions change.
   C. Your portfolio's expected rate of return might drift, making its performance less productive.
   D. All of the above.

   Answer: D. All of the above. Your portfolio should be mathematically calculated to the efficient frontier so you are more likely to achieve the highest gains for the specified risk you are willing to accommodate. As the portfolio's value changes, your portfolio may drift from its original efficient frontier, requiring new calculations to reposition your portfolio on a new efficient frontier so you can continue earning the most return for your predetermined level of risk.

3. The danger of investing too conservatively is:

   A. Market risk has your portfolio performing at the benchmark indices.
   B. Your portfolio may not outpace inflation.

C. The credit risk with BBB-rated bonds is too risky.
D. Interest rate risk can slow your portfolio's return.

Answer: B. Your portfolio may not outpace inflation. Inflation grows at approximately 3% per year, so costs double approximately every 20 years. Your portfolio must grow at a rate that gives you true purchasing power in the future, after years and years of inflation.

4. A portfolio with an "optimized return" means the portfolio:

A. Is optimized to capture the highest returns in the market.
B. Has investments working synergistically for the highest return for the least risk.
C. Is correlated to index benchmarks for limited risk.
D. Has the ability to adjust its return based on shifting market trends.

Answer: B. Has investments working synergistically for the highest return for the least risk. You always want your portfolio to operate at its most effective efficiency. This can be accomplished through mathematical calculations to determine the efficient frontier.

Chapter 7
Blueprinting Your Investment Plan

When you have finished reading this chapter, you will:

- Be able to name your short term, mid-term, and long-term financial goals
- Have a strong understanding of the purpose of the RRR
- Know the four steps to crafting your RRR
- Possess a solid introduction to writing your own IPS

Introduction

In the last three chapters we laid the groundwork to help you self-identify the type of investor that's most appropriate for you. Keep in mind that even though you may have chosen to consider yourself as either a conservative investor, a moderate, or an aggressive investor, your circumstances may preclude your having the latitude to be the type of investor you most desire. Your current financial situation may dictate a role outside your comfort zone. If so, we urge you to seek the professional services of a Registered Investment Advisor (RIA) because this expert may be able to provide critically important information that might otherwise go unseen.

Chapter 4 asked you to consider which of the variety of investors or traders seemed most compatible with your own interests and personality. Chapter 5 inquired about your placement within the span of the three investment stages, while providing some foresight on the stages that yet lie before you. In Chapter 6, a discussion developed about the different objectives your investments and your portfolio might choose to include, based on the financial goals that are mirrors of your financial needs.

Now, in this chapter, we will use the information you learned about yourself and your goals to create the blueprint for your financial plan.

We will discuss an amazing tool called the Required Rate of Return (RRR), and we will also create a solid draft of your Investment Policy Statement (IPS). Now it's time to get (even more) serious!

Your Financial Plan

Having a written plan is essential. It's not everything, because you still have to take action with your plan, but you can't take truly sensible action until you have a written plan. The plan must be written because this organizes your thoughts in a cohesive structure and provides easy reference as often as needed. Besides, without a written plan as a guide, there is a tendency to mishandle your funds and invest frivolously.

Goals

Now is a good time to get a piece of paper and a pencil or your laptop, and start writing down your goals. You've set goals before and know they must be clear and precise. For this activity, your goals should be broken into three units, one for your short-term goals, another for your mid-term goals, and the third for your long-term financial goals.

SHORT TERM GOALS:

Typically a short-term goal is a one or two-year goal, but you may want your short-term goals to also cover the basics of meeting your immediate financial necessities. While you may already be past this point with your current financial wellness, this segment is worth reading as a reminder and just-in-case.

1. Have sufficient cash flow to pay all monthly living expenses.
2. Have an emergency fund with six months cash in case of an emergency or job loss.
3. Purchase an appropriate amount of medical and dental insurance, or supplemental insurance if additional coverage is needed.
4. Purchase a $25,000 life insurance policy for survivors in case of unexpected death.

5. Purchase a disability insurance policy to protect against loss of income.
6. Research long term care (LTC) insurance and buy a policy if affordable now.
7. Pay down credit card debt by 25% this calendar year.
8. Start a monthly savings account and deposit no less than $100 per month.

MID-TERM GOALS:

Mid-term goals are goals for 3-5 years from now. Here is an assortment of goals you might consider for your list:

1. Pay off all non-mortgage debt.
2. Interview and select a fiduciary advisor.
3. Plan for a wedding.
4. Provide funds for advanced education.
5. Set aside funds for a down payment on a home.
6. Accumulate funds for the costs of having a child.
7. Increase personal income to achieve goals sooner.
8. Replace vehicle or add a second vehicle.
9. Save for home furnishings.
10. Fund a special travel vacation every three years.

LONG TERM GOALS:

These goals are for the future when your income has increased and you are more capable of setting aside funds for these purposes.

1. Begin saving for retirement.
2. Consider purchasing long term health care if not done yet.
3. Develop a plan for the possibility of helping aging parents.
4. Pay off the mortgage.

5. Start making plans for retirement living.
6. Enhance standard of living.
7. Provide funds for children's college education.

These are just a few examples of goals that you might choose to place on your own list. Once your list is formed, you should then prioritize your goals so you can clearly see the order of their importance. It would also be very helpful if you can assign a time horizon for achieving each goal because this will add more credibility to your intentions and will probably cause you to achieve them more rapidly.

Setting your goals is not simply an exercise, but a very significant activity. Take the time necessary to carefully think about your future and realistically determine the lifestyle you want to enjoy. It may be amusing to think of yourself as the lead guitarist of the next world-famous rock 'n roll band, or the world's best head chef in Paris, or a movie producer in Hollywood, or... The list goes on, and while it may be alright to entertain these versions of your future self, this is the time to be realistic and determine which financial goals are credible given your current circumstances and immediate potential for a good and contented life. Keep your dreams, but also build your foundation.

Therefore, set aside some quality time to seriously consider the goals you want to achieve during your life. Some are necessities, and some will add joy and satisfaction to the life experience you will have over the next 20, 30 or 40 years or more. Most people have the similar goals of getting married, having children, buying a home, traveling and enjoying a hobby, and preparing for the years in retirement. These may or may not be your goals, but whatever you choose, writing your goals and developing a plan will help you reach and enjoy them that much sooner.

Once you've determined your goals, the next step is to develop a plan. This might at first appear to be a horrendously difficult process, but if you do it in the right way, you will see that with the right attitude and the right help, making your financial plan can actually be both an entertaining and a rewarding experience.

We've all stepped into a commercial passenger jet and taken a quick look into the pilot's cockpit; our eyes have boggled at the number of dials, switches, colored panels, blinking lights, levers and sticks. Our rational mind told us that flying an airplane is a complex process, and with a sigh of relief we've acknowledged with gratitude that there is a pilot and a copilot assigned to the journey that will use all the tools and indicators to take us to our destination. We also know that if you know how to fly an airplane, the task is not quite as unnerving as it appears. Our rational mind tells us that if someone else can do this, then it is certainly within our own abilities, with enough information and training, to also fly the plane.

The situation is the same with your financial plan. Yes, there is a lot to know, and training and experience will expedite your arrival at your financial destination. Can you do this by yourself? Well...what do you think? How well do you know the markets, strategies, individual investment instruments, and the mathematical correlations within a portfolio of assorted stocks, bonds, and cash? How willing are you to step into your financial aircraft and fly the years between where you are today and where you want to be 30 or more years from now?

If you're not sure you can get your financial airplane off the runway and into the air on a safely calculated flight plan that assures the most direct route to your financial freedom, you should be happy to take a passenger seat.

This is not to say you couldn't do this by yourself, because you probably could with the right amount of training and experience. You can choose to be a jet pilot, and you can choose to be a professional financial advisor, but both occupations mandate required instruction and actual experience to pilot the airplane and guide the portfolio toward its terminal expectations. This is too important for risky behavior. You do not want to crash and burn!

Now, just because you might need a pilot to help you arrive safely and on time at your financial destination doesn't mean you have to purchase an expensive ticket. You can choose to fly first class or coach...and you can choose to have several stops along the way.

The point is that hiring the services of a financial planner does not mean exorbitant and ongoing costs. You can choose the services as you need them. A financial planner can help you get started, and can meet periodically throughout the years when you need advice. Do you have a doctor on retainer? Probably not. You visit when necessary; it's the same with a fiduciary advisor. Of course, you might see value in retaining these services on a continual basis, and you might not...but the choice is yours.

There is one caveat, however, and that is to work with a financial planner who offers fee-only services; you want a professional who is paid by fees, not by commission (fee-based) because a commission/fee-based advisor may direct you toward investments that earn him or her a commission. This is neither good nor bad, but by working with a fee-only advisor the potential for this bias, however intentional or unintentional, is avoided.

Let's take a look at a unique proprietary process Synergy developed, one which may strengthen your financial planning. It's called the Required Rate of Return (RRR) and it's the cornerstone of your financial plan.

Required Rate of Return (RRR) and the Lifestyle Return Benchmark

The required rate of return (RRR) is the percentage by which your portfolio should be increasing every year to keep you on course to achieve your goals in the time prescribed. In essence it is your Lifestyle Return Benchmark. It is the number by which you need to measure your portfolio returns, not the S&P 500. One problem we frequently encounter is that investors focus on the S&P 500 as their portfolio benchmark. The problem here is that the S&P 500 has nothing to do with your lifestyle. Your benchmark needs to be specifically calculated for your lifestyle.

Let's back up a little bit. You've identified a variety of financial goals you wish to achieve over the course of your life. Each of these goals represents a specific dollar amount. You, or you and your financial planner, have estimated a reasonable price for each of them.

One of your goals is to buy a home in a certain neighborhood, and you estimate your future home will cost $900,000. You'll need 20% for the minimum down payment, which is $180,000. You want to be able to move into your future home in five years, so you'll have to set aside an average of $36,000 per year for each of the next five years. In order to have $36,000 each year, you will need to earn "X%" on your investments. Let's say you have $500,000 invested in the market; you would need to have a required rate of return of about 7.25%. This is your required rate of return for each of the five years, providing the $180,000 in time for your down payment.

Granted, this is a simplistic example because the invested funds will compound, and they may also have transaction fees or capital gains taxes if individual assets are sold, etc., but this is an abridged and simply presented example of what the RRR (LRB) is and does.

Key:

Your required rate of return (RRR), or your Lifestyle Return Benchmark (LRB), will help you track your portfolio's progress toward meeting your financial goals. Every year, you know if you are on target or not. This information reduces your anxiety and provides the opportunity to adjust your portfolio's performance if necessary.

The next step is to take what we have learned about you and your lifestyle, and to establish your Lifestyle Return Benchmark™ (LRB). The LRB is the number that you need to earn on your portfolio to make your lifestyle goals and aspirations come true.

The LRB process will convert your lifestyle goals and aspirations into your personalized return objective. Additionally, it will act as your custom return benchmark as opposed to a relative and often random benchmark like the S&P 500. The S&P 500 has nothing to do with who you are, so it is a mistake to measure your investing success by it.

We establish your LRB through our proprietary required rate of return (RRR) process. Each year we will compare your LRB with the actual return on your portfolio to ensure you are moving in the right direction. If you are not on track, we will reevaluate your plan and make any necessary portfolio adjustments that are economically possible. Moreover, we will educate you on the other options you have to stay on track.

Investing success hinges on the integration between the investor's unique circumstances and the prudent identification of long-term strategies that are positioned to achieve client goals with the highest probability of success.

At Synergy Asset Management, we take a different approach to constructing your portfolio by reverse-engineering your required rate of return (RRR) and using it as your Lifestyle Return Benchmark™.

Use your LRB to build your portfolio.

Okay, your lifestyle has been converted into a real number that actually means something to you. So now what? Now it is time to take your LRB and use it to build your portfolio. The goal is to build you a portfolio that has a good chance of achieving your LRB with as little risk as possible.

Remember that there is a trade-off between expected return and risk and that some investors are strongly risk-averse, while others are more tolerant of risk. Therefore, it is very important that we build you a portfolio that is respectful of your ability and willingness to take risk while also providing you with an above average chance of meeting your LRB objective.

Figure 30: The RRR Process.

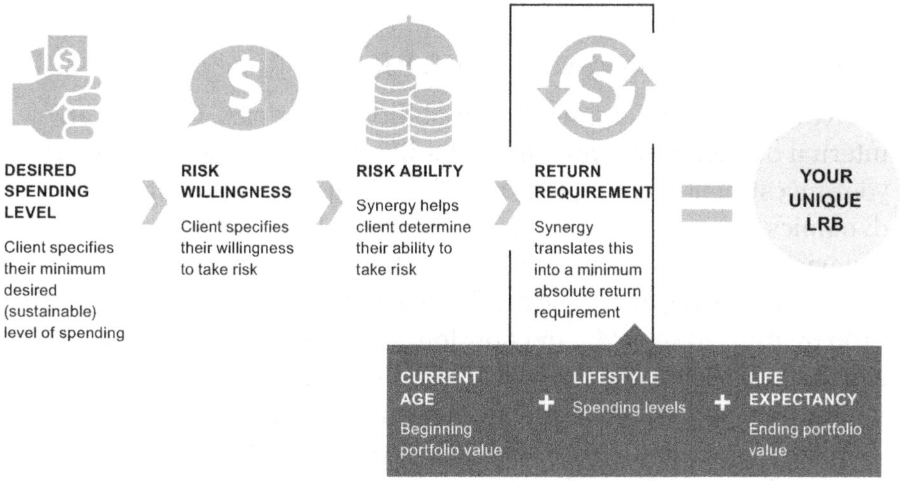

Definition:

The Required Rate of Return (RRR): The minimum percentage an investment must earn annually to achieve the investment's goal for growth. The RRR can be different for different people.

Now you have a basic understanding of the RRR concept. Let's review its elements so you can clearly see how this would work when discussing these ideas with your financial planner, or when you are crafting your own calculations.

STEP 1: SPENDING LEVEL

Decide how much money you need to achieve the goals on your list. Your calculations should include costs for inflation, taxes, and a reasonable estimate on any fees and expenses your portfolio may be required to pay. You should also include any reasonable expectations you have for receiving funds from sources other than your investment portfolio, such as insurance premiums, the sale of a home and/or business, and a future inheritance; while these may not be guaranteed, they are part of your potential future picture and can be included in the calculations.

STEP 2: WILLINGNESS TO TAKE RISK

Arrive at an understanding of your ability to take risk. Conduct an internal dialogue with yourself about living with financial loss if your investment is too aggressive. This discussion must engage the dynamics of how much money you currently have, how much money you wish to have, how many years you have available for investing before you'll want to use the funds, how you'll feel if your investments drop by 10%, 20%, 30%...and how long you realistically estimate it will take for your portfolio to recover from that loss. This self-exploration, if done honestly, will give you an excellent barometer of how much weather you can stand. It will also help you more clearly understand how to adjust your portfolio as your many years of investment begin to diminish as you approach retirement. This discussion is not intended to give you cold feet, but rather to assist you with determining the fictitious reality of what might happen and how it will affect you if it does. Remember, also, that you can always have a portion of your portfolio in an aggressive range, while the bulk of your portfolio can be moderate or conservative. This is not an all or nothing scenario, but it is essential that you understand your ability for taking risk and the fallout from that risk position.

STEP 3: ABILITY TO TAKE RISK

If you have decided to work with a financial planner, and once you have determined your own tolerance for risk and the degree to which you are willing to suffer if your portfolio experiences loss, you should have the same conversation with your financial planner. In Step 2 you calculated the degree to which your emotions would come into play. In Step 3, the discussion between you and your financial planner will be more rational, and focused on a realistic view of how loss will affect your portfolio. The combination of your emotional response and the coldly calculated reality of portfolio loss will help you refine your understanding of the true effect of lost cash and lost time, and is likely to define your diminished willingness to take risk much more clearly.

Of course, you may be in circumstances in which you need to take a higher degree of risk, but at least now you have a clear picture of what this means.

Your ability to accept risk depends on these four factors:

1. A portfolio with a large amount of assets.
2. A lengthy time horizon.
3. A guaranteed fixed income of sufficient size so lifestyle is not affected by loss.
4. Controlled spending limits.

STEP 4: CALCULATION

This is the step where you or your financial planner reverse-engineer the calculations to determine your required rate of return (RRR), arriving at the annual percentage your investment portfolio should achieve every year to acquire the sums needed to purchase your goals. In some years your portfolio will exceed your RRR, and in other years your portfolio will fall short. As long as over the course of time your portfolio averages your RRR, you are on course.

Here is an illustration of the process:

Figure 31: Required Rate of Return.

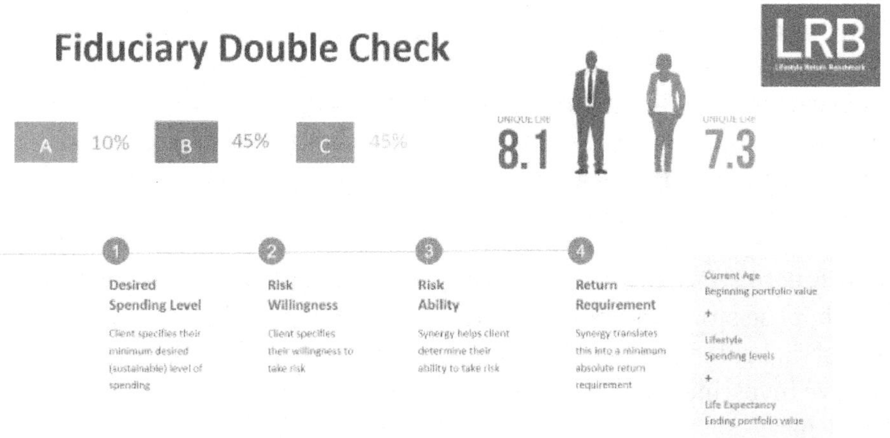

Remember that you must monitor and analyze your portfolio to make sure your portfolio continues to have the appropriate diversification of assets. If it doesn't, you must seriously consider making adjustments either to the portfolio if market conditions allow, or from the alternatives discussed above.

Remember, the purpose of establishing your LRB is for proper and precision portfolio construction.

We will build your portfolio based on your goals instead of around the jolts of the market or some qualitative risk classification such as conservative or aggressive.

Our objective is real wealth accumulation, preservation, and distribution through portfolio construction practices that are inherently sensible and thoroughly tested, resulting in market-like returns with a reasonable level of risk. If your lifestyle planning calls for a more conservative approach, we can achieve that, too. This tactic may result in a slightly lower rate of expected return, but will have better protection in the event of a severe bear market.

In the end, most investors prefer a plan that will ensure their standard of living against severe short-term loss while allowing them to maintain and improve their lifestyle over time. Remember, the goal is not to beat the S&P 500, it is to earn your Lifestyle Return Benchmark™ (LRB).

To accomplish your objectives, we will use a mix of safe and conservative investment strategies, core investment strategies, alternative investment strategies and, if appropriate, a mix of real estate and small business assets. Annuities and insurance can also play an important role in a broadly diversified portfolio to buffer sudden shocks and unexpected perils.

Our mix of strategies will keep you sleeping tight at night regardless of what the stock and bond markets are doing. And based on your Lifestyle Protection Plan, we can adjust the size of your safe and secure investment so that you can afford to withstand more risk elsewhere.

In the end, the LRB/RRR planning process will build your solid goals-based portfolio by integrating investment management with the math and science of cash flow-based financial planning, helping you feel safe about your lifestyle regardless of what the market is doing. This is significant!

The process will help you better understand why you own risky investments in the first place. It will also help you find a balance between investments that possess return characteristics, and investments that possess risk management characteristics.

As you know, we have discussed the two approaches of a coin, heads on one side and tails on the other. The investing coin has risk on one side and return on the other. Or, think of stocks for risky investments and bonds for less risky investments.

Finding the right combination of these two types of assets, while monitoring and adjusting them on a continuous basis, is what leads to success.

We are not recommending that you only invest in stocks or bonds. We recommend that you allow our process to integrate your appetite for risk and return with your lifestyle goals and aspirations.

The IPS, Your Investment Policy Statement

After establishing your financial goals and then calculating your required rate of return, the investment policy statement is the third most important part of your financial plan. We touched on this briefly in Chapter 3, noting that the IPS is the blueprint for your investment plan.

Another underlying theme of this book is that a successful investor requires dedication to purpose. Becoming wealthy is not a haphazard occurrence; making money, taking calculated risks, keeping an eye on your goals, being willing to sacrifice many hours in reflection by reading and studying independently and/or discussing investment strategies with your financial planner, staying in touch with your emotions and working through fear and greed, and maintaining your patience through a decade, or two, or three to ultimately achieve security and comfort of a lifestyle you've envisioned for perhaps half your lifetime, requires steadfast focus, a character capable of discipline, an optimistic attitude, and the ability to make serious decisions under pressure. This is not child's play, but rather the survival of the fittest.

To say that the IPS is the blueprint of your financial success is to hear a call to action for the engagement of your utmost attention because within the parameters of this strategic plan lie the precisely measured steps of your financial success, the success of your family, and possibly your family's future generations. Whatever you decide to include in your investment policy statement should be regarded seriously, like the game plan for your Super Bowl run, the menu for your five-star celebrity chef Parisian restaurant, the training for your position on the Olympic gold medal podium... your strategy for becoming a Wall Street wizard.

Here is a diagram that provides a clear synopsis, explained by the paragraphs which follow:

Figure 32: Investment Policy Statement Objectives and Constraints.

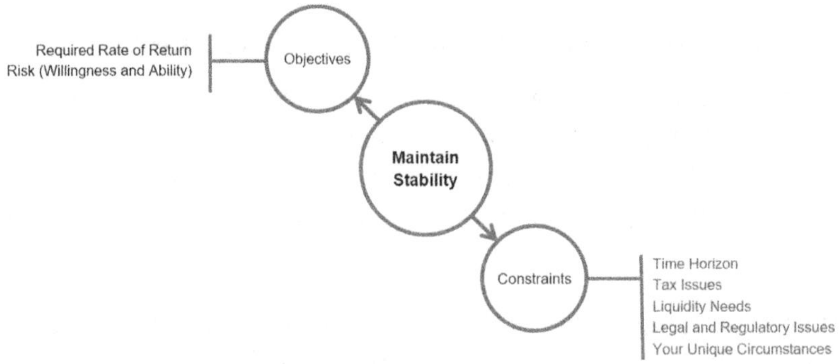

Several of the following segments of an investment policy statement have been discussed previously, and are repeated here in capsulated form. Others are newly introduced and explained in more detail.

INVESTMENT OBJECTIVES:

Make a list of your short term, mid-term, and long-term goals; price each goal so you know exactly how much money you'll need to attain all of them, as if you were requiring them today.

RISK TOLERANCE:

Based on the conversation you've had with yourself, and hopefully with a financial advisor, how much risk are you willing to accept? Remember the danger of investing too safely because the result may be an underperforming portfolio. Given that time is your ally and inflation your enemy, you can't be too conservative because you may wind up running in place, or worse. On the other hand, if your portfolio is too aggressive, you could lose years of gain. Rather than be sorry later, be carefully clever and wise now.

REQUIRED RATE OF RETURN (RRR):

The required rate of return is the annual percentage of return your portfolio must achieve to fund all your financial goals during the course of a set period of time. The RRR is composed of the combination of all the investments in your diversified portfolio working together efficiently. We'll discuss the diversification of these assets later in the book.

TIME HORIZON:

This is the number of years available for reaching your goals, and is a constraint to your portfolio's growth. Most people regard 65 as the year to retire...and some people extend this ceiling to 70 or later; it may be a personal choice to increase monthly Social Security benefits, or the desire for working longer and benefiting from company-paid wages for a few more years; if you own your own business, there may be benefits to working for your own company beyond 65 as well.

TAXES:

Taxes are another constraint. Every investment plan needs to heed the effect of taxes on a portfolio's growth. The more your portfolio buys and sells assets, the more the likelihood exists for capital gains taxes, which can devour your portfolio's growth. Your IPS should have a statement that guides your decisions on incurring taxes, and how you will strategize to defend against taxes that could be avoided. If you expect to file in a high tax bracket, tax-deferred investments might be a smart decision.

FEES AND EXPENSES:

The same is true about the fees and expenses the assets in your portfolio could contract. Studies show that fees and expenses can be deleterious to the growth of your portfolio's assets, so a statement that defines your philosophy and your fiscal limits to including assets with fees and expenses greater than what you regard as reasonable should be clearly stated in your IPS.

LIQUIDITY:

Liquidity is an important issue as well. In most cases, you want to be able to buy and sell an asset quickly and not be coerced into holding an undesirable asset until an eventual buyer saunters into view. Some real estate holdings might present this situation, for example. Consider the value of easily liquidating your assets when you are ready to do so, and make this a part of your IPS if it suits you. Another liquidity issue might be needing access to cash to buy your home; in this case, liquidity is a constraint on your investments because you'll need to have the funds available at a certain time.

LEGAL:

Assets selected for your portfolio may have legal or regulatory compliance issues that could affect the performance of the asset, or your access to the asset. Be sure your IPS identifies the preferred features you want your assets to have so you don't receive an unwelcome surprise that impedes their sale or value. An example is your requirement to retain an asset for 10 years or suffer a penalty for its premature sale, which is the case if you owned a 10-year certificate of deposit.

UNIQUE CIRCUMSTANCES:

A constraint that might be unique is your self-imposed restriction not to ever purchase assets that harm the environment, like oil or coal company stocks or bonds. Or perhaps you are opposed to companies that encourage poor health, so you could choose not to include companies that sell products with high fructose corn syrup.

These are all important considerations when writing your IPS. An IPS can be as detailed or as casual as you wish...but the more you define your ideas of how your portfolio will be designed, the more completely you will benefit from its guidance, especially when the markets are shifting and you must make decisions to buy, hold, or sell. The more prepared you are, the more capable you become with making decisions that advance your purpose.

Summary

There are three essential elements to your financial plan. First of all, you must know your financial goals; most people never identify them and so they live in a hazy maze of their own making. The more precisely you identify what you want, the more likely you are to acquire what you envision.

Once you know where you're going, you have to calculate what it takes to get there, so knowing the annual return percentage you need for every year of the years in which you will be investing is the key factor to knowing if you're on a course of action that will bring you to your destination in the time you have available.

The third element of your financial plan is your Investment Policy Statement (IPS) because this is the guidelines or rulebook, you'll use to achieve the annual return percentage needed to reach the destination on time.

The trio of your goals, your annual rate of return, and your guidelines compose the principal structure of your financial plan, and the more completely you construct your plan, the better it will serve you. Most basketball coaches don't have a thin playbook; your financial playbook should be carefully reasoned, thorough, and capable of providing you with clearly defined choices as financial circumstances rise and fall, offering new opportunities for your advantage.

Chapter 7 Review Questions

1. Are these short-term, mid-term, or long-term goals? Have sufficient cash flow to pay all monthly living expenses; have an emergency fund with six months cash in case of an emergency or job loss; purchase a $25,000 life insurance policy for survivors in case of unexpected death; pay down credit card debt by 25% this calendar year.

   A. Short term.

   B. Mid-term.

   C. Long term.

2. The cornerstone of your financial plan is the:

   A. Binary technical indices.

   B. Asset diversification.

   C. Efficient frontier helix.

   D. Required rate of return.

3. True or false? Your ability to accept risk depends on these four factors:

   A. A portfolio with a large amount of assets.

   B. A limited time horizon.

   C. A guaranteed fixed income of sufficient size, so lifestyle is not affected by loss.

   D. Controlled spending limits.

      A. True.

      B. False.

4. The blueprint for your investment plan is the:

   A. IRS.

   B. RRR.

   C. IPS.

   D. MPT.

Chapter 7 Review Answers

1. Are these short-term, mid-term, or long-term goals? Have sufficient cash flow to pay all monthly living expenses; have an emergency fund with six months cash in case of an emergency or job loss; purchase a $25,000 life insurance policy for survivors in case of unexpected death; pay down credit card debt by 25% this calendar year.

   A. Short term.

   B. Mid-term.

   C. Long term.

   Answer: A. Short term. These are a few of the short-term financial goals that lay the foundation for financial health.

2. The cornerstone of your financial plan is the:

   A. Binary technical indices.

   B. Asset diversification.

   C. Efficient frontier helix.

   D. Required rate of return.

   Answer: D. Required rate of return. The required rate of return (RRR) is the percentage by which your portfolio should be increasing every year to keep you on course to achieve your goals in the time prescribed.

3. True or false? Your ability to accept risk depends on these four factors:

   A. A portfolio with a large amount of assets.

   B. A limited time horizon.

   C. A guaranteed fixed income of sufficient size, so lifestyle is not affected by loss.

   D. Controlled spending limits.

      A. True.

      B. False.

Answer: B. False. A lengthy time horizon is needed, not a limited one.

4. The blueprint for your investment plan is the:

   A. IRS.

   B. RRR.

   C. IPS.

   D. MPT.

   Answer: C. IPS. Your investment policy statement is your investment guide, a predetermined set of investment rules you will follow at all times, especially when under emotional duress with fear and greed. The IPS is your safety net, guiding your decisions so you reap your rewards and curtail your losses.

Chapter 8
Measuring Your Progress

When you have finished reading this chapter, you will:

- Know the difference between relative and absolute benchmarks
- Be able to determine which benchmark is best for your situation
- Understand why it's important to agree with your financial advisor on which benchmark to use
- Be familiar with the seven components of selecting a good benchmark
- Explain the value of creating a valid custom benchmark
- Be introduced to the concept of attribution analysis
- Appreciate the difference between fundamental and market cap indexing

Introduction

One of the challenges of being an investor is monitoring your portfolio so you can confirm that it is growing at a pace that is expected, or better. Yes, you have the advantage of the required rate of return as a measuring stick, so every year you will know whether or not you are meeting your own personal benchmark...and there are other ways to measure your progress, too.

As we said before, in some years you'll be better and worse than the RRR you need to meet your goals on time. As long as, over the course of time, your RRR's average equals or exceeds your desired annual percent return, all is well. Therefore, with the RRR you have a built-in benchmark based on the desired outcome for your individual financial goals.

Even so, your portfolio, which is an aggregate of multiple assets all working together synergistically, might be performing better than it is. Most investors want to know if their portfolio is performing at a peak level or is inefficiently leaving money on the table. Truly, if you could be earning a greater return for the same risk, wouldn't you want to? Aside from the transaction fees and taxes you might have to pay for buying and selling your assets, if everything was equal, a higher rate of return with no additional risk is a welcome advantage.

This raises the question of how to measure your portfolio's performance. This is not a simple task because a portfolio with a variety of assets does not match up properly with the benchmark indices that are typically used. To provide a simple example that clarifies the issue, many investors mistakenly compare their portfolio's performance to the S&P 500. It may be that these investors do so because they are familiar with the S&P 500, or somehow believe the S&P 500 is a universal benchmark for measuring annual growth, which it is not.

The comparison lacks value because the S&P 500 is a stock index and investors may have a diversified portfolio that has a combination of both stocks and bonds. In addition, their stock portfolio's risk and return calculations could be higher or lower than the S&P 500's risk and return expectations, depending on the assets in the individual portfolio. To add insult to injury, the S&P 500 is not a sensible index for measurement because the S&P 500's performance does not include the cost of management fees, loads, or commission costs which all investors pay! Typically, these costs, which are called frictional costs, can slow a portfolio's annual return by 1.5%, which is considered a conservative estimate. Anyone comparing their portfolio's performance to the S&P 500 is using a compass that only points east. More inconsistencies could be entertained here, but the point is made.

How then, should an investor measure the progress of their portfolio?

Relative vs. Absolute Benchmarks

There are two types of benchmarks, relative and absolute. Both benchmarks have value for the investor, and they are used in different ways. As an investor, you should consider employing both of them.

A matter of importance to consider, whether you are doing your own investing or have hired the services of a professional advisor, is recognizing whether or not a relative benchmark is an appropriate measurement tool. You may be selecting a tool that is inappropriate for the task. The task may require a screwdriver, but if you need a Phillips screwdriver and all you have is a flat-head, you won't get the results you want.

Key:

Select a benchmark that truly measures the assets in your portfolio.

If you are using the services of a financial planner, you need to ask which benchmark he or she is using because there may otherwise be a big and unhappy disconnect between you. Your expectations for measurable results may be entirely different from your advisor's reasoning for selecting and using another benchmark than the one you envisioned. This can create a lot of confusion and make your business relationship with each other very difficult. Knowing how your portfolio will be assessed is a great discussion to have with your financial advisor so you have an accurate understanding of how to judge your portfolio's growth or loss.

Here is a clever thought to determine if a benchmark is a good contender for your use. Chartered Financial Analysts regard a benchmark as valid if it has the following seven components, known by the mnemonic lettering, SAMURAI:

Figure 33: Samurai.

SAMURAI	
Specified in advance:	The benchmark is known to all at the start of evaluation period.
Appropriate:	The benchmark should accurately reflect the manager's performance style.
Measurable:	You must be able to measure the results.
Unambiguous:	A good benchmark's components should be known.
Reflective:	Reflects manager's current investment expertise.
Accountable:	Manager should agree that the benchmark is an appropriate measure.
Investable:	You should be able to replicate and invest in a benchmark. *

* Chartered Financial Analysts; http://www.cfainstitute.org

Relative Benchmarks

A relative benchmark provides the opportunity to compare your portfolio's performance against the performance of a benchmark like the S&P 500. The challenge will be finding benchmarks that are similar enough to your portfolio to validate a worthy comparison.

Absolute Benchmarks

An absolute benchmark is the benchmark you use to assess your performance toward achieving your financial goals. In essence, this is the required rate of return (RRR) you are already using. Your absolute benchmark could be 5.67% or 7.23% ... whatever you need to achieve your financial goals.

Custom Benchmarks

A custom benchmark is what it sounds like, a benchmark that is custom designed to accurately reflect the investment strategies and specific asset allocations of various asset classes and ratios in your portfolio. The custom benchmark is as similar to your portfolio as possible so it can provide an accurate measurement of your portfolio's performance.

Unlike most of the generic market benchmarks, the custom benchmark must be constructed so it has the same systematic risk as the strategy or strategies employed by your portfolio. The custom benchmark must also be similar in asset classes and asset subclasses. Furthermore, the custom benchmark must also represent an equivalent asset allocation that equates with the diversification of your personal portfolio. The constraints in your portfolio must match the constraints in the custom benchmark as well.

Note:

Always test your custom benchmark to ensure its validity as a measurement.

Finally, the custom benchmark will need to be tested so it can be confirmed as a valid measurement tool. Obviously, great care must be taken to construct a custom benchmark that can be appropriately used to measure your portfolio's performance. If you are a good mathematician and have experience with this level of portfolio construction, this is a necessary task worthy of your time. If this is not within the range of your expertise, you should hire the services of a professional financial planner.

The key point is that most investors are incorrectly comparing their portfolio's performance with benchmarks that will give them inaccurate findings. Therefore, the only real way to know how well your portfolio is performing is to design a custom benchmark that is completely aligned with your portfolio so your progress can be accurately measured.

Of course, the reason you want your portfolio to be accurately measured is because you want your portfolio to be as efficient as possible so you can adjust your portfolio as needed to earn as much as possible within the limited time of your investment horizon. Time is an important factor in the mechanics of building wealth; time is a resource that is precious and limited. If your portfolio is losing time, then you are losing the opportunity for the efficient accumulation of wealth. The best way to know that your portfolio is performing efficiently is by comparing the results of your portfolio with the results of a custom benchmark, and then, as necessary, adjusting your portfolio to meet or exceed the benchmark's performance.

Remember that if you change your portfolio's asset mix, you have to change the benchmark as well. For example, if your portfolio begins with 50% U.S. equities and 50% U.S. bond positions, it may be appropriate to measure your portfolio's performance against the S&P 500 and the Barclay Bond Index. Should you decide to adjust your portfolio to 33.3% U.S. equities, 33.3% U.S. bonds, and 33.3% international equities, you have to adjust your benchmark to have an accurate evaluation.

Attribution Analysis

Attribution analysis allows the investor to determine which assets have affected the portfolio by becoming either overweight or underweight. This analysis shows what can happen if you decide to either experiment with your allocations, or your portfolio becomes unbalanced over time.

Here is an example of what can happen if you overweight or underweight an asset in your portfolio:

Example 1. You decide to include the stock of a company that's not in the S&P 500, and the stock does very well; your portfolio outperforms the S&P 500 benchmark, but you've invalidated your benchmark because you're using a stock that is not in the index.

Example 2. You decide to use a benchmark that includes Apple, but do not include Apple in your portfolio. Months later, Apple is the top-performing stock in the benchmark, but because it wasn't one of the stocks in your portfolio, you now realize why your portfolio underperformed the benchmark.

This little diversion in our discussion on benchmarks can help you see how important it is to align your benchmark in your portfolio as closely as possible so you have an accurate reading of your portfolio's performance, assuming you value the data you will receive from having a relative benchmark. Even though you may be totally focused on an absolute benchmark, that is, your required rate of return (RRR) which you must achieve over the course of years to have the funds for your financial goals, using a relative benchmark has its merits because it will broaden your perspective as an investor and may provide insight on how you can refine and accelerate your portfolio's performance within the time horizon that remains.

Fundamental vs. Market Cap Indexing

Market capitalization indexing is the traditional method for benchmark indexing. Typically and generally speaking, the S&P 500 Index is used to measure stock performance, the Russell 3000 with its 3,000 stocks measures a broader swath of the stock market, the Lipper indexes are used for mutual funds, Morgan Stanley indexes are the traditional benchmarks for international investors, and a few other specialty indexes are respected benchmarks as well, even though they are flawed as noted.

Along with the popularity of exchange-traded funds (ETF), there have been developments with new concepts for benchmarking. This gave birth to the practice of using a fundamental index, which measures key components of a company's performance rather than only the market value of the company's shares, which is the focus of market cap indexing. Here is a short description of both:

Fundamental Index

With fundamental indexing, securities are measured by a variety of different factors such as cash flow, sales, revenue, dividends, number of employees, company valuation, and book value, which are many of the elements of a company's fundamentals that truly should matter. With a fundamental index, you're looking deeper into the economics of companies. You can find existing fundamental indices that weight and rank specific fundamental criteria in a number of different industry sectors such as mid-cap or small cap stocks, and international stocks as well. These indices are regularly updated to keep their data current and reliable.

Information:

A fundamental index can measure such factors as cash flow, sales, revenue, etc.

One of the advantages of using a fundamental index is that it may reduce your exposure to the flaws of market cap benchmarking which favor only one factor: the singular focus is on a company's share value in price and quantity. A potential disadvantage of using a fundamental index is the risk of underperforming traditional indexes whose market value data may be more precise at given moments in the markets' cycles.

People who don't like fundamental indexing are likely to criticize it as a form of active management, and they discount it as a worthwhile form of indexing. Whether that's the case or not, it's important to remember that the Big Picture is to achieve a certain return, and if fundamental indexing is another path toward that end, then there is every reason to consider it as a valid tool.

Market Cap Index

Market capitalization indexing, also known as classic or traditional indexing, is an index benchmark composed of the aggregate of its components, each company individually weighted by the value of its outstanding shares. The average of this combination of multiple companies, based on the outstanding shares and share prices, results in the index's value. This value changes daily, and can provide daily, weekly, monthly, quarterly and annual averages that individual assets can use for comparable performance.

One of the advantages of market capitalization indexing, depending on the index used, is the generally low turnover of the companies included in the index; this provides stability to the index and makes it a more solid benchmark because its components largely remain the same. Another advantage is that the market determines each component's weight, so the average daily price of the index is not subjective.

There are several potential disadvantages as well. One of them is that an index can underperform when compared with other indices that are weighted differently because of their different strategies. A second disadvantage is that the larger indices may under-represent companies that have smaller capitalizations.

Both forms of indexing have their value and their drawbacks. As a successful investor, you may want to do some additional reading on this topic so you have additional methods for comparing the performance of your assets with other assets having similar characteristics. The more information you know and the more comparisons you make, the more informed you will be with gauging the performance of your assets.

Summary

There are times when active management works best, and times when a passive role is the proper choice. The choice is between alpha vs. beta; over-performance vs. mirroring the markets' returns. At Synergy Asset Management we typically split between the two and use both a fundamental index and a market cap index. This helps ensure a good diversification model. There are times when the market favors the use of both, or one or the other. Because they have different properties and characteristics, they bring value to the portfolio's assessment at various points in time, which help us more precisely measure our clients' portfolios.

While fundamental indexing might be regarded as a flawed measuring tool by some because it's perceived as a filter and not a measure for investment decisions, those who favor the market cap indexing model should also consider the fallibility of their own champion, given that they are using a benchmark based on the market's arbitrary pricing of shares; the S&P 500 is a price-weighted index and thus has its own shortcomings. The truth of the matter is that no tool is perfect, so an investor needs a tool chest with sufficient variety to construct a portfolio that serves their bottom line.

Whether selecting an industry-standard benchmark that truly measures your portfolio's performance, or designing a benchmark that's customized to precisely gauge your portfolio's progress, a valid means for measuring your assets is paramount so you can determine the productivity of your funds and earn the most return for your investment.

Chapter 8 Review Questions

1. A relative benchmark is:

   A. Like the S&P 500 against which a portfolio compares its performance.
   B. A combination of several indices, of which elements of each are in your portfolio.
   C. Custom designed, reflecting the strategies and asset allocations in your portfolio.
   D. Like your required rate of return, assessing progress toward your financial goals.

2. Market capitalization indexing is an index benchmark:

   A. Measures key components of a company's performance.
   B. Composed of the aggregate of its components, with weighted values.

Chapter 8 Review Answers

1. A relative benchmark is:

   A. Like the S&P 500 against which a portfolio compares its performance.

   B. A combination of several indices, of which elements of each are in your portfolio.

   C. Custom designed, reflecting the strategies and asset allocations in your portfolio.

   D. Like your required rate of return, assessing progress toward your financial goals.

   Answer: A. Like the S&P 500 against which a portfolio compares its performance. A benchmark like this can only be relative because it only approximates your portfolio's design, and must be used cautiously.

2. Market capitalization indexing is an index benchmark:

   A. Measures key components of a company's performance.

   B. Composed of the aggregate of its components, with weighted values.

   Answer: B. Composed of the aggregate of its components, with weighted values. Market capitalization indexing weights each company individually by the value of its outstanding shares. Answer A is the fundamental index, measuring key components of a company's performance.

Chapter 9
How to Build the Best Portfolio

When you have finished reading this chapter, you will:

- Have a broader understanding of how diversification and asset allocation work together
- Understand why not diversifying has value for some investors
- Consider whether asset allocation or focus investing is a better choice for you
- Know about the value of asset rotation as an investment strategy
- Understand the underlying concepts of passive management versus active management
- Be able to describe the difference between a strategic and tactical investment decision
- Identify the most essential factor when building a portfolio

Introduction

The best portfolio is different for each investor, based on their individual needs. The design of your portfolio, the selection of your assets, and your allocation of those assets depends on whether you subscribe to an efficient or inefficient market, to passive or active management. This chapter will guide your thinking on which underlying principle is the preferred foundation of your portfolio's focus.

Diversification and Asset Allocation

About 2,600 years ago Aesop told the tale about the farm maid who was taking her basket of eggs to market. She imagined selling her eggs, using the profit to buy a goose, and selling the goose for enough profit to buy a cow. Before she got to market, she dropped her basket and provided us with the moral of not putting all our eggs in one basket. This is the essence of diversification.

Then there was Aesop's story of the bundle of sticks in which a father taught his quarreling sons a lesson about unity. Each son received a stick that was easily broken, but when the sticks were in one bundle, the bundle could not be broken. Allocating your assets is like the bundle of sticks; as a group, the allocations have more strength than if your allocation was only singular. This is the essence of asset allocation.

Diversification

The general concept of diversification is simple. Your money should be in a variety of investments so if any one investment does poorly, your other investments, one hopes, will not suffer as much. Again, simplistically, if you have a portfolio composed of only large cap stocks, and you buy 20 of them, your portfolio is diversified. If any one company falters, the others may not. One egg might break, or two, but the others will probably survive. Remember, this is just the concept of diversification, not a practice you should necessarily follow.

When we invite a conversation about diversification, it is also important to realize that our conversation includes the recognition of systematic risk and unsystematic risk. We have no control over systematic risk, which is the risk of the market system. The market will do what the market will do; when we enter the environment of the market, we are subjecting ourselves to the rules and behavior of its special and separate universe. Systematic risk is also known as beta risk; this risk cannot be diversified. Unsystematic risk is another matter entirely. This is the risk we take by investing in different companies, and this is the only risk for which we are rewarded.

Three out of four stocks trend with the market; this is the beta effect. You've heard the expression that a rising tide floats all boats. No boat is immune to the tidal effect; every boat in every slip is affected by the tide's movement. The boat in slip 15 is not immune to the tide. You don't see the boats in slip 14 and 16 rise and fall while the boat in slip

15 stays the same; that's not how it works! And, just as the tide lifts all boats, the tide will also lower all boats.

Important:

Remember that diversification and asset allocation are not the same, and both are necessary to protect your portfolio.

Many people get diversification and asset allocation mixed up. If you have 20 to 40 large cap stocks, assuming that each of the stocks is different by virtue of their distinctly different features, you're diversified. If you own 20 to 40 bonds, you're diversified. If you own 20 to 40 international stocks, you're diversified. Diversifying is a mathematical way of reducing the unsystematic risk. You can also diversify within an asset class.

Asset Allocation

Asset allocation is taking the concept of diversification and applying it to asset classes such as large cap stocks; small cap stocks, U.S. bonds, global bonds, emerging markets, cash, and commodities. These are a few examples of different asset classes. Your portfolio should be diversified among several asset classes as well as diversified among the securities within each asset class.

In 2008 when the markets had a huge tumble and dropped by 40%, many investors said that asset allocation hadn't worked and they declared the practice dead...but asset allocation was never intended to protect your portfolio from all loss; the value of asset allocation is that your money will probably diminish less than it would if you didn't allocate your assets.

Note:

Asset allocation is a good tool for protecting your portfolio from loss, but not from all loss.

Asset allocation actually did what it was supposed to do. Not every portfolio dropped by 40%. If you had owned the 500 stocks of the S&P 500, you would've been diversified because you owned all 500 stocks, but your portfolio still went down 40%. Instead, however, if your portfolio had been in an asset allocation model, your portfolio may have gone down maybe only 20%...a big difference. Asset allocation, when done correctly, would also have protected your investment funds by diversifying within the asset classes themselves; your portfolio might not have been composed of 100% U.S. equities.

Diversifying among a variety of asset classes is one step, and diversifying within the asset classes is the other.

This is a good time to bring up the essential theme of this book, which is represented by the title, "Investment Insight: Getting to Diversified... Or Not!" Is diversification a good practice, or isn't it?

There are two primary ways to invest: asset allocation and focus investing, and they are opposite sides of a coin. Asset allocation was made famous by Harry Markowitz, a Nobel Prize winner, for his work in the 1950s. Focus investing has been made popular by the world's best investor, Warren Buffett.

Buffett maintains that investors who diversify are missing significant opportunities for accelerated wealth. His strategy is to buy just a few of the right companies' stocks, focusing on those that are most likely to grow steadily and safely. However, since not everyone has the time, talent, skill or resources to engage in focus investing, asset allocation is a bona fide alternative.

Important:

There are two primary ways to invest: asset allocation and focus investing. Which one is right for you, or are both right for you?

To use a metaphor, asset allocation is like a tugboat while focus investing is like a speedboat. These are two different tools formed from two different theories. We live in a society that always places demands on us to make choices, but we don't have to accept that these choices are mutually exclusive; they can coexist. Investors can benefit from both practices when they understand how each model works and specifically, how each would work toward your best interests within your portfolio.

If you're working with an advisor, it's also important to know what your advisor prefers and is most strongly suited to doing. Is your advisor an asset allocator, or is your advisor a focus investor? Perhaps your advisor is a little bit of both? Both theories are "right", it just depends on the method that suits you best, or the best combination for you. Some investment advisors recognize the value of both asset allocation and focus investing, and can blend both theories into their practice and their clients' portfolios.

Even though you can have a 4,000 horsepower dragster, that doesn't mean it's the right vehicle for you. You could crash it, while a professional driver could win the first-place trophy. It's not the car that's bad, it's that the driver isn't equipped to drive it. The theory isn't good or bad, it's whether or not the investor is equipped to accept the conditions and execute the theory. One size does not suit all.

Please keep in mind that when we review active investing and passive investing in a few pages, we'll be discussing Robert Shiller, the Nobel Laureate, for his work on active management, and Eugene Fama, the Nobel Laureate, for his work on passive indexing. So again, we have two world-renowned Nobel Prize winners with competing theories, and one is heads as the other is tails. One advocates the theory while the other advocates the tugboat theory. What's an investor to do? There is no magic answer, and this is one of the conundrums of the investment world.

The key point here is that if you become really good at managing one style or the other, stick with it. Or, if you get really good at managing a little bit of both, stick with that. Know your objectives, know your tools, use the right tool for the job, and apply the theory as it was intended. Both these theories have tremendous merit, and like so many other situations you can find yourself in, it's not about one theory being right and the other being wrong. Nothing ever works 100% of the time and both have indisputable value in different circumstances. It's up to you as an investor to decide which one works best for your particular style of money management.

The great news is that you have a well-stocked toolbox; now you need to learn more about these tools, find out which tool you're more skilled at using, and know when and how to apply your expertise. Once you determine which strategy you prefer, or if you like a combination of the two, stick with your selection; the majority of your gains may not come so much from your choice of strategy as from picking and sticking with your preferred and most comfortable choice.

ASSET ROTATION:

Whether you are a disciple of asset allocation or focus investing, asset rotation might be appealing to you. Asset rotation is employed when you can guesstimate that a certain asset class will be favored in the months to come. A little bit of knowledge is a wonderful thing, and while you might be wrong, your information and instincts are suggesting a strong short term play could result in additional profits... so you decide to rotate your assets so you have a larger percentage of the favored assets in your portfolio.

This is a bit like focus investing because you are selecting assets based on their strong potential for sudden growth, but it's focus investing with a little bit of asset allocation mixed in because it's also about being in the right place at the right time.

At Synergy Asset Management, we have three different types of diversified portfolios. Whichever portfolio is the best one for you depends on our conversations to determine your philosophy of investing combined with your goals for financial growth, which then guides us with customizing the perfect portfolio for you.

Let's continue the discussion on active and passive investing by looking at the hypotheses of each:

Efficient Market Hypothesis

Passive investment managers agree with Eugene Fama and believe in the efficient market hypothesis. This hypothesis states that assets offered in the market are fairly valued because all relevant information has been processed, resulting in a price that is efficiently set. They contend it is impossible to outperform the stock market and managers that attempt to do so cannot do it consistently over the long term, plus they also charge fees that further limit the investor's return.

Passive Management

Investors who subscribe to the passive investment style argue that their time is better spent concentrating on the underlying asset allocation of their portfolios instead of searching for undervalued stocks. Passive investors buy index mutual funds or ETFs (exchange-traded funds) that replicate a market index like the S&P 500 or the Russell 2000. Rather than deciding whether to buy Chevron or Exxon, which they believe are both efficiently priced, passive investors choose to focus on whether to buy stocks or bonds, or domestic versus international assets.

Note:

As an investor, are you a hunter or gatherer? It's okay to be either.

By buying an index fund or ETF that tracks an index as closely as possible, expenses are much lower than the costs with active managers. The passive manager doesn't have to spend hours and hours researching the fundamentals of hundreds of companies to identify qualified funds for purchase. The intention of passive investing is to replicate the market, not beat it; since the underlying philosophy is that the market's prices for all assets have been efficiently valued, an index fund is the perfect solution.

Even though the passive investor's portfolio has the benefit of reduced costs, this portfolio will not have the opportunity to acquire significantly higher returns than the index. When certain asset classes and sectors are underperforming, the portfolio will also underperform in these areas. A passive investment portfolio's value can only increase and decrease based on the performance of the underlying assets in the index.

On the one hand, passive investors have less costs and trend with the market; on the other hand, passive investors are unlikely to achieve growth above the index to which they subscribe. They rise and fall and rise and fall according to the dictates of the asset index they own.

Beta

Beta is the name of the descriptor that measures an investor's risk according to the market's average. A beta of 1 is the precisely neutral point of risk an investor accepts for just being in the market. If an asset has a beta of less than one, then the asset is less volatile than the market. For example, a beta of 0.8 means the asset is 20% less volatile than the market. If an asset has a beta of more than one, then the asset is more volatile than the market. For example, a beta of 1.3 means the asset is 30% more volatile than the market.

Definition:

Beta is the name of the descriptor that measures an investor's risk according to the market's average.

Beta is a good indicator to help you determine the degree of risk your asset would have; remember that the downside of risk is that you are more susceptible to loss. This is why knowing your tolerance for risk is so important; you can be clear with yourself on what is and is not acceptable.

Inefficient Market Hypothesis

Active investment managers dismiss the efficient market hypothesis and believe that the market has many price inefficiencies that make it entirely possible to outperform the market in the long term. They agree with Robert Shiller and believe they can discover securities that are undervalued; they are willing to do the research to identify and purchase a stock, for example, that is trading at $70 but is worth $90.

Active Management

The advantage of active investment is that these investors can often generate higher returns than the benchmark they are seeking to exceed. They know that if they can discover more winning stocks than losing stocks, they can beat the index and sometimes quite significantly. Active investors also have the capacity to generate good returns even when the markets are trending downward.

For example, a mutual fund manager is attempting to exceed the returns of the S&P 500, which measures U. S. large cap companies. The S&P 500 contains companies from all 10 sectors, from Consumer Discretionary to Utilities. Assuming that the telecommunication sector was underperforming by 10%, the entire market would suffer and would lose profitability because of telecommunication's drag on the performance of the S&P 500 as a whole.

The passive investor's portfolio would decrease in value accordingly because the passive investor is mirroring the entire index. However, active managers have the ability to sell their telecommunication positions and can invest in the sectors that are outperforming the S&P 500, thereby cutting potential losses and accelerating potential profits. When managers have the ability to make active decisions, they are potentially capable of beating the market.

Of course, there are criticisms of active investing. A primary criticism is that outperforming the indexes year after year is difficult. With a more focused portfolio, an active investor could significantly underperform, and this could result in the loss of both time and money. Another criticism is that the active management of a portfolio is more costly than the management of a passive portfolio. Management fees are higher because they are used to support the manager and the research team; there are also more transaction fees with an active portfolio. Fees can become expensive and could seriously deplete the return, negating the value of having an actively managed account.

There is, however, a way to employ the best of both hypotheses. There are occasions when active investing is more rewarding than passive investing and vice versa. It's also true that the different asset classes perform variously during different market cycles. Some asset classes, such as the U.S. large cap equities, are typically a very efficient asset class because information about these equities is usually very complete.

On the other hand, an asset class like emerging market bonds is not familiar to very many investors. It could be a good strategy to passively invest in the U.S. large cap equities, but hire an active investment management team to research and manage the emerging market bonds. A blend of the two investment styles could result in the benefit of drawing on the strengths of both by outperforming in the asset classes that are less efficient while enjoying lower fees in the asset classes where efficiency is more likely.

Alpha

Alpha is the descriptor that describes a fund's excess returns when compared with the returns of a benchmark index. For example, an alpha of 4 means the fund performed 4% better than the benchmark index; an alpha of -2 means the fund performed 2% less than the benchmark index. An alpha of 0 means there was no differentiation between the performance of the fund and the market's movement. Alpha is the return on your investment in excess of the market's fluctuation.

Definition:

Alpha is the descriptor that describes a fund's excess returns when compared with the returns of a benchmark index.

While a positive alpha is obviously highly desirable, it is also not easy to attain, which relates to the continuing debate about efficient and inefficient markets. Is it possible to beat the market consistently year after year, with the additional fees and possibly additional taxes? Or is it best to go along with the crowd and accept the market's ups and downs, and only trade based on the indexes? Or is there value in a third choice, the blending of these two practices? You have now seen the failings of both, as well as the promise of both...so could this third option be a viable solution for you? More on this soon.

Strategic Decisions vs. Tactical Decisions

When you make decisions to invest your money, you'll find yourself in the position of having to make strategic and tactical decisions. A strategic decision is one that sets the structure of the Big Picture, such as when an investor decides to build a portfolio that is 50% stocks and 50% bonds, or 60% stocks and 40% bonds; this is a key foundational decision. A tactical decision is important but less significant, such as when an investor makes a decision that's different from normal policies because the investor believes information or an insight suggests a promising reward when this modification is made...such as: "Hmmmm...the European markets are starting to improve; maybe I need to establish a stronger position there..."

Strategic Decisions

Strategic decisions are about the Big Picture, about setting up the structure of your investment plan and portfolio. Strategic decisions include determining the percentage of your portfolio which will be stocks and which will be bonds; what percentage of your stocks will be U.S.-based, and of the stocks that are U.S.-based, what percentage will be large cap, medium cap, and small cap companies? What intentions do you have for being an asset allocation investor or a focus investor, or a combination of both? Are you going to set up your financial plan for a projected retirement at age 65, or age 70? What is your required rate of return (RRR), and what is your Plan B if you begin to fall behind? What is your annual commitment to adding new funds to your investment portfolio? What is the exact dollar amount you need to ensure the comfortable lifestyle in retirement that you envision?

These questions provide good examples of strategic decisions that set the structure of your investment plan and subsequently of your investment portfolio.

Tactical Decisions

Tactical decisions are best described as variations to the overall strategy that defines the structure of your plan and portfolio. An example of this would be your decision to buy bonds to augment your existing portfolio. Instead of buying U.S. bonds, you decide to purchase international bonds because the European market is now beginning to decline. The investor makes a decision outside their normal investment policy. Even though the portfolio's guiding strategy is to own 60% stocks and 40% bonds over the next 20 years, the investor will make tactical decisions that support influences that are already working to potentially accelerate the returns. In essence, the investor makes a little bet when he or she think rates will go up or down, or a little bet when the investor thinks he or she has some knowledge that might work in their favor. These little bets don't always work out as hoped, but the risk is reasonable considering the potential for the reward.

Here's another example. An investor built a strategic portfolio with 13 asset classes, and one of these asset classes was commodities. Last year, commodities performed terribly so the investor makes a tactical decision to reduce commodities from a 3% position to a 0% position. In the long-term, the investor values commodities and knows commodities should be in the portfolio, but has temporarily removed commodities because data indicate commodities will perform poorly again this year. Here is a variation. The investor believes that emerging markets equity should be in his or her portfolio, but because it was trending so poorly, the position was reduced from a 10% weight, which is what the portfolio's recipe called for, down to a 5% weight by selling off a number of those assets. The tactical decision was to keep emerging markets, but to temporarily reduce its proportion from 10% to 5%.

Cash can also be employed as a versatile and tactical asset within an investment portfolio. By holding cash, investors have the liquidity to weather storms and preserve capital during especially uncertain market conditions while also facilitating swift action when opportunities arise. In times of market distress, asset prices may plummet, providing investors with the chance to acquire quality assets at discounted prices, bargains that may lead to growth and capital appreciation. The availability of cash also allows investors to reallocate capital to sectors that are poised for performance without first having to sell other assets, providing flexibility. In these ways, cash provides options for investment processes when managed with prudence.

Strategic decisions are largely based on the future, looking down the road 20 or 30 years, or more, and making choices that avoid serious problems later. Tactical decisions are those that make modest modifications to suit a temporary condition for potential gain with limited risk. An experienced investor knows not to play around with the strategic foundations of the portfolio unless major cracks are showing, and in which case it would be wise to consult with a professional financial planner before making any changes. An experienced investor also knows how to calculate the effect of tactical decisions, and whether or not to take the risk for the reward of the gain.

Summary

There is no argument about whether diversification is wise or unwise. 2,600 years ago, Aesop made the point with a basket of eggs. The real issue is how to select and diversify your assets among the 22 main asset classes, and then how to diversify among the securities included within each of your selected asset classes. This will be the topic of the next chapter.

We also spent a moment defining the nature of the investment world's debate over the dichotomy between two opposing philosophies which attempt to determine whether the market is efficient or inefficient. Each philosophy has its own practices, and both philosophies have their own Nobel champion; thc luminaries of the Nobel Economic

Sciences Prize Committee, in honoring the intellectual and experiential results of both pioneers, have profoundly recognized the individual validity of these opposing approaches to investment.

What's an investor to do? Passive management? Active management? Both styles have their positive and negative features.

The attraction of passive management is that investors have less work to do because they trust the efficiency of the market's ability to price securities. There are also likely to have less transaction costs and management fees because this style of investing is passive; all one needs to do is follow the benchmark index as closely as possible. Yes, the markets will go up and down, but this is an acceptable given because in the long run, investors will bring home sufficient profits with limited risk. A passive investor is a gatherer, not a hunter.

Oh, but wait! There are also investors who do not want to be a satellite orbiting a sleepy planet, accepting profits and losses doled out by the market. These are hunters, not gatherers. Active management promises a more exciting and more rewarding result when price anomalies appear in the bush. Why accept a steady diet of automatic profits and losses when the opportunity exists to advance one's portfolio value at a more rapid pace, offering the potential of achieving one's goals sooner and with increased results? Yes, there are likely to be more transaction and management fees, and potential capital gains costs, but the risk is amply compensated by the vast potential for accelerated returns.

But is there a third choice? Is it possible to be both a hunter and a gatherer? The answer is yes, it's possible if an investor has the time and personality to become knowledgeable in the best practices of both, or is willing to employ the professional services of a financial management team that has the expertise and track record for doing the same.

We live in a culture that appears to demand either a yes or a no, probably a product of the binary code of our time. But our choice of investment philosophy does not have to be limited to one or the other; we CAN have our pie a la mode and eat it, too...if we are willing to make the effort and invest our time in becoming proficient with both investing practices, or hire an investment firm that already is. We don't have to accept the narrow restrictions of either/or; we can enjoy an investor's frame of mind that permits us the lucrative pleasure of harvesting the benefits of both/and.

Chapter 9 Review Questions

1. Which of the following is not true about systematic risk?

   A. Systematic risk is also known as beta risk.

   B. An investor has some control over systematic risk.

   C. Systematic risk can be diversified.

   D. Systematic risk is the risk of being in a system with its own rules and behaviors.

2. Diversification and asset allocation are the same thing. True or false?

   A. True.

   B. False.

3. Which statement is true?

   A. The market is efficient.

   B. The market is inefficient.

   C. The efficiency of the market depends on the philosophy of the investor.

   D. The market is always inefficient, but tries to become efficient.

4. The passive investment style is for investors who:

   A. Choose to actively manage their portfolio.

   B. Prefer to concentrate on the asset allocation of their portfolio.

   C. Enjoy searching for undervalued stocks.

   D. Are hunters, not gatherers.

Chapter 9 Review Answers

1. Which of the following is not true about systematic risk?

   A. Systematic risk is also known as beta risk.
   B. An investor has some control over systematic risk.
   C. Systematic risk can be diversified.
   D. Systematic risk is the risk of being in a system with its own rules and behaviors.

   Answer: C. Systematic risk can be diversified. Actually, systematic risk cannot be diversified because it is the risk an investor accepts by investing in the market, and environment with its own rules and behaviors.

2. Diversification and asset allocation are the same thing. True or false?

   A. True.
   B. False.

   Answer: B. false. Asset allocation is the allocation of your assets into different investment classes, but your portfolio can still be undiversified if those asset classes or assets are too similar. Diversification is selecting your assets so if one asset declines in value, others may increase in value to offset the loss of the declining asset.

3. Which statement is true?

   A. The market is efficient.
   B. The market is inefficient.
   C. The efficiency of the market depends on the philosophy of the investor.
   D. The market is always inefficient, but tries to become efficient.

   Answer: C. The efficiency of the market depends on the philosophy of the investor. The answer is based on the philosophic preference of the investor. This philosophic viewpoint determines whether an investor will prefer an alpha or beta portfolio performance.

4. The passive investment style is for investors who:

   A. Choose to actively manage their portfolio.
   B. Prefer to concentrate on the asset allocation of their portfolio.
   C. Enjoy searching for undervalued stocks.

   Are hunters, not gatherers. **Answer: B.** Prefer to concentrate on the asset allocation of their portfolio. Believing that the market is efficient, they see no point in comparing companies, and would rather accept the gains and losses of a passive management style.

Chapter 10
Asset Allocation

When you have finished reading this chapter, you will know:

- The essential concept upon which Modern Portfolio Theory is based
- The process for developing an asset allocation model
- Why it's important to combine investments with different expected returns and risks in your portfolio
- The importance of the mean variance
- The process for analyzing investment options
- The six steps for building an asset allocation model
- The three elements for developing asset class inputs
- The difference between static and dynamic rebalancing
- How to improve the monitoring of your portfolio
- Why it's important to rebalance your portfolio, and when not to do so

Introduction

Asset allocation is an approach to investment selection that involves diversifying among different types of investments called asset classes to reduce risk.

As we established in the last chapter, asset allocation is the essential factor when building a portfolio. Whether you are an active or passive investor, you will need to make a decision about the best mix of assets for your portfolio. This strategic decision will be based on the degree of your risk tolerance, your ability to accept risk, and the asset allocations you are willing to make.

To obtain the benefit of diversification, the first and most important step is to select several asset classes which are fundamentally different and, therefore, likely to vary above and below their expected return rates at different times.

The second step in the process is to apply a mathematical analysis called Modern Portfolio Theory. This application identifies a range of best-diversified mixes of asset classes that offer various expected return rates, each with the least possible volatility and risk. If, during the year, one asset class goes down, others are likely to offset that decline by going up. The objective is to optimize your account through portfolio construction practices that are thoroughly tested and designed to minimize risk while maximizing returns.

Let's take a look at Modern Portfolio Theory and the work of Harry Markowitz because this will explain why so much care must be taken with selecting differentiated asset classes, and differentiated assets within each asset class.

Modern Portfolio Theory

The name Harry Markowitz may be familiar to you now. He was mentioned briefly in the last chapter. Markowitz is an American economist who earned the Nobel Memorial Prize in Economic Sciences in 1990, and who, in the 1950s, pioneered modern portfolio theory. Modern Portfolio Theory is the study of the effects of risk, return, diversification, and the correlation of assets within portfolios.

The essential concept underlying modern portfolio theory is that an investment portfolio's assets should be selected based on a projection of how the changing price of each individual asset will affect the price of the other assets in the portfolio. In other words, every asset in a portfolio should be selected not just on their individual capacity to generate return and limit risk, but also on how each of the assets in the portfolio affect the other assets relative to their combined effect on the entire portfolio's risk and return.

Key:

An investment portfolio's assets should be selected based on how the changing price of each asset may affect the price of the other assets.

Markowitz's modern portfolio theory is intended to help investors select the assets for their portfolio that will result in the highest possible expected return. Looked at from the other angle, this theory helps investors who want to achieve a specific return and create a portfolio with the least possible risk. Modern portfolio theory is therefore a theory about diversification because it provides you with guidelines on how to make varied asset selections that work together, cohesively, to achieve a higher potential return with the least possible risk. This is why it was so important to determine your risk tolerance in Chapter 7; any return can be fashioned, but it's the investor's tolerance for risk that dictates the investor's preference for return.

This brings us to a topic we barely mentioned in Chapter 6, the efficient frontier. It's time now to more closely review this important concept and how it relates to modern portfolio theory.

The Efficient Frontier

The efficient frontier is the dynamic relationship between an asset's risk and return in which the investor seeks the knife blade edge of an asset's potential to earn the highest return for the least risk. This concept is usually presented in a graphic depiction.

When you think about it, this is the activity that engages most people with just about everything in their lives. In the Big Picture, we all want to have the most for the least. That's why we favor one gas station over another or one restaurant over the other. That's why most people like two-fers, or buy airplane tickets on Wednesdays. It's the reason why people date a variety of people before choosing The One, or why we purchase this car and not that car, or this home here and not that home there. We spend a good part of our lives seeking the efficient frontier so we have more return for less risk in almost every aspect of our lives.

Note:

The efficient frontier: More return for less risk.

Selecting assets for your portfolio is no different. When your portfolio is efficiently earning the maximum dollars it possibly can while keeping the threat of loss as low as possible, you are achieving a monetary form of investment perfection. We all want the most possible money with the least likelihood of loss. This is the whole point of investing!

When our portfolio is efficient, and assuming we have made good decisions with our tolerance for risk, have carefully calculated the exact price of our financial goals, have properly factored the number of years that our investments can work for us, have protected our financial health from the unknown with various forms of insurance, and have knowledgeably selected assets both individually and collectively because we are rationally convinced they have the ability to earn our required rate of return, we will be practicing the same expertise as the tight rope walker on the high wire.

Welcome, then, to the efficient frontier! It's called the efficient frontier because your portfolio is on the balanced edge ("frontier") between the best return and the least risk, and performing at its optimal level ("efficient") on that balanced edge. As noted in Chapter 6, calculating the efficient frontier for the collection of assets in your portfolio will require a capable mathematic ability. This is one of those instances when you don't want to make a mistake, and it may be well worth your while to consult with a fiduciary advisor if you've been resistant to doing so until now.

The following figure shows the charted results of a financial planner's calculations for arriving at a fictitious portfolio's efficient frontier. Note that the risk is the same, at about 10.0, but the result is an increased return of about 4%, from the Problem's initial 7% to the Solution's conclusive 11%. As you can see, calculating a portfolio's efficiency is a critically important and rewarding task!

Figure 34: The Efficient Frontier.

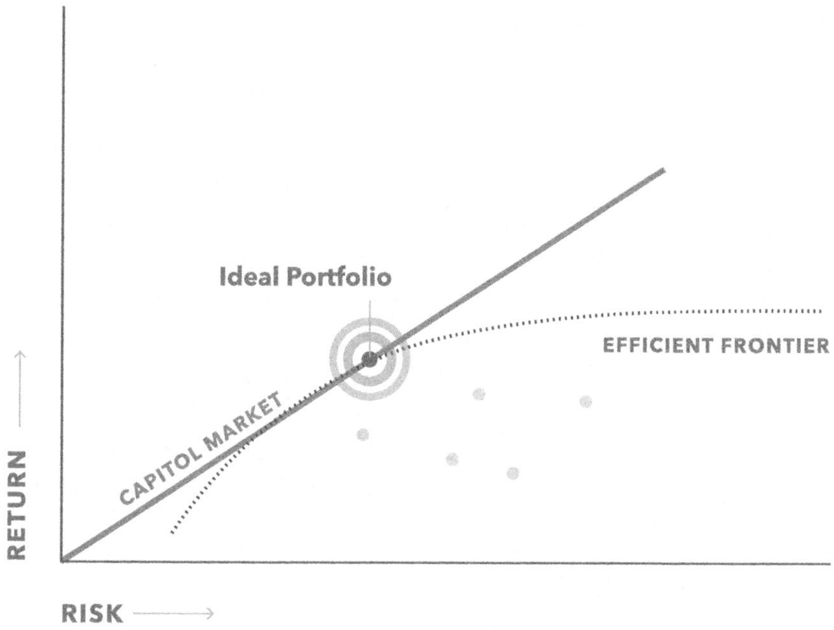

Building Asset Allocation Models

We are now going to present the process of building an asset allocation model step-by-step. This will reveal the essential considerations that must be part of your thinking and planning when you design your own portfolio, or, if you decide to use an investment management firm, this knowledge will provide a basic understanding of how your financial professionals constructed a portfolio they believe will serve your expressed needs.

Step 1. Develop Asset Class Inputs

The investment team at Synergy Asset Management begins by analyzing a global set of asset classes, and applies our unique proprietary process to forecast each asset class's expected return, risk measurement (standard deviation), and the relationships between the asset classes (correlation).

A. SELECT ASSET CLASSES:

The most important step is selecting several asset classes that are fundamentally different and, therefore, likely to vary above and below their expected return rates at different times. If one asset class goes down, other asset classes are likely to offset that decline by going up.

As commented upon previously, many investors have the misconception that they are sufficiently diversified if they have placed their investments in large cap stocks, sector stocks such as energy and healthcare, and international stocks. Their error is that they are not diversified because their investment is completely in the equities asset class, and these securities will rise and fall together, not separately. The first step in diversifying is to diversify across asset classes which do not simultaneously move in the same direction. When a portfolio is thus represented, the value of the portfolio is more capable of defending against volatility and has a better potential of compensating for the asset classes that are underperforming.

B. ESTIMATE LONG TERM EXPECTED RETURNS:

The study of probability theory claims there is a discrete set, not a continuous set, of likely outcomes. Professional financial advisors calculate the expected return of each security that is a candidate for your portfolio to mathematically determine the potential annual return. Based on the annual return, further projections and calculations are made to establish the potential growth of the security on a long-term basis, typically 10 years. Based on these calculations, the security can be compared to other candidates for your portfolio. There are no guarantees that the security will perform as projected because the formula is influenced by the factors used in the equation, which are circumstantial and limited.

While the measurement of future performance is tentative, tactical forecasting is typically based upon historical data on returns, standard deviation, financial and behavioral theories, and the correlation for each asset class under consideration; furthermore, Synergy Asset Management analyzes and applies more robust forecasting methods to build better portfolios.

C. ESTIMATE EXPECTED RISK:

The risk is that the securities in the portfolio will not perform as expected, and either they will underperform, either remaining neutral in value, or losing value. After completing thorough research to determine whether a security is a worthy candidate for your portfolio, your next step is to set target highs and target lows based on the security's current price. This information will establish what you believe is the capacity for the security to achieve a decent return, and the degree of your risk tolerance for this particular security.

Important:

When investing your money, at least a 4:1 return over risk is preferred.

Once you've established the range of the security's potential high as well as the potential loss you are willing to accept, you can now conduct the calculation by dividing your estimated profit by the cost of the risk you are willing to accept. The higher the risk/reward, the better the opportunity for you. Using this methodology, you can limit your downside risk with securities that promise a decent return for the risk you've established.

Normally a 2:1 return for the risk is the minimum an investor should accept, though many experienced investors will only seek 4:1 returns or better. Remember to include the costs of all related expenses, and if the security you've examined doesn't meet your required ratio, let it go and find another candidate.

ESTIMATE CORRELATIONS:

Defining the correlations between the selected assets is a critically important task because this determines the synergetic relationships with the potential for maximizing return and minimizing risk, providing a truly diversified portfolio. This is a mathematical process that blends the effect of all the individual assets, calculating their risk/return outcome as a single dynamic.

Step 2. Create Asset Class Models

After we have selected the optimal number of asset classes and forecasted their expected return/risk characteristics, we build robust models by applying the Nobel prize-winning mathematical optimization process originally developed by Harry Markowitz, which identifies the range of best-diversified portfolios or mixes of the selected asset classes.

Regardless of the number of asset classes to be included in a portfolio, for every different combination it is possible to calculate the mix that will result in the lowest possible variance of returns (risk) while still yielding the highest possible expected return.

One of the basic tenets of modern portfolio theory (MPT) is that a combination of investment vehicles with different expected returns and risks can have less risk than the weighted average risk of the combined investments...or even less risk than the least risky asset class in the portfolio. This is due to the dissimilarity in patterns of return across the asset classes.

The general mean variance optimization process is typically based upon log-normal historical data that relies on arithmetic expected returns, historical standard deviation as its risk measure, and historic correlation coefficients that match the periodicity of the returns' data. This data is used to form a single period view of the efficient frontier.

At Synergy Asset Management we build our portfolios with more sophisticated optimization techniques that do not necessarily rely on log-normal historic return data, and the other biases of general mean variance optimization. Additionally, we conduct back-testing procedures, sensitivity, and scenario analysis to ensure our models present stable recommendations through complete economic cycles.

MEAN VARIANCE OPTIMIZATION:

The mean variance optimization refers to the calculations that result in the efficient frontier that describes the "sweet spot" at which a security has the most return for the least risk. Obviously, this calculation is critical when selecting a security because it maximizes return while limiting risk.

Definition:

Mean variance: The calculations that determine which investment will provide the highest return for the least risk.

SENSITIVITY AND SCENARIO ANALYSIS:

These two analyses help an investor understand how attractive a company might look under varied circumstances. By changing a factor, or multiple factors, the company's productivity, and therefore its risk and return values, might change significantly, informing an investor on whether or not the company is a worthy candidate for the portfolio.

Sensitivity Analysis. With sensitivity analysis, a potential investor could adjust a single variable to determine how this one modification might affect the performance of his or her investment in the company. For example, the potential investor might change the company's cost of production of their primary product, or consider what might happen if employees received a 10% annual raise. This helps the interested investor view the company from the perspective of possible performance changes to determine if the company is still a viable investment choice.

Scenario Analysis. A scenario analysis is more of a Big Picture analysis of a company being considered for potential inclusion in the portfolio. With a scenario analysis, multiple variables are used to shift the current scenario into any number of other potential scenario conditions. Again, this helps an investor understand how the company might perform given significant changes to its current set of circumstances.

Monte Carlo Analysis. This is a system of calculations designed to help investors calculate the probability of percentage gains and losses by using scenarios composed of a group of standard deviations and assumptions. While certainly not flawless, a Monte Carlo analysis is another tool that can be implemented to indicate the mathematical likelihood of achieving profit and loss. Conducted by computer, hundreds of possible outcomes can be forecast so the investor has a modest idea of how different factors might play out over the course of time, suggesting whether an investment is worthy or not. The Monte Carlo analysis is subject to its own set of assumptions, but as a tool for probability analysis, it is regarded as one more indicator that could play a part in selecting a strong security for the portfolio.

Step 3. Analyze Investment Options

Synergy Asset Management's global investment universe review integrates both quantitative and qualitative factors in our analysis and selection of investments. A combination of returns-based and holdings-based style analysis is used to help us determine which investments will be best suited for successful implementation in our models, thereby resulting in consistent and accurate performance when compared to our custom objectives and the appropriate benchmark. Moreover, fundamental and technical analysis is used to give guidance on investment selection along with the examination of passive and active investment considerations.

Global Investment Universe. The global investment universe comprises fixed income, hybrids, cash equivalents, and many other investments around the globe. The variety is enormous but with its enormity, the investor has the opportunity to invest in practically any type of business anywhere in the world.

Screened Investment Universe. The global investment universe is different from the screened investment universe, which are the investments that the investor or the investment management firm has identified as worthy and potential candidates for the investor's portfolio. From the screened investment universe, the investor can compile a list of recommended securities, and from this recommended list the final selection can be determined for inclusion in the client's portfolio.

Mutual Funds. A mutual fund is an investment fund which is professionally managed, and composed of money provided by thousands of investors who wish to invest in the mutual fund's investment objective. There are thousands of mutual funds from which to choose, representing a wide variety of investment objectives.

Electronically Traded Funds (ETFs). ETFs are investment funds that are traded through stock exchanges, very similar to the way stocks are traded. An ETF holds a variety of assets which may include or exclude stocks, bonds, commodities, or cash instruments.

Information:

At the end of 2014, the U.S. ETF market consisted of over 1,000 funds and almost $2 trillion in assets, the largest in the world.

Step 4. Construct the Portfolio

After developing asset class inputs, creating asset class models, and analyzing investment options, Synergy Asset Management constructs the portfolio. The result is a finely tuned portfolio that is ready to meet its objectives. In bringing all the ingredients together, we take advantage of our analytical insights by applying both strategic and tactical implementation strategies.

Fine Tune. After the portfolio has been constructed, there is always the need for fine tuning to make sure the securities in the portfolio are fulfilling their role and performing as expected. Together, strategic and tactical decisions will result in final portfolios that are expected to maximize returns for the investor's acceptable level of risk.

Strategic Decisions. These are the high-level decisions that take a long-term view to investing, and incorporate both investor specific objectives and constraints with the factors that compose the capital market assumptions: expected risks, expected returns, and expected correlations.

Tactical Decisions. Tactical decisions are made when we believe that in the short term, one asset class will perform better than another. For example, we may believe U.S. stocks will outperform U.S. bonds, or international equities will outperform domestic equities.

Step 5. Monitor the Portfolio

At Synergy Asset Management we take a dynamic approach to monitoring and adjusting our portfolios. As time goes on, the market's continual change must be monitored and adjusted to maintain optimal portfolio characteristics. Simple calendar year rebalancing will not do the job and exposes the portfolio to unnecessary risk.

Portfolio Performance. In conducting our monitoring process, we dynamically monitor and evaluate our portfolios on a monthly basis to determine the most appropriate portfolio strategies for the current market conditions. We apply back-testing strategies alongside statistical procedures such as Monte Carlo analysis to help guide our portfolio adjustments. We rebalance the portfolios as little or as much as necessary to keep them on track, and we are always considering trading cost and taxes in our decision-making process.

Capital Market Assumptions. As with every projection, assumptions are made when the calculations are formulated. While the assumptions are intended to define the unknown, they may prove to be inaccurate because of the changing conditions in the market. For this reason, Synergy Asset Management defines the assumptions that were made when the portfolio was constructed so the client understands the basis upon which the portfolio was founded, allowing the client to preview and evaluate the factors that led to the investment decisions.

Expected Returns. Returns may be higher or lower than anticipated depending on the investment instrument valuations, dividend yield, interest rates, the price/earning ratio, the rate of inflation, changes in the unemployment rate, and assumptions related to global economic conditions.

Expected Risk. Similarly, the anticipated risk may prove to be either higher or lower than initial assumptions. While every effort is made to build a portfolio customized precisely to the intentions and needs of the client, the markets are fluid and the underlying assumptions must be monitored; changing conditions require portfolio review and the potential for adjustments.

Expected Correlations. Due to the changing conditions in the market and the influence these changes may have on the securities in the portfolio, the anticipated correlations may become skewed. When this happens and the correlations are out of balance from the original expectations, the originally anticipated results are likely to be to the detriment of the investor and will need to be corrected.

Economic Conditions. Both domestic and international economic conditions must be regularly monitored to ensure that these influences remain reasonable and do not cause a serious change on the portfolio's performance. Domestically, an increase or decrease in inflation, unemployment figures, cost of commodities, severe weather conditions and many other factors can have either an adverse or positive influence on a portfolio's securities. If the investor has international securities, similar aspects can augment or decrease a portfolio's value, in addition to a change in government, the threat of war or civil disorder, and sudden currency changes. Monitoring economic conditions may provide you with an advanced decision-making capability. Here are some more areas that bear observation:

Interest Rates. As interest rates rise and fall, the cost of money will vary, and because of these fluctuations the economy of a country will also shift, either making it easier or harder for business interests to expand. When interest rates drop, the cost of money is less, and conversely when interest rates rise, the cost of borrowing becomes restrictive.

Inflation. Inflation is another prohibitive factor to growth. As the cost of goods and services increase, efforts must be made to reduce expenses, cut waste, and possibly increase prices. As prices rise, business costs also rise which puts pressure on the market to continue the upward spiral. Keep in mind that inflation may be positive or negative for your portfolio depending on how your portfolio is structured. What may be good for your portfolio may be abysmal for someone else.

Corporate Conditions. The corporations in which you are invested may also experience major adjustment. The management could change, or a once profitable division could close. A large lawsuit settlement could have a significant impact on the growth of the company, or new government regulations might hamper progress the corporation once enjoyed.

Your Personal Circumstances. Events in your life may also experience unanticipated changes. Personal adjustments such as a death in the family, a marriage or a divorce, an increase or decrease in personal wealth, the establishment or loss of a business, or even a change in your personal financial goals can all be the source of a major change that may require changes in your investment portfolio.

Willingness Toward Risk. Because of some of these changes, you may find that your willingness to take risk has either increased or subsided. You may be more eager than ever to accept more risk if the death of a loved one has brought you a large inheritance, or you may be much less willing to take risk when you realize you have a new and sudden need for your money but your time horizon has shortened.

Ability to Take Risk. Likewise, your ability to accept increased risk may have grown or fallen depending on the vicissitudes of your financial or personal circumstances. When your current portfolio's intentions no longer suit your previous capacity to accept risk, whether higher or lower, your portfolio is no longer in sync with the new purpose and influences in your life, and relevant changes must be made.

IPS Factors. Remember, your investment portfolio statement (IPS) should also be reviewed periodically to keep it current with any changes in your personal or financial circumstances. Your IPS is an essential tool, your financial action plan, your play book, the roadmap to your financial goals, your flight plan, treasure map...the path to your financial freedom. When your IPS is current, your focus is tighter and decision-making is easier because distractions will fall away with the focus of your clear lens.

Step 6. Rebalance the Portfolio

Rebalancing your portfolio is standard practice, and this activity should be conducted when the correlation of your investment assets shift. Monitoring your portfolio closely will expose the unbalancing of the interrelationship of your assets; there is a range of acceptable distortion, but it's not very wide. As the imbalance broadens, your portfolio's performance becomes less efficient, so your potential returns decrease as the threat of risk increases.

The Reason to Rebalance. This should be evident. The more the assets in your portfolio diminish in their synchronicity, the less efficient your portfolio becomes with manifesting the money you are in the market to gain. There are many influences in the marketplace that cause constant change, so it's normal for your assets' composition to shift. With such a fluid environment, you can guarantee that your portfolio will experience a degree of drift from its original intentions.

When your assets are out of balance with their ability to work communally and with the precision your portfolio originally established, your portfolio is leaving money on the table. With extra effort, which is the purpose of professional investment managers everywhere, analyzing the right time to rebalance the portfolio, with an eye toward transaction fees, expenses, and taxes, your portfolio will perform at a higher level. When you begin to hear a pinging sound in your car's engine, it's a brilliant idea to bring your car to a mechanic. Whether that mechanic is you or a paid professional, you should never ignore the signs.

Asset Weights. Some assets grow and some assets diminish; the effect of this disparity from your original allocations creates the imbalance you wish to avoid. It could be that the asset weighting changes are in your favor and that's always a pleasant and welcome surprise. This, of course, creates its own situation, because now you'll need to monitor this condition just as closely so you can benefit from the increased productivity before it reverses and your paper profits evaporate.

On the other hand, if the asset weights are contradictory to your best interests, you'll need to assess the divergence and determine if it's time to correct the imbalance, based on your assessment of the attendant costs.

Correlations. The correlations are another key component of your portfolio's profitability. When your portfolio's assets have drifted from their intended synchronicity, you have lost the fine edge between risk and return and your efficient frontier is no longer as efficient as it could be, which means that either your return is diminishing, or your risk is increasing, or a degree of both has manifested...none of which is desirable.

Volatility. Another reason to rebalance your portfolio is to take advantage of the volatility if a specific sector of the market is doing well. There are occasions when rebalancing your portfolio to the original weightings may cause an investor to sell their winning assets and increase their losing assets. Obviously, this is counterproductive.

Since you always want to let your profits run and cut your losses, the decision to rebalance must be carefully considered. You may have reason to let a particular asset in your portfolio continue unhindered; just keep a sharp eye on it and prepare to take profits before the volatility and the trend reverses.

Static Rebalancing. There are two different styles of rebalancing. The first style is static rebalancing, which is the process of rebalancing a portfolio to its original percentage mix. For example, an investor might say that the right portfolio is a 60-40 mix. After six months or a year the investor recognizes that it's time to rebalance the portfolio because the portfolio has shifted to a 50-50 mix. Because the portfolio must be 60-40, the investor adjusts the asset allocation so the portfolio is once again at 60-40. This is an automatic decision because it's what the investor's investment policy statement (IPS) requires.

This is the static rebalancing process, and it's an unwise practice because this investor is always going back to the 60-40 mix...which was the right choice at some point in the past, but it may not be the right choice for today or the future. Making this assumption based on criteria from the past could be a source of inefficiency and potential loss; a more dynamic approach is the wiser path when engaged in the process of rebalancing your portfolio.

Dynamic Rebalancing. A dynamic asset allocator will reconsider the portfolio mix based on the new data and any other situations that have arisen that suggest the need for an adjusted rebalance. Instead of a 60-40 mix, perhaps a better recipe is 50-50, or 65-35... Once the new determination is made, the investor invests into that new ratio mix because it's more efficient, given the circumstances presently in the market. The key here is that it's being done as part of a dynamic assessment of what will work best for the current factors in the marketplace, not just because originally the strategic asset allocation mix was a set-and-forget decision.

There is no value with institutionalizing a decision that was made in the past when a better, more-considered choice appears.

Periodicity of Rebalancing. Of course, another consideration is the periodicity of the rebalancing activity, because this can make a big difference. Should the rebalancing activity occur every month, or quarterly, semiannually, or annually? This depends on the degree of circumspection the investor wants to have. There is no right answer except that which is best for the investor.

Something else to keep in mind is that even though the investor is willing to regularly engage the dynamic asset allocation process does not mean that a rebalancing will actually occur. At Synergy Asset Management, we employ a five-factor algorithm to determine the influence of how the portfolio's weight has drifted, the effect of taxes, the cost of fees, the effectiveness of correlations, and the influence of volatility. These five factors must all be in accord before a trading decision is reached.

Even though the five-factor algorithm may recommend a trading decision, it's important to remember that rebalancing the portfolio and adjusting the assets will incur transaction fees, and possibly a number of other expenses, one of which may include capital gains taxes. Therefore, even though the value of adjusting the asset allocation mix of the portfolio might clearly advocate a rebalancing, a savvy investor must also pay attention to the associated costs that could diminish the value of making the strategic changes. If the potential reward is really not there, given the additional costs that are involved, then there is no point in making the changes.

As an example, let's assume that a new 50-50 portfolio is expected to improve its performance with an expected return of an additional 1% over the old 60-40 portfolio. On the surface, this seems like a valid reason for rebalancing the portfolio to 50-50 because a 1% return improvement is a significant sum of money. However, once the transaction costs, fees, taxes, and other details are assessed, the cost may have a negative value of 2%, which may preclude the decision to adjust the assets to the new allocation mix. Closer circumspection is necessary before deciding whether or not the rebalancing is appropriate given the long-term prospects for a 50-50 portfolio.

Just as we questioned the value of static rebalancing, so also must we question the value of committing to a dynamic rebalancing event if there are debatable factors. Prudent, rules-based active management is much more advantageous in the long term than the automatic static rebalancing to the same strategic weight over and over again using an original decision that may be outdated. Trading decisions should never be made blindly; there are many factors that must be considered before a trade is authorized.

Tax Considerations. Taxes are always an important factor when considering the rebalancing of your portfolio. The benefit of harvesting capital gains could be subverted by the cost of taxes you may have to pay. You might consider timing your rebalancing to offset your capital gains against other capital losses you may have incurred; this may at least diminish the effect of your potential tax bill. Of course, always consider the value of speaking to a tax professional and having a conversation with your professional investment advisor, if you have one.

Trading Cost Analysis. You must also consider the cost of conducting trades, as the transaction fees or penalties you may have to pay could be prohibitive given the advantage you are expecting to receive from trading. Fees and penalties can be very expensive and can erode your portfolio's profits; calculating your costs before taking action is always a wise step. Make sure your trade is cost-effective and will save or make you more money than the cost of the transaction.

Risk Models and Return Models

Models are very convenient and helpful when analyzing a course of action. The previous section of this book focused on building asset allocation models; now a brief discussion on the importance of developing risk models and return models is appropriate.

Risk Models

The purpose of a risk model is to describe the interaction of the components of risk. The risk model might include such factors as the macroeconomic risk, market risk, the sector risk, operational risk, liquidity risk, credit risk...to identify just a few. When the applicable risk factors have been identified and quantified, an investor, or his or her professional advisor, can calculate different aspects of the risk and its impact on portfolio losses.

Return Models

Similarly, the purpose of a return model is to calculate and represent the return on investment with sufficient information for an investor to make the choice for an investment purchase. The return model analysis is intended to provide the investor with projected data on price movement over a selected period of time. A calculation of return on investment can help an investor decide between several different investment choices.

Summary

Asset allocation is a critically important process and decision because the assets you choose to include in your portfolio must work together to provide your portfolio with return based on your acceptable level of risk. In this chapter, we reviewed the six steps of allocating assets which are (1) developing your asset classes, (2) creating asset class models, (3) analyzing investment options, (4) constructing the portfolio, (5) monitoring the portfolio's performance, and (6) rebalancing the portfolio so it performs as expected. We also considered the concept of risk models and return models...because we know that it's the interaction of the different components in the portfolio that together create the risk...and the returns desired. Careful assembly of the components in your portfolio can spell success...or...disaster.

Chapter 10 Review Questions

1. Which of these statements is not true about the Modern Portfolio Theory?

   A. This theory was developed by Harry Markowitz.
   B. This theory was developed by Warren Buffett.
   C. This theory proposes that the market is efficient.
   D. This theory developed a mathematical formula for achieving increased return without increased risk.

2. Which statement is not true about the efficient frontier?

   A. The efficient frontier has nothing to do with Daniel Boone.
   B. The efficient frontier is a mathematical concept for calculating risk at 25% less than a portfolio's potential return.
   C. The efficient frontier seeks to earn the highest return for the least risk.
   D. The efficient frontier is the relationship between an asset's risk and return.

3. Identify the ratio of return for risk an investor should accept.

   A. 2:1.
   B. 3:1.
   C. 4:1.
   D. 5:1.

4. Which of the following best describes the Monte Carlo Analysis?

   A. This analysis indicates the mathematical likelihood of achieving profit and loss.
   B. This analysis is based on its own set of assumptions.
   C. This analysis is not flawless.
   D. This analysis calculates the probability of percentage gains and losses using scenarios composed of standard deviations and assumptions.

Chapter 10 Review Answers

1. Which of these statements is not true about the Modern Portfolio Theory?

    A. This theory was developed by Harry Markowitz.
    B. This theory was developed by Warren Buffett.
    C. This theory proposes that the market is efficient.
    D. This theory developed a mathematical formula for achieving increased return without increased risk.

    Answer: B. This theory was developed by Warren Buffett. Warren Buffett is an advocate for focus investing, not the Modern Portfolio Theory.

2. Which statement is not true about the efficient frontier?

    A. The efficient frontier has nothing to do with Daniel Boone.
    B. The efficient frontier is a mathematical concept for calculating risk at 25% less than a portfolio's potential return.
    C. The efficient frontier seeks to earn the highest return for the least risk.
    D. The efficient frontier is the relationship between an asset's risk and return.

    Answer: B. The efficient frontier is a mathematical concept for calculating risk at 25% less than a portfolio's potential return. The efficient frontier is a mathematical process for increasing a portfolio's return for the precise amount of risk the investor is willing to accept.

3. Identify the ratio of return for risk an investor should accept.

    A. 2:1.
    B. 3:1.
    C. 4:1.
    D. 5:1.

Answer: A. 2:1. Normally a 2:1 return for the risk is the minimum an investor should accept, though many experienced investors will only seek 4:1 returns or better. If you picked C instead of A, regard your answer as correct.

4. Which of the following best describes the Monte Carlo Analysis?

   A. This analysis indicates the mathematical likelihood of achieving profit and loss.

   B. This analysis is based on its own set of assumptions.

   C. This analysis is not flawless.

   D. This analysis calculates the probability of percentage gains and losses using scenarios composed of standard deviations and assumptions.

   Answer: A or D.
   (A) This analysis indicates the mathematical likelihood of achieving profit and loss.

   (D) This analysis calculates the probability of percentage gains and losses using scenarios composed of standard deviations and assumptions. All the answers are correct about the Monte Carlo Analysis, but we think A and D are the most complete responses.

Chapter 11
Building a Focused Portfolio

When you have finished reading this chapter, you will:

- Possess a confident understanding of focused investing
- Be able to explain the difference between focused investing and asset allocation investing
- Know the 22 recognized asset classes
- Realize that focused investing requires a consistent investment of your time
- Be familiar with the concepts of top down research and bottom up research
- Understand the purpose of macro screening and micro screening
- Have a strong understanding of how a factor model assists with selecting investments

Introduction

Earlier in this book we discussed the two sides of the investment coin, the two differing investment theories. On one side, heads, there is asset allocation. On the other side, tails, you have focus investing. The last chapter was dedicated to the virtues of the asset allocation model, which is also known as the Modern Portfolio Theory. You'll recall this was developed by Nobel Prize winner Harry Markowitz.

This chapter will be devoted to a discussion on focus investing to help you determine if this philosophy and practice is a good choice for you as an investor. "When you choose focus investing, you're choosing fewer investments, ones that may have the potential to grow rapidly. Focus investing does not seek average growth, as with asset allocation, but is more aggressive because it seeks funds that are more likely to have a higher than average return.

Focus investing applies investment science to identifying companies, carefully and rationally, that are poised for accelerated growth and value. This is not speculative investing, but rather cogently applied strategies and tactics that provide the focus investor with a strong opportunity for expanded investment results. Focus investing is not for everyone because it is more aggressive than the asset allocation model, and therefore carries an increased risk, but this risk can be managed. The real issue is whether this type of investing suits your temperament as an investor. Let's find out.

Asset Classes

There are 22 recognized asset classes under the five main categories of stocks, bonds, cash, real estate, and commodities. Each of these five categories has subcategories with which you are familiar. For example, in the category of stocks, there are large cap, mid-cap, and small cap stocks...as well as the other subcategories of stocks.

We can build a focus portfolio with any subcategory of stocks, or bonds, or real estate, or any of the 22 asset classes. The point of a focus portfolio is to find the best of whatever category or subcategory is likely to provide increased returns, so whether the asset class is international stocks, domestic fixed income, ETFs, currencies...a focus investment portfolio can be constructed with any of them, and with combinations of them. The investment universe is so broad that a wide variety of options and opportunities is available...however, the point of focus investing is to find the best of the best, and as an investor, you can select those investment vehicles that most suit your temperament, your timing, your resources, and your personal interests or restrictions.

Note:

Here is a list of the core asset classes:

- Cash Equivalents
- Equities
- Bonds
- Real Estate
- Gold and other Precious Metals
- Commodities
- Alternative Investments

A playful analogy is to think of yourself as an NFL coach. You want to find and sign the top 11 football players to your team because you know they are likely to outperform on the field and earn a steady stream of solid wins. It's the same thing with focus investing; you want to find the best investments available so you can outperform the market average in a significant manner.

Because of the nature of asset allocation, the downside risk is limited because risk is spread among a large variety of investments, resulting in average returns. Focus investing is different because a higher degree of risk is accepted for the intended benefit of higher returns. At first glance, focus investing appears to carry more risk because instead of building a portfolio that limits risk by relying on a wide variety of investments that lead to average risk and average returns, focus investing seeks only high return, not a balanced and diversified set of investments, and therefore each element in the portfolio could either accelerate or diminish the portfolio's performance. One of the investments in a focus portfolio could gain 40%...or lose 40% without proper monitoring.

Key:

Focus investing accepts a higher degree of risk for the opportunity to capture higher than average returns.

Continuing our analogy of the NFL coach, one of the top 11 players you've signed could break a leg and is out for the season. On the face of it, this would be tragic, but this is not the case for a focus investor; there are many tools that may prevent such losses. One of the critical characteristics of a focus investor is to either afford the time to carefully monitor your portfolio on a regular basis, or hire the services of a fiduciary advisor to monitor your portfolio for you. Focus investing is not a passive, or beta, form of investing in which you "set and forget"; focus investing is active, or alpha, investing and requires more dedicated time on task. The results can be outstanding, as you'll subsequently see. For now, however, let's take a look at how investments for a focus portfolio are identified.

Fundamental Analysis

When evaluating candidates for a focus portfolio, both fundamental analysis and technical analysis should be conducted because they both provide different forms of valuable data. This section is on fundamental analysis. Fundamental analysis can be conducted using either of two research methodologies, either a top down approach or a bottom up approach.

Top Down Research Approach

A top down approach means starting at the top, with a global view. We start by looking at all the investment possibilities worldwide, without restriction. We want to have an unbiased view about where in the world to invest, we want the Big Picture of financial circumstances affecting economies around the world. We would study the general health of the world economy and determine the current phase of the economic cycle, and how this affects individual national economies. The economies of developed countries would be regarded as well as those of emerging countries; the gross domestic product growth is a key indicator of economic performance and would be one of the key elements that attract initial interest.

Further study would consider the potential for national or regional conflict that might undermine investment results. Once we have determined which regions and countries should not be included, we can then study the remaining universe of possibilities. We would look at the economies of Great Britain, Italy, Lithuania, Russia, China, Japan, Argentina, the United States, Canada...the economies of every country to determine where our investment is best placed. In a sense, we are trying to identify our 11 best football players, so we have a winning team.

Definition:

Top down research begins with a global economic analysis, filtering financial information leading to specific companies of investment interest.

Once we've determined the right place in the world to be, then we have to decide the best industry. Should we be in telecommunication, energy, health care, consumer staples? Well, perhaps the right industry is energy because the indicators led us here! Now that we know the right industry, what sector of this industry is the best one? Should we be in energy equipment and services? Or oil, gas and consumable fuels? Based on our research, perhaps the best place is in energy equipment and services! Which of these services is the hottest? It looks like drilling services are in demand! Now we have to decide which companies in this industry's sector are the best, and there are 100 of them. What do you know? There is this new company in Russia...and their drilling services are in high demand. This is the company we should be in!

This is the top down approach.

Bottom Up Research Approach

A bottom up approach works in the opposite direction. From this perspective, we don't care where in the world the best choice is for our investment money. We also don't care about the industry or the sector. All we care about is looking for companies that are showing growth and potential for continued growth. Guess what? We found this great little drilling oil services company and of all the places in the world, they happen to be in Russia. Who would have thought? But there they are, in Russia, and gosh, are they good! It looks like they're going to be a great investment, but before buying this company, let's conduct a top down overlay; we want to be as sure as we can that their fundamentals are not going to be sabotaged by what's going on in their sector, industry, and country. We need to make sure we're not making some huge mistake by not seeing something outside the relatively myopic view of only studying this company's data. With a top down overlay, we can make sure we're not buying stock of a buggy whip company just before Ford's automobile factory starts producing cars.

This is the bottom up approach.

Definition:

Bottom up research begins by finding companies that have investment potential, and then checking sector, industry, and global financial conditions to confirm an investment choice.

WHICH APPROACH IS BEST?

The top down approach is starting with the global view and burrowing down to find the treasure, and the bottom up approach is burrowing along and then popping up to make sure there won't be any unfortunate surprises. The financial analysis is the same, focusing on cash flows, growth rates, return on equity, return on assets, etc., so the two approaches are exactly the same except they are performed in reverse order.

Both can be deployed equally well. The approach you choose will most likely be based on your personality as an investor, and by using what is most familiar to you. There really is no point in employing tools or an approach with which you are either unfamiliar or uncomfortable. Remember, there is no best way to do this; both approaches are equally valuable and should help you arrive at the same conclusion. However, an asset allocation investor will likely prefer a top down approach, and a focus investor will likely prefer a bottom up approach because of the different ways they look at the market and hunt for opportunities.

Technical Analysis

With technical analysis, there is no differentiation on the approach, whether top down or bottom up. Technical analysis is technical analysis. This means a company that is a candidate for your portfolio will be analyzed by its price resistance and support channels, moving averages, stochastics, Bollinger Bands, trends, etc. This, of course, is critical work because it substantiates the quality of the investment opportunity.

Screens

Screening a company helps an investor determine more details about whether or not the company is a good investment. There is macro screening, and micro screening, explained below. Being able to identify the impact of external and internal forces that have the potential for shaping the company's ability to perform is necessary before buying the company's stocks or bonds.

Macro

Macro screening is used to discover the variety and impact of external forces affecting the value and growth of the candidate company. Some examples of macro influences are market demand for the company's products and services, the ability of the company to acquire the supplies it needs for production, existing or potential legal issues that may either emancipate or burden the company's performance, cultural restrictions, economic conditions, and technological influences.

Micro

Micro screening focuses on the company's internal data such as market share, experience of the management, production capabilities, sales forecasts, price to earnings ratio, the amount of stock owned by the company's senior management, etc.

Figure 35: Fundamental and Technical Analysis.

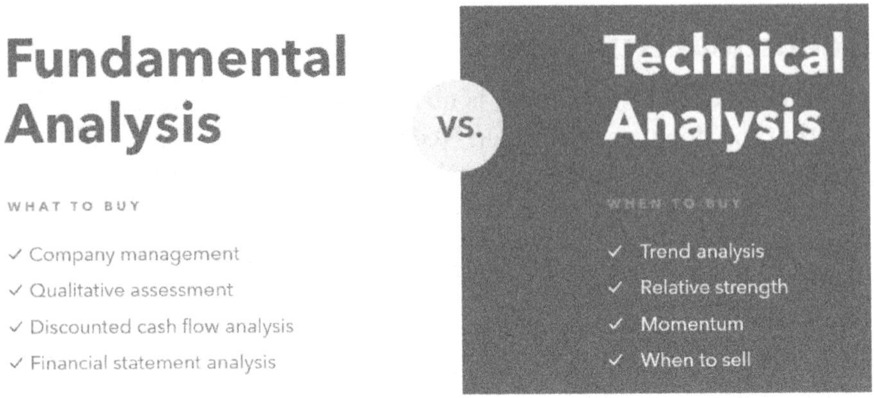

Other Indicators

There are occasions when other sources may guide you with whether or not a company is a good financial investment. Interest in a company may be generated or dissuaded by the following:

Events

Following the news can often result in your perception that a specific industry sector will become a good resource for finding companies that may generate investment profits. For example, new developments in rubber production might signal an interest in tire manufacturing; new treatments or medicines in the health care industry might lead to considering investment in a pharmaceutical company. Similarly, a downturn in the economy could call for the wisdom of selling stock in airplane and tourist service companies.

Opportunities

Sometimes opportunities can appear unexpectedly such as when a nation's economy is experiencing a downturn that results in deflated prices for the country's goods and services. An example is when a country deflates its currency and the cost for its goods and services decline; healthy companies should maintain their value, making this a good opportunity to purchase reliable companies for a lower price. Another example of a possible opportunity might be the impact of weather fluctuations on an important global crop such as coffee, cocoa, or oranges.

Newsletters and Other Information Systems

Newsletters and other communication devices might also be the source of information that leads you to consider investing in a company. You might learn that a regional grocer is planning to purchase a number of stores from a competitor, or that a new retail coffee store is expanding its market reach through new outlets and a new designer coffee line. By keeping current with the news, opportunities will regularly appear, providing you with a constant series of worthy investment possibilities. The investment world is always evolving with new products and services, continually changing market influences, the continual ebb and flow of economic cycles, advancements in technology and healthcare, the redistribution of demographics, currency adjustments, global weather pattern changes, the shift from fossil fuels to alternative energy forms... Today's investment universe is a rapidly transforming flow of wealth-making opportunities that invite your attention and your cash.

Important:

New investment opportunities always become available. The savvy focused investor continually reviews information that may result in an exciting and lucrative investment.

Factor Models

A factor model is a mathematical measurement that identifies how much a portfolio of stocks is being influenced by a variety of economic factors. Some of the economic factors that might be considered are the impact of inflation, the cost of energy, and interest rates.

Factor models can be categorized according to three basic types. The first type is a statistical factor model which attempts to understand investment returns from the investment's exposure to risk such as currency risk, sensitivities to cash flow, and the potential for a decrease in purchasing power. The second type is a macroeconomic factor model which intends to explain investment returns from a mathematical analysis of the economy. The third type is the fundamental factor model which is focused on the impact of financial factors pertinent to a specific industry or market.

Using factor models can be helpful with determining which investment candidates could be appropriate for your focus investment portfolio.

Asset Rotation Strategies

Employing asset rotation strategies can also lead to the returns a focus investor seeks. As circumstances change in the markets, a focus investor can mirror those changes with the sale of the portfolio's assets in those asset classes that are moving into disfavor, and buying assets in the asset classes that are showing momentum, and therefore demonstrating growth and the potential for increased returns.

Important:

Investment is a process; some people like to call investment an art and a science, but more than an art or science, it's a craft, and a great investment management company must do their craft well.

Summary

Building a focus portfolio requires an alpha temperament because as a focus investor you must always be on your toes looking for the best of the best companies that are outperforming the average returns that an asset allocation investor is satisfied with having. Focus investing means you want your portfolio to have only the assets that are the best performers in the best performing asset classes.

Of course, you must do your due diligence and analyze your investment candidates with fundamental analysis, choosing either the top down or bottom up research approach, and complement your analysis with rigorous technical analysis. This chapter mentioned a variety of tools you can use to initially identify stocks, bonds, cash, and alternative investment instruments for your portfolio.

Remember, also, that if you are seeking increased returns and don't have the dedicated time it takes to do the required research, you can always hire the services of a fiduciary advisor who advocates for focus investing. If focus investing is the right investment style for you, finding a financial consultant that will do the work for you for a fee could be a brilliant solution...with brilliant results.

Chapter 11 Review Questions

1. The purpose of focus investing is to:

   A. Invest in the best of the best companies.
   B. Avoid all risk by focusing on the most secure high performing stocks.
   C. Seek alpha returns that double the value of the portfolio in one year or less.
   D. Combine alpha and beta investment practices to avoid risk and increase return.

2. What is the value of top down research?

   A. Good companies can be immediately spotted.
   B. Biases lead the investor to lucrative opportunities.
   C. The companies in emerging countries can be quickly dismissed.
   D. All the worldwide investment possibilities are available for consideration.

3. The purpose of a factor model is:

   A. To identify how much a portfolio of stocks is being influenced by a variety of economic factors.
   B. To identify the factors that make a company a good investment.
   C. To identify the effectiveness of factors in the Modern Portfolio Theory.
   D. To identify the correlations of factors between the Modern Portfolio Theory and your portfolio for increased efficiency which lowers your risk and raises your returns.

4. The purpose of asset rotation is:

   A. To change your assets and lower your taxes.
   B. To protect your portfolio from excessive returns.
   C. To have as many assets as possible to demonstrate momentum.
   D. To always keep your assets balanced.

Chapter 11 Review Answers

1. The purpose of focus investing is to:

   A. Invest in the best of the best companies.
   B. Avoid all risk by focusing on the most secure high performing stocks.
   C. Seek alpha returns that double the value of the portfolio in one year or less.
   D. Combine alpha and beta investment practices to avoid risk and increase return.

   Answer: A. Invest in the best of the best companies. Focus investing requires an investor to spend substantial time identifying the best currently performing companies, or companies poised to become the best of the best. The rationale is that the investment will be rewarded by rapid profits. By closely observing the investment after purchase, the investor can eliminate the holding when the investment begins to lose its profitable features.

2. What is the value of top down research?

   A. Good companies can be immediately spotted.
   B. Biases lead the investor to lucrative opportunities.
   C. The companies in emerging countries can be quickly dismissed.
   D. All the worldwide investment possibilities are available for consideration.

   Answer: D. All the worldwide investment possibilities are available for consideration. When investigating investment opportunities, the top down approach is all inclusive, allowing the investor to search from the benefit of seeing the Big Picture.

3. The purpose of a factor model is:

   A. To identify how much a portfolio of stocks is being influenced by a variety of economic factors.
   B. To identify the factors that make a company a good investment.

C. To identify the effectiveness of factors in the Modern Portfolio Theory.

D. To identify the correlations of factors between the Modern Portfolio Theory and your portfolio for increased efficiency which lowers your risk and raises your returns.

Answer: A. To identify how much a portfolio of stocks is being influenced by a variety of economic factors. A factor model reviews such economic factors as the impact of inflation, the cost of energy, interest rates, etc.

4. The purpose of asset rotation is:

A. To change your assets and lower your taxes.

B. To protect your portfolio from excessive returns.

C. To have as many assets as possible to demonstrate momentum.

D. To always keep your assets balanced.

Answer: C. To have as many assets as possible to demonstrate momentum. Asset rotation is a process that allows the investor to benefit from the highest performing asset classes in the current market. Asset classes have their own cycles, and as one asset class declines, another asset class grows predominant. After assessing the cost for fees and taxes, the investor should make the changes if the profitability is still clear.

Chapter 12
The Top-Down Approach

When you have finished reading this chapter, you will:

- Have a strong understanding of the top down research approach
- Possess introductory knowledge about the eight elements that drive the economy
- Be able to identify the four stages of the market cycle
- Understand the 11 quantitative factors when researching an investment
- Recognize the value of using the six qualitative factors when analyzing an investment
- Know the advantages of a top down research approach
- Be familiar with Porter's Five Forces and how they affect competitive advantage
- Consider whether top down research analysis is something you would like to use

Introduction

The top down approach is the analysis process for identifying investment candidates for your focused portfolio, and it is the method most familiar to investors. For this reason, a larger portion of the book is dedicated more to reviewing the top-down analysis than the bottom up analysis, which follows in the next chapter. Remember that whether you are drilling down or burrowing up, the process will be the same... except it's in reverse.

Here is the process for top down analysis, presented in more detail.

Global Research

Top down research begins at the top...with the largest, most global view available. When conducting focus investment research, you want to have the complete universe of possibilities available to you. Because you want the "best" of the "best", and since you can't be sure where you will find the best investments for your portfolio, you want to approach the field with an open mind and be all-inclusive.

There are three drivers when conducting global research: economic drivers, quantitative drivers, and qualitative drivers.

Economic Drivers

Eight elements drive the economy, each of them contributing to either opening the economy for expansion or limiting the economy with contraction.

1. CYCLE:

Every market economy has a continually repeating cycle composed of four stages; therefore, the first task is to identify the current economic stage. The first stage is expansion in which the economy is growing, and prospects are optimistic. The second stage is when the economy peaks and the continuing upside becomes extremely limited and begins to turn. After an economy peaks, recession sets in and the third stage begins as the economy starts a downward path. Once the recession has run its course, the fourth stage develops, and this recovery stage leads back to the expansion stage. These stages are accepted as reasonably predictable, and can be measured by the gross national product of a country.

Note:

It's generally agreed that a market economy will complete a full cycle in about five years, though there is variety and exceptions.

---

2. SPENDING:

When consumers and businesses are spending money, the flow of this money supports and may expand the number of jobs as well as the continued production and development of products and services. A strong financial position encourages consumers and businesses to increase their spending and the result is that the economy expands, building toward its peak; however, when spending increases to a point where debt becomes a burden, spending is curtailed. The economic peak has been reached and a recession commences, leading eventually to a recovery.

Important:

Too much debt curtails spending and slows the economy. The economy then slows down until debt pressures ease or the economy falls into a recession.

---

3. IMPORTS:

The purchase of goods and services from other countries stimulates a country's economy. For example, a country importing oil may use that commodity to produce more goods. The exchange of trade between countries is good for the global economy because it invigorates production and the potential for continuing or expanding consumption.

4. EXPORTS:

Exports are the other side of the coin from imports. Selling goods and services to other countries has a positive impact on a country's economy because it encourages production and may lead to innovation, job growth, an influx of increasing revenue, and the subsequent stimulation of the country's economy.

5. POLICIES:

Policies that control the economy can significantly affect a country's financial well-being. Controls on imports and exports, restrictions on trade relationships, adjustments to the national currency's value, mandates on the use of natural resources, imposed ceilings and floors for loans and the flow of money...well, you get the picture. Some policies support economic growth and other policies do not; when conducting your research, a careful look at a country's policies, together with its historical and political pattern, will help you make a determination of whether or not it's sensible to invest.

6. INFLATION:

The impact of inflation is another key economic driver, marking the increase in the costs of goods and services. The average annual inflation rate is around 2%, but given the wrong circumstances, inflation can rise to 10% or more and it then becomes more expensive to conduct business and riskier to invest. Determining the interest rate, as well as the potential interest rate in the future, must be carefully considered.

Important:

Though the average annual inflation rate is around 2% per year, products and services in some industries could be remarkably higher. For example, medical costs and college costs far exceed the average annual inflation rate. The cost of oil and gasoline also varies widely.

7. RATES:

The cost of borrowing money is the seventh essential factor. When money is costly, economic growth is usually more limited because people and businesses have to accept more indebtedness, and this burden weighs on the economic potential of the borrowed funds. When rates are low, people and businesses are more inclined to spend because the resource is affordable, and economic engagement is typically heightened. Businesses can be created or expanded, and consumers are more willing to purchase homes, cars, and nonessential goods and services.

8. ECONOMIC INDICATORS:

Such economic indicators as the Consumer Price Index (CPI) and the Gross Domestic Product (GDP) are weathervanes that point toward an economy's growth or decline. Unemployment figures are another good tool for measurement, as well as the price of crude oil since oil is currently so essential to economic production.

Quantitative Drivers

Now that you've made an assessment of the global influences acting on global regions and individual countries, and you have a solid idea about which asset classes are showing growth or the imminent likelihood of growth, the next step is to analyze companies in these regions and asset classes. Remember that you are looking for the best of the best, and the 11 quantitative factors that appear below are good mathematical tools for narrowing the scope of your search. These factors are excellent as a means for comparing one company with another because they are mathematical representations of economic activity.

1. ROE:

Return on Equity identifies the profitability ratio of a company. The ROE shows how much profit each stockholder's dollar has generated. Look for historic stability and trends.

2. ROA:

Return on Assets is a ratio indicator that measures the percentage of a company's profits compared to its total assets. Generally, an ROA over 5% is considered good.

3. ROIC:

Return on Invested Capital is a metric that expresses financial performance by measuring a company's profit based on the company's total investment dollars. This shows shareholders and interested parties the ability of a company to employ its money to generate returns.

Definition:

Quantitative drivers influence value and price based on numerical data.

4. SALES GROWTH:

Sales growth indicates a company's ability to increase its sales through any combination of expanding its market, producing new products, lowering prices to increase sales, supporting customer service, etc. Increasing sales volume over an extended period of time is a good indication of past performance, and may presage future growth.

5. MARGINS:

Profit margin is the amount of revenue remaining after all expenses have been paid. The net profit margin is a measure for determining the overall ability of a company's fiscal health, retaining more funds for its use than it expends.

6. GROWTH RATES:

A growth rate is the advance or decline of any selected fiscal variable over a set period of time. There are several types of growth rates that should be monitored, and among them are such key factors as a company's earnings, dividends, revenues, sales, etc.

7. REINVESTMENT:

Another important factor in determining if an investment is one of your best possible choices is to determine how much of a company's profits are being reinvested in the company to expand its growth. Known as "plowback", or the "Plowback Ratio", this is a calculation of the amount of retained earnings used to expand the core business rather than paying out those earnings (Payout Ratio) to its shareholders. Reinvestment is typically a good sign because it indicates the company's management is focused on expansion...which could result in growth and more profitability.

8. TURNS:

When a security's price trend reverses, this might indicate an opportunity to invest in the company as its price advances, or, should you choose, it may be a good time to short.

9. LEVERAGE:

The degree to which a company is leveraging its debt could be indicative of financial danger or well-being. Companies require both the shareholders' equity and business loans to conduct their operations. If a company has too much debt, the company may be in trouble; if a company has too little debt a question arises about the company's interest or ability with increasing its profits. Looking at the leverage ratio of a company can be revealing.

10. FUNDAMENTALS:

Some of the usual fundamentals that should be studied are assets, liabilities, revenue, earnings, and growth. A review of these measurements help investors determine if the asset is a good investment for your focus portfolio.

11. RATIO ANALYSIS:

Conducting a ratio analysis of the key factors of a company will highlight the intrinsic value of a company's worth in the market. Ratios will be helpful when used to analyze the company's health, and also when comparing companies in the same industry or sector. The DuPont analysis is a calculation that separates ROE (Return on Equity) into three categories. The three categories are operating efficiency, asset use efficiency, and financial leverage.

Qualitative Drivers

When trying to calculate the intrinsic value of a company, quantitative factors are generally easier to work with because they are already in a numeric form. Qualitative factors, however, also offer a high degree of information that's important to analyze. The challenge is that not every value represented by a company's performance can be measured numerically. Here is a brief commentary on the six qualitative drivers that should feature in your analysis of a company you're considering for your focus portfolio.

1. INDUSTRY ANALYSIS:

Every industry has its own unique set of business proclivities. These include types of customers, the distribution of market share among the relatively many or few firms in the industry, the history of growth and its potential for more, regulations, business cycles, competition, etc. When considering an investment in any industry, the investor should learn more about how the industry is structured in order to have a more complete understanding of an individual company's performance and financial health. One of the more important details to contemplate is whether the company demonstrates the likelihood of continuing growth because its goods and services will be desired by the market.

2. NEW PRODUCTS:

One of the ways a company continues to command market share is by bringing new goods and services to market. If the company has a good research and development department with a history of continual invention and innovation, your investment may be warranted.

3. MANAGEMENT:

Good management is essential. Leadership, careful administration, sensible policies and practices, and the ability to execute in a timely manner are all good indicators of a company's ability to perform well during constantly changing circumstances.

Definition:

Qualitative drivers influence value and price based on qualities that are not measured with numerical data.

---

4. OWNERSHIP ANALYSIS:

The lower the total cost of ownership, the more potential value there is in holding the company. As a shareholder, you are a part owner in a business. If that business has costs that appear excessive in relation to other businesses in the same industry and sector, then the profits that will be shared with you through the company's price adjustment will be less than a different investment made in a company with less owner costs.

5. COMPETITIVE ADVANTAGE:

When a company has a competitive advantage, such as a lower cost for supplies or a large and loyal customer base, more profitability is likely than with a company that lacks a competitive advantage. A company's competitive advantage can be gauged by using Porter's Five Forces. This system of analysis assumes there are five forces that underlie competitive advantage in a business situation as follows:

a. **Bargaining Power of Suppliers:** If suppliers can drive up prices, competitive advantage may be weakened. If there are a limited number of suppliers, their strength and control could damage profitability.
b. **Bargaining Power of Customers:** Buyers like to spend less money if they can. If a company only has a few buyers, they may be able to control the company's sales and limit profitability by driving the price down.
c. **Rivalry Among Competitors:** The number and quality of competitors may eliminate all competitive advantages. If customers can choose among several competing companies, the company you're interested in will probably have to offer attractive deals to retain their market share... Unless they also have an inventive research and development department and can break away from the herd. Competition is a two-edged sword because competition can help a company eliminate waste and improve its competitive edge, but competition can also eliminate market advantage. An investor should look closely at the products and services offered by the candidate company and decide if competition

does or doesn't weigh too heavily on its prospects, both in the current market and with its potential for future profits.

d. **Threat of Substitution:** If a product line can be replaced or duplicated, the market may choose to purchase the company's products and services from the new competitor. If, however, no other company can replicate the product or service, then competitive advantage remains strong.

e. **Barriers to Entry:** It might be possible for another company to enter the market and compete, resulting in unexpected competition and a diminishment of the market share. On the other hand, if a new competitor will be greeted by numerous obstacles that your company has already weathered, the entry of new competitors may be restricted.

6. STRUCTURE AND STRATEGY ANALYSIS:

The careful investor will also benefit by analyzing the company's structure and strategies. By studying strengths and weaknesses, the value represented by the company can be more keenly observed and be used in comparison with other candidate companies in the same industry and sector to help the investor decide on the selection of one or another for inclusion in the focus portfolio.

Summary

The top down approach is the most common method for identifying the active global regions, asset classes, industries, sectors and companies in which to invest as a focus investor. Taking the time to study global economic conditions and identifying where the economic drivers are most fertile will lead you to those companies that appear to be the best of the best. Then, drilling down with a detailed analysis of the quantitative and qualitative factors that measure a company's financial health and promise, investment candidates will begin to surface, allowing you to make sensible selections based on the data you find. The focus investor is always looking for companies that are outperforming in their sector, in the asset classes that are outperforming all the other asset classes. This investment of research is likely to result in the greatly increased possibility of securing financial reward for your diligence.

Chapter 12 Review Questions

1. Which is the third of four stages in a market cycle?

   A. The economy recovers and leads to a new expansion stage.
   B. The economy is growing, and prospects are optimistic.
   C. The economy peaks and recession sets in.
   D. The economy peaks and the upside becomes limited.

2. True or false? Quantitative factors are mathematical tools for determining comparative values.

   A. True.
   B. False.

3. The value of an industry analysis is:

   A. It helps an investor understand factors peculiar to the industry.
   B. It helps an investor understand if the management team is top-heavy.
   C. It helps an investor learn everything about a specific industry.
   D. It helps an investor learn more about the bargaining power of customers.

4. Rivalry among competitors is good for business because:

   A. Customers typically benefit with better products.
   B. Customers typically benefit with better prices.
   C. A, only.
   D. A and B.

Chapter 12 Review Answers

1. Which is the third of four stages in a market cycle?

   A. The economy recovers and leads to a new expansion stage.
   B. The economy is growing, and prospects are optimistic.
   C. The economy peaks and recession sets in.
   D. The economy peaks and the upside becomes limited.

   Answer: C. The economy peaks and recession sets in.

2. True or false? Quantitative factors are mathematical tools for determining comparative values.

   A. True.
   B. False.

   Answer: A. True. Some quantitative factors are ROE (return on equity), ROA (return on assets), ROIC (return on invested capital), sales growth, margins, etc.

3. The value of an industry analysis is:

   A. It helps an investor understand factors peculiar to the industry.
   B. It helps an investor understand if the management team is top-heavy.
   C. It helps an investor learn everything about a specific industry.
   D. It helps an investor learn more about the bargaining power of customers.

   Answer: A. It helps an investor understand factors peculiar to the industry. Every industry has elements that are peculiar to itself; by performing an industry analysis, an investor can better determine an individual company's performance and financial health, and the likelihood of continuing growth.

4. Rivalry among competitors is good for business because:

   A. Customers typically benefit with better products.

   B. Customers typically benefit with better prices.

   C. A, only.

   D. A and B.

   Answer: D. A and B. customers typically benefit with both better products and prices. A company's competitive advantage can be gauged using Porter's Five Forces: The bargaining power of suppliers, bargaining power of customers, rivalry among competitors, the threat of substitution, and barriers to entry.

Chapter 13
The Bottom Up Approach

When you have finished reading this chapter, you will:

- Have a strong understanding of the bottom up research approach
- Be able to identify the four investment styles
- Know the six factors to study when conducting an analysis for investing in a company
- Understand how ratios can be used to determine the financial health of a company
- Possess an understanding of how a security's value is reflected in its price
- Recognize the advantages of a bottom up research approach
- Consider whether bottom up research analysis is something you would like to use

Introduction

In the last chapter you read a presentation about the top down approach when conducting research to identify alpha-grade investment opportunities for your focus portfolio. This chapter will discuss the methodology for finding investment candidates from the bottom up. Whether you choose the top down or bottom up approach, the process is the same except conducted in reverse. Most investors are more familiar with the top down approach, but there are also many focus investors who prefer to find their investment opportunities by proceeding from the bottom up. This chapter will be less detailed because much of the material has already been described in the preceding chapter. For those of you interested in the bottom up approach, here is a recommended strategy for identifying the companies that may earn higher than average returns.

Pick Your Style

As a focus investor, one of these four investment styles is likely to define your preferred method. Being a proponent of these investment styles is a function of your investing temperament, and your education and experience as an investor. These are not exclusive to each other because there may be occasions when one or the other of these styles is best suited for the investing environment or for a particular opportunity. Focus investors often move between these different styles.

Growth

When looking for companies that evidence strong growth, a focus investor is interested in companies with high earnings, high ROE (return on equity), and low dividend yields. A company with these financial metrics is probably reinvesting much of its profit to advance its growth.

Value

There are also focused investors who prefer finding underpriced industry and sector leaders, and they research the market to find healthy companies offered at a good price. In this case, an investor is looking for a company with low price to earnings ratio and low price to sales ratio. Another good indicator is how the company performs during periods of volatility; if the price drops during volatility and then restores itself during periods of stability, a focus value investor may be able to benefit from accelerated investment return.

Important:

When evaluating investment opportunities, Warren Buffett says," Growth and value investing are joined at the hip". Many investors try to separate the two and distinguish them as different factors. Mr. Buffett believes they work together.

Aggressive Growth

An aggressive growth strategy accepts a higher degree of risk for a higher degree of return. Capital appreciation is the main investment objective, and an aggressive growth investor will study equity asset classes to find those classes and companies that have the most potential for explosive growth, knowing that the risk of loss is strong. Of course, there are a number of ways to limit loss which will be discussed in the section on placing stops in Chapter 14.

Momentum and Growth

Some investors prefer momentum investing, which is the practice of buying securities that have a history of high returns during the preceding three to twelve months. Assuming there are no perceivable negative factors in the near future, a company that is showing consistent high returns over a reasonable period of time and places well in an analysis of its growth factors could be an excellent candidate for your focus portfolio.

Analyze the Company

Once you decide on your investment style, the next step is to analyze the companies that fit the specifications you've outlined. As a focus investor, you are looking for the best of the best in the style category that appeals to you. So, if you are looking for companies that are demonstrating strong growth, then you want to start combing the charts of companies that are performing well in the factors that determine strong growth. Here are some ways to analyze the candidate companies.

1. Growth

When analyzing a company's growth, the primary factor is to confirm continual growth based on a history of steadily increasing annual revenue. If the company has strong historical earnings growth sustained over at least five years, the company is displaying good growth. The next criteria is to review the company's projected five-year growth rate, which should state at least a 10-12% expectation, though 15% is preferable; this projection should be made by unbiased analysts or valued sources. Though these are only estimates, they will at least provide assurance of a progressive future. Next, it's important to establish that management is controlling the company's costs and revenues; you can determine this by studying the company's pretax profit margins. While high annual revenue growth is desirable, it doesn't mean much if the company's expenses are crushing the profit.

Key:

When selecting an investment, your expectation is that the stock price should double in a five-year period, which is 15% growth per year.

You'll be able to tell if the company's management is operating the business efficiently by the return on equity (ROE); the ROE will tell you the net income or profitability based on a percentage of the shareholders' invested money. Another indicator is determining if the stock price will double in a five-year period; at 15% a year, price would double. If the stock cannot realistically do this, it's not a growth stock. As a focus growth investor, your job is to identify those companies with strong growth potential, and which continue to reinvest their profits to support growth and produce new products for an expanding market.

2. Profitability

Focus investors seek companies that will return high profitability as measured by profitability ratios. Profit margin, return on equity (ROE), and return on assets (ROA) are examples of profitability ratios used by analysts to compare the profitability between companies. Conducting a profit margin analysis will give a good indication of whether the company should be considered in your portfolio.

3. Financial Health

There are numerous ways to evaluate a company's financial health. One common method is the liquidity ratio; there are several components to this ratio, but generally an analysis will reveal a company's ability to stay abreast of its debts. In some industries, liquidity is dependent on seasonal changes, so it's important to know the elements that compose an industry's cycle, so your evaluation generates appropriate conclusions.

Another ratio used to measure financial health are efficiency ratios such as, but not limited to, inventory turnover and the average collection period ; both of these relate to the availability of resources for operations and for reinvestment. A third set are the profitability ratios just discussed. Then there are the leverage ratios which establish the ability of the company to manage its debt and sustain its solvency for the long term. Remember that ratio data will vary by industry, and interpreting the information will require expertise.

4. The Case For and Against

Once you have gathered and assessed the data, you'll need to decide whether or not to invest in the company you've been researching. It's time to list the pros and cons of the research you've just completed and, in comparison to the other choices you have, decide to invest or not. Even if a company looks really good, it may not be as good as another. Remember that as a focus investor you are looking to select the best of the best; your goal is to rapidly appreciate the capital value in your portfolio; you have room for only the top performing securities. You may find that those securities which did not make the cut might be choices in the future, so set them aside and keep your eye on them because these might be a pool from which you can draw later after your first string investments have cycled through their profitability.

5. Management

The quality of the management to guide the company and execute profitable policies and practices is essential to company performance and investor profits. Without good leadership and the ability of senior management to create new products, create new markets, cut costs, curtail waste, and effectively compete for an increase in market share, a company cannot thrive.

When researching the company's management, you want to see experienced hands knowledgeably steering the company through the shoals of market obstacles. Be sure to take a close look at the management team and determine the value of giving them your money. Will they use your funds so wisely that they will double your cash in five years?

6. Valuation vs. Price

As a candidate for your focus investment portfolio, investors must ask themselves whether a company represents a good value for the price. All the research you conducted was necessary to bring you to the point of decision: buy or not? Is it worth the risk of your capital to invest in a company you've ascertained is likely, but not guaranteed, to provide high returns?

VALUATION:

The issue is how well you have estimated the value of the company. You've considered the company's growth potential, profitability, financial health, and management. You've examined its ROA, ROE, ROIC, and all its financial data. You have determined that its value is there; this is a good, solid company with strong prospects for profit. Now you have to decide if the price of this security is reasonable.

PRICE:

According to what you've discovered, does the price accurately reflect the inherent value of the security? Is the price distorted in some manner, either to your favor or detriment? Then, assuming the price is reasonable based on its value, you now also have to decide if it's reasonable for you. How much should you purchase? How much can you afford? How large a position should you purchase in comparison with the other positions in your portfolio? The price of the security creates another whole set of questions that need to be answered in the context of the focus portfolio you are building or adjusting.

The dynamic between value and price brings you to the point of decision.

Summary

The bottom up research approach is the opposite of the top down research approach; both will bring you to the same point of decision after conducting the necessary research. In the bottom up approach, the first task is to decide which of several investment styles most suits your temperament and your purpose. Once determined, the second task is to review charts of securities to identify initial candidates with the specifications you desire...specifically, the potential for accelerated portfolio profits.

Analyzing the candidate companies for their potential to reward your investment, it is then a necessary step to confirm that the Big Picture is aligned with the research you've conducted, confirming that the company's sector and industry is healthy and in an expanding business cycle, and that its asset class mirrors this forward progress. When all these factors are aligned, and you are satisfied and confident that your research is complete and bona fide, there is nothing left to do except make the decision to purchase the security so your portfolio can rapidly increase in wealth.

Chapter 13 Review Questions

1. True or false? A company with low dividend yields is a metric that attracts focus investors because it's an indicator that the company is probably reinvesting much of its profit to accelerate its growth.

   A. True.

   B. False.

2. The top down and the bottom up approach to researching good investments are:

   A. The same.

   B. Very different.

   C. The same but in reverse.

   D. Complement each other.

3. The term momentum investing is the practice of buying securities the history of high returns during the preceding:

   A. 3-12 months

   B. 1-9 months

   C. 1-12 months

   D. 1-3 months

4. When selecting an investment your expectation is that the stock price should double in:

   A. A five-year period.

   B. A six-year period.

   C. A seven-year period.

   D. A 10-year period.

Chapter 13 Review Answers

1. True or false? A company with low dividend yields is a metric that attracts focus investors because it's an indicator that the company is probably reinvesting much of its profit to accelerate its growth.

   A. True.

   B. False.

   Answer: A. True. Low dividend yields are only one factor a focus investor seeks. Two other factors are high earnings, and high return on equity (ROE).

2. The top down and the bottom up approach to researching good investments are:

   A. The same.

   B. Very different.

   C. The same but in reverse.

   D. Complement each other.

   Answer: D. Complement each other. Top-down and bottom-up accomplish the same purpose but start from the opposite ends of the spectrum.

3. The term momentum investing is the practice of buying securities the history of high returns during the preceding:

   A. 3-12 months

   B. 1-9 months

   C. 1-12 months

   D. 1-3 months

   Answer: A. 3-12 months. The short-term period of 1-2 months is too limited to make a judgment about the company having momentum; this is why a company that has a history of high returns from 3-12 months is a good candidate for momentum growth.

4. When selecting an investment your expectation is that the stock price should double in:

   A. A five-year period.
   B. A six-year period.
   C. A seven-year period.
   D. A 10-year period.

   Answer: A. A five-year period. The price should double in five years, which is 15% growth per year.

Chapter 14
Making the Decision to Buy, Hold or Sell

When you have finished reading this chapter, you will:

- Value the importance of having an exit plan before making an investment
- Know how a margin of safety protects your investment when purchasing a security
- Understand why an investor needs a smaller margin of safety when purchasing the stock of a large cap company than a small cap company
- Recognize the importance of closely monitoring your investment's value drivers when you are a focused investor
- Be familiar with five common situations that signal it's time to sell your position
- Be able to explain the advantages and disadvantages of using a stop loss
- Discern the differences between four stop loss types
- Have an introductory understanding of when to buy, hold, and sell your position

Introduction

We've done all our research. We've been as thorough as possible and out of the universe of several hundred securities that first caught our attention, we now have a qualified short list of 30 or 40 securities we think are the best in the world and we want to make a selection from these final contenders. We can't buy all of them; we only want 10 or 15 securities, and we only want the best of the best. We've assured ourselves that each of these high-quality stocks has a strong value proposition and we won't be buying a stock for more than it's worth. Also, we've looked closely at the fundamental and technical indicators and can see that now is the right time to buy these securities. These are the ones!

Now we have to make a buying selection. How do we choose which of these final candidates are the best choice for our focus portfolio?

Buy

The first stock on our list is IBM. IBM is a safe large cap company and we want to purchase the stock with a margin of safety. A margin of safety provides a buffer in case, in spite of our best efforts, this choice turns out to be a mistake.

At Synergy Asset Management we always want a margin of safety when making a purchase. A reassuring margin of safety for a large cap company is 8% to 15%, so if IBM was trading at $100 per share, we want our estimation of the company's value to be between $108 to $115 before considering its purchase.

Note:

A margin of safety:
For a large cap company: 8% – 15%.
For a mid-cap company: 15% – 20%.
For a small cap company: 20% – 25%.

Mid-cap companies carry a little more risk, so for this size company, we like a 15% to 20% margin of safety. If the company is worth $100, we need to calculate its value at $115 or $120 before we see a buy signal. Small cap companies carry a lot more risk than a goliath like IBM; in many cases these companies are unproven performers without a lengthy performance track record. An even bigger discount, or margin of safety, is necessary before we would risk our own or our clients' money. To be enticed into making an acquisition of this size company's stock, we would need a 20% to 25% margin, meaning we would have to be assured the company is valued at least between $120 and $125.

Knowing that we need a healthy margin of safety before risking our clients' money, we need to decide how to make not only an appropriate choice, but also the best one. How do we do that? The first step is to do some "comparison-shopping" using a broad market index as a measurement for selecting the companies we want for our clients' portfolios.

When investing on your own, you'll want to use a broad market index appropriate for investment selection. If you are seeking a variety of company sizes, the Russell 3000 contains large cap, mid-cap, and small cap companies, making this a good index for your purpose. Any reliable index will work well; for example, if you are only seeking large cap companies, you could use the S&P 500.

Let's assume we are only looking at large cap companies, and therefore we are going to be using the S&P 500. In this example our fictional prognosis for the S&P 500 is 7%. Since our goal as focus investors is to beat the market average, we would only be selecting securities that were high quality companies with a value proposition we believe could exceed 7%. We are looking for companies that will perform 8% or higher, otherwise we might as well buy the broad-based market index; if we're going to get the same return as the index, buying the index carries a lot less risk. Focus investors need enough return over the benchmark to be enticed into buying an individual stock.

In the universe of large cap companies, we've identified 10 that are all highly qualified. The timing is right to purchase all of them, but we only want to buy three. Clearly, we could rank them in the order of their highest potential return and purchase the top three. Remember, we want to make sure we have a sufficient margin of safety because we need to hedge our bet when making a buying decision. We are always looking for the highest risk-adjusted opportunity, the highest risk-adjusted returns within the universe of securities we've screened and researched.

When we've identified a high-quality company with realistically projected returns that are expected to exceed the benchmark and which include an appropriate margin of safety, it is a serious contender for selection. We will compare it with the other securities in this final group, and buy the best of them.

Hold, Monitor, and Adjust

Once we have purchased our chosen securities, the best of the best from our perspective as a focus investor, we are now in the position of holding them in our portfolio. As we know from our experience, the only thing we can expect is that everything will change. These securities will lose value, maintain value, or gain value. As there are no other possibilities, our task as an owner of these securities is to monitor them closely and adjust our portfolio as changing circumstances require. So, the next question is "What are we watching for, and how often do we watch?"

Monitor Value Drivers

You want to monitor the value drivers. The value drivers are the growth in the value of the security and its return on investment capital (ROIC). This is the measure of a company's financial performance, assessing the amount of profit for every dollar invested in it. The measurements are both technical and fundamental; we want to make sure our initial readings of the company's security are advancing in the direction we predicted, and staying within the range of acceptable performance based on the entry specifications we delineated in our decision-making process.

At Synergy Asset Management, our monitoring and ongoing research assigns a 10% value to economic drivers, a 60% value to quantitative drivers, and a 30% value to qualitative drivers. If these different readings on the pulse of the company's profitability continue in favor of our sustained ownership, we hold the security until we receive a sell signal, discussed a few paragraphs below.

Important:

When monitoring your investment, assign values to the economic drivers, quantitative drivers, and qualitative drivers as a tool to help you determine your sell signals. This provides a mathematical calculation that guides your decision-making process.

Monitoring is nothing more than keeping a close eye on the value drivers, and deciding at predetermined time periods that the security is or is not performing as anticipated. The monitoring process is conducted at a less robust level than the process we used for selection. The key idea here is that we've done our homework and we deliberately chose to purchase a security we believed had significant financial value for our portfolio. At this point, we are content to monitor the security's performance to assure ourselves periodically that the security we've purchased is increasing in value for our portfolio. We don't need to do deep research now because the security has already been carefully considered and chosen.

When circumstances change and the security is either advancing toward its upper sell level, or the position has deteriorated and the security is descending toward its lower sell level, this is when a deeper degree of reflection becomes necessary, as the decision to sell becomes imminent. As an example, we determined that a stock could have a price range between $95 and $115. We bought the stock at $100, and we think the stock is worth $115. We'll be happy to sell the stock at $115, which was our predetermined sell price based on our determination of its intrinsic value. During one of our regular monitoring activities, the stock is up to $113, so we know a decision will be needed soon because the stock is very close to our targeted value. Similarly, should the stock not be faring well, and its price is $96, we also know that a decision to sell the stock is imminent because of its nonperformance.

MONTHLY:

Monitoring the securities in our portfolio on a monthly basis is a very good idea because this short time period will help us identify securities that may need to be put on probation, i.e., securities that are nearing a sell signal. Some securities may arrive at this termination point, for good or ill, rather rapidly, while others will meander within their expected price range for several months or longer. Checking the securities in our portfolio every month is a great way to sleep well at night, rather than being rudely shocked with the unexpected results of a quarterly review.

QUARTERLY:

A quarterly review, which is more typical, should engage us a little more completely than the monthly review. A quarterly review allows us to compare the progress of our portfolio with the benchmark we selected as a measurement, and will also allow us to assess the performance of each security with their measurement from the prior quarter, as well as the same quarter in the previous year. Reviewing this data may not always be pertinent because our decision to invest in the security was based on the value drivers that were specific to the economic circumstances and technical indicators at a precise time. Even so, a quarterly review will provide a longer perspective than just the monthly review, and trends and circumstances may be more evident in this three-month range than they would otherwise be visible within the limitations of a monthly time period.

ANNUALLY:

The annual review offers the value of an even greater time perspective, providing us with a 12-month view in which to consider the importance of the annual high and the annual low for each of our securities. As we have been keeping notes on the performance and pertinent news of each of our securities during our monthly and quarterly monitoring sequences, an annual review will inform us of the larger picture, and may cause us to consider whether or not our original investment monies were well-placed; the realistic prospects for continuing to hold the security; and the challenge of making a decision about holding or selling.

Trigger Research Review

When we notice that our security is getting close to a decision point, it may be wise to conduct a research review to determine our next step. There are only four outcomes:

1. Hold our position. Since the security is meeting expectations, we maintain our position.

2. Sell our position. We are approaching a sell signal; we should get ready to divest.

3. Increase our position. Based on new research, our security shows additional potential value for our position; we should consider increasing our investment.

4. Extend our acceptable trading range. We may calculate that the trading range we established on entry now deserves a wider girth, and instead of a range of $95 to $115, our new calculations indicate a potential to $130; we should consider letting our winner run.

Here are two scenarios:

1. In the first scenario, let's assume that a deeper level of research confirms the security is still worth only $115. We'll move up our stop and commit to selling when the price reaches $115, taking our originally anticipated profits.

2. In the second scenario, our research determined there is more upside potential. In our new estimation, it's actually not worth $115; now we think it's worth $119. $119 is higher than our originally expected value of $115...and we might decide we'll stay with the position and pick up the additional value. But is it worth it to keep holding the security for the additional 3.5%? Perhaps not.

   This additional return may not be attractive enough, because if we've been watching and screening other candidate-stocks for our portfolio, and there is a security we like equally well that

> has a potential return of 8%-15%, it's best that we sell at $115 as we planned and buy the other security that has a much higher upside. We need to always be looking for the best risk-adjusted opportunity, and we don't want to tie our money down in any investment that is being outperformed by another. In most cases it's probably sensible to see the commitment through, and then cash out and move on to better prospects.
>
> Of course, we may decide to cash out at $113, too... This will be a discussion we'll have to have with ourselves as our sell signal gets close. Some factors may lead us to wait for the $115 price, while other factors may indicate the wisdom of selling and moving on to the next outstanding opportunity. When investing on your own, you will certainly benefit by developing your own set of selling rules on a situation like this so you can act with the strength of logic rather than wrestling with the peaks and valleys of fight or flight emotions.

In this example, someone might ask, "Why did you sell at $113 when you thought the stock was going up to $119? And why didn't you wait until the stock reached your original estimated value of $115? You left so much money on the table! You could've made more profit."

Key:

You are an investor in the business of buying and selling securities for a profit. Since this is not your hobby, you must regard every task...identifying, analyzing, selecting, purchasing, monitoring, selling...as a critical function of your business...the business of increasing your wealth as rapidly as reasonably possible with the tools you are expert at using.

Your response would be, "Well, I'm reinvesting. I'm rebalancing my position with a stock that has more upside potential. My calculations indicate that I may only earn about 5% by holding the position a little longer, but with my new position my calculations indicate I can earn a minimum of 8% return, and maybe as much as 12%."

Of course, you have to be intellectually honest and do your robust research, confirming you are making the right decision at the right time. If you still get a strong buy signal from the candidate-stock, this would clearly be a good decision. If you can't find a security that offers you a return in excess of 5%, then you are wise to hold your position as long as it is appropriate to do so. Remember that you must always include the cost of transactions in your calculations about whether to hold or sell.

Investors subject to taxable transactions should always be mindful of the effect of taxes on their returns. These investors should look at investments that can be held for at least a 12-month period because when the security is held for 12 months, the investor will benefit with long term capital gains. In some cases, though the investor recognizes the value of holding their position for at least 12 months, the calculated gain may occur rapidly when you suddenly earn a 15% or 20% gain; the security reached its target value faster than expected, a welcome surprise. In a case like this, when you've already realized the expected return, it may make the most sense to sell the position and pay the short term taxes because you will still have a higher after-tax return than originally expected, and there would be no point in tying up your money in a position that has already reached the projected level and may stagnate or reverse.

Though an investor would like to hold a position for 12 months to reduce the capital gains rate, sometimes you find serendipity. If the after-tax adjusted return meets your requirements, accept the gift with grace and vacate the position.

Sell Rules

Most investors know how to buy securities, and enjoy the thrill and promise of owning a security with the potential for increasing their financial wealth. Unfortunately, few investors know how to sell a security well, and typically have an unhealthy perception of the process. On the one hand, buying a security is rather like hunting...the excitement of the chase, the prey within the crosshairs, and bagging a prize. On the other hand, selling a security for most investors can be a traumatic experience of uncertainty, not knowing exactly when to withdraw, and associating the selling process with loss and missed opportunities.

Key:

Always create an exit plan before you enter a trade. By setting the sell signals when you are dispassionate about the outcome, you can spare the anxieties of being ruled by fear or greed. An exit plan is mandatory. Then, when the time comes to sell your position, obey the signals you have set!

Always create an exit plan before you enter a trade. By setting the sell signals when you are dispassionate about the outcome, you can spare the anxieties of being ruled by fear or greed. An exit plan is mandatory. Then, when the time comes to sell your position, obey the signals you have set!

It doesn't have to be this way; in fact, selling a position could have an even more exhilarating emotional context than buying a position. When you sell a position according to your preestablished rules, you are likely to be locking in your profits, or saving most of your investment resources from the agonizing pain of steady erosion. Both of these experiences are positive!

As with everything related to investing, an investor can run around the meadow like a rabbit being chased by a fox, or an investor can have a calculated plan of action for every scenario so the steady accumulation of profitable returns is as securely managed as a farmer at harvest time. This should be a deliberate choice, not a ticket on a roller coaster. When it comes to selling your position, you should have a set of rules that provide you with a dispassionate and thoughtful extraction. Investing becomes a business, not a hobby. You are in the position of harvesting profits and each of your fruit-bearing trees will probably offer different complexities, but your mature and professional response is based on pre-calculated behavior.

One of the most important responsibilities of an investor is to premeditate the set of circumstances that signal when to exit a position. This rational decision must be determined before the security is purchased. Every entrance requires an exit sooner or later, and an exit decision related to your investments should always be based on a carefully devised plan of action. As we've acknowledged before, money can make people act spontaneously when they are under duress. Therefore, it's financially sensible to spend as much time planning how to get out of an investment position as you spend getting into one. When the heebie-jeebies are let loose in the interior of your noggin, you don't want to be compromised into making an irrational slip and sudden descent into the pit of financial sacrifice, despair, and doom.

You need an exit strategy. There are five common situations that may arise and signal that it may be time to sell your position.

1. You made a mistake in your analysis. This will happen every once in a while; you may have misread a technical chart, or misunderstood some fundamental news. Perhaps an unexpected weather or supply change will dramatically alter your original calculations; maybe a new report is issued that changes everything or the company's board suddenly decides to withhold dividends for the next two quarters. Whatever the reason, it's clear that your expectations are diminished and there is no point locking up your investment resources on a horse that won't run.

2. The company's value drivers have deteriorated. While it looked like the technicals were forever in your favor, the trajectory of this security's path toward profitability have completely diminished, and just like a baseball that looked like it was headed out of the park becomes an infield pop fly, you've been thrown a curve ball and are now sitting on three strikes. It's time to find another pitcher.

3. The security has met its predicted value target and has no more upside. Your calculations were accurate and that's a reason to celebrate! This was a profit-maker you nailed on the head, and

now it's time to take all your marbles and go home because you're the winner. Calculations indicate that this particular horse has run its race; enjoy the taste of victory!

4. You found a better investment opportunity. As discussed earlier, the investment you're currently in has an upside of maybe 4%, but one of the securities you've been quietly watching has now come into the full focus of its potential and may yield an upside of 10% or even 20%. If you are as sure of your calculations as possible, have acknowledged your taxable costs, and this opportunity still seems to have an aura of golden promise, trading-up becomes a rational risk with legitimate promise.

5. The security has done really well, and it is now time to rebalance your portfolio. When a position approaches 15% - 20% of the portfolio, it might be a good time to trim back and rebalance. There is a dilemma here, of course; you always want to let your winners run, and sell your losers, so you have to have a discussion with yourself about whether or not to rebalance. If the security is continuing to be profitable, you may want to continue holding the position knowing your imbalance is creating a risk for your portfolio. Rather than selling your position, you could always employ stops, a safety tool reviewed in the next paragraph. This is an occasion to remember...while carefully reflecting upon the never-ending flux between heads and tails, and your choice of accepting more risk for more upside with a less diversified portfolio, surrendering a degree of security in exchange for a hoped-for larger degree of return. Make this a rational and calculated decision, though, so the greed-monster does not come alive.

Stop Losses

Using stop-losses in your investment practice can be worthwhile. They are not for everyone, but they are a useful tool to have available. Stops are a market order to sell your position when the price you indicated is reached. For example, if you have a security which you bought at 120 and it is presently trading at 135, you can place a stop at 130 so if the price of the security drops to 130, the market receives an order to sell.

In this case, you lock in your profits of "10". Stops are a convenient way of reasonably securing a sell price.

Definition:

Stop Loss: A stop loss is a market order to sell your position at an exact price.

The market cannot always sell at your predetermined price level and you may discover that when the market finally does sell your security, the sale price may be somewhat lower than 130 because of a price gap, but usually the markets will accommodate your order to sell. The reason the market cannot always sell at your stop level is because there may be a frenzy of trading and your stop is consumed in a rapid descent, or a buyer for your security was not immediately available and the price drifted until a buyer could be found.

A TWO-EDGED SWORD:

Employing a stop-loss can be either beneficial or detrimental depending upon the circumstances. A stop-loss can extricate you from a depreciating position, it's true. Sometimes, however, a stop-loss can also take you out of an opportune position too early. If the market is unsettled and there are regular occasions of extreme advance and decline during the course of a day or a week or a month, if you've set your stop-loss too tightly, the market may hit your stop-loss and release you from your position. The market may then reverse and proceed in the direction you desired, but without you. When using stop-loss orders, be wary of placing your stop too close, yet not too far away so your return isn't sacrificed.

INITIAL STOP:

An initial stop is the stop-loss you place on your security, ordering the security to be sold at the specific market price you've set, if possible. The stop is fixed, and can only be changed by a further order from you.

TRAILING STOP:

A trailing stop moves in the same direction as your security. For example, you can have your trailing stop shadow your security by remaining 10 points behind; as your security increases in value, the trailing stop also advances, staying 10 points behind the current market price. If your security reverses and its value decreases, the trailing stop does not reverse but maintains its highest position; if the trailing stop is hit by the security's price reversal, your security is sold. The trailing stop is usually used at first to minimize losses, but then, as the security increases in value, the trailing stop secures profits.

MOVING STOP:

A moving stop moves in tandem with the price, maintaining a specific trading range, protecting the investor from a sudden shift against the position.

PHANTOM STOP:

A phantom stop is a mental reminder you provide to yourself to sell one of your positions at a given time and circumstance. There is no market order to sell your security. The benefit of this type of stop-loss is that you will not be prematurely eliminated from your position; however, you will need to be alert to the daily vicissitudes of your security's price and prepared to take action immediately when a sell signal is reached. Because the only protection you have is your own diligence to the price fluctuations of your security, you will need to pay attention throughout the trading day.

Summary

This chapter reviewed the process for buying, holding, and selling securities. When buying a security, you must include a margin of safety in your calculations so you can protect yourself when making the initial investment; we discussed how to gauge the size of your margin of safety and select a reasonably appropriate benchmark to determine the right purchase price.

When holding an investment position, you should periodically monitor the value drivers that led you to make the investment in the first place.

If the value drivers are holding firm and your further research and reflections confirm the continued profitability of the security, you should maintain your position unless a better opportunity is apparent. As your security nears the predicted extent of its value, additional research and reflection may be necessary so you can determine whether to continue holding the position, or prepare to sell.

When the time finally comes to sell, a positive mental attitude about your outcome is beneficial, remembering that you are an investor conducting a business activity with calculated and unemotional decisions based on a set of selling rules, your exit plan, that guide your unbiased predilection for steady financial growth. Greed and fear have no place in your decisions; you are dispassionately making your choices based on a set of selling rules you established when your emotions were disengaged. Five common selling situations were recounted, and the use of a stop-loss mechanism as a tool to curtail the loss of investment capital or ensure the capture of profits was presented.

Now that we have reflected upon the circumstances for buying, holding, and selling the securities in your portfolio, we are thoroughly prepared to investigate the most important aspect of investing which is, using all the previous information in this book, deciding on which Core Satellite solution provides the best investment choice for your unique circumstances and preferred investment style. As an informed investor, which strategy is best for you?

Chapter 14 Review Questions

1. A margin of safety when purchasing an investment must always be included. Which of the following margins of safety are advisable?

   A. For a large cap company: 8% – 15%.
   B. For a mid-cap company: 15% – 20%.
   C. For a small cap company: 20% – 25%.
   D. All of the above.

2. To which of the following should you assign values that will help you determine your sell signals?

   A. Economic drivers.
   B. Quantitative drivers.
   C. Qualitative drivers.
   D. All of the above.

3. Which of the following situations would not signal that it's time to sell your holdings?

   A. You made a mistake in your analysis.
   B. You are working on a home renovation project and need immediate cash.
   C. The company's value drivers have deteriorated.
   D. The investment has met its predicted value target and has no more upside.

4. Which of the following is not a recognized stop loss?

   A. Ghost stop.
   B. Trailing stop.
   C. Moving stop.
   D. Initial stop.

Chapter 14 Review Answers

1. A margin of safety when purchasing an investment must always be included. Which of the following margins of safety are advisable?

   A. For a large cap company: 8% – 15%.
   B. For a mid-cap company: 15% – 20%.
   C. For a small cap company: 20% – 25%.
   D. All of the above.

   Answer: D. All of the above. You never want to make an investment without allowing a margin of safety so in case the market turns against your position, you've included some flexibility, so you won't immediately take a loss. The larger the company's capitalization, the less a margin of safety is required.

2. To which of the following should you assign values that will help you determine your sell signals?

   A. Economic drivers.
   B. Quantitative drivers.
   C. Qualitative drivers.
   D. All of the above.

   Answer: D. All of the above. One of the most important tasks when purchasing an investment is to know when to sell it. Identifying those factors that were attractive to you and then giving them a numeric value, you will be better able to identify when it's time to divest from the investment.

3. Which of the following situations would not signal that it's time to sell your holdings?

   A. You made a mistake in your analysis.
   B. You are working on a home renovation project and need immediate cash.
   C. The company's value drivers have deteriorated.
   D. The investment has met its predicted value target and has no more upside.

Answer: B. You are working on a home renovation project and need immediate cash. Needing cash is not a signal to sell; it is simply a personal need for cash. Other sell signals are that you've found a better investment opportunity, or the security has done very well, and it is now time to rebalance your portfolio.

4. Which of the following is not a recognized stop loss?

   A. Ghost stop.
   B. Trailing stop.
   C. Moving stop.
   D. Initial stop.

   Answer: A. Ghost stop. There is a stop called the phantom stop, which is a stop you keep in your mind rather than register as a market order.

Chapter 15
The Core Satellite Solution

When you have finished reading this chapter, you will:

- Recognize the value of using both asset allocation and focus investing in your portfolio decisions, and how to do it
- Feel confident explaining the asset allocation optimization process
- Be familiar with the concept of the "Core Satellite Strategy"
- Understand the difference between a portfolio's core and satellite investments, and how they can work together to decrease risk or increase return
- Have gained a powerful insight to three proprietary asset allocation strategy models
- Know how a portfolio can be structured so it is risk-based, or return-based, or both risk and return-based
- Observe the five steps to building an asset allocation portfolio
- Be able to explain how strategic and tactical allocations can modify a portfolio's risk
- Remember that trading should only occur when your analysis of five factors indicates action is necessary
- Possess introductory knowledge about how the Tugboat, , and Sailboat portfolios are the same...and different
- Realize why some portfolios should be monitored daily, and some only quarterly

- Identify at least one important fact about the value of momentum in a trend
- Discern how constructing an asset allocation portfolio is different from constructing a focused portfolio

Introduction

This is the chapter that brings everything together to help you become an exceptional investor. During the course of this book we have discussed alpha and beta strategies, also referred to as active and passive strategies. We have discussed both risk and return and their corollaries of downside protection and upside capture. We've taken a look at strategic decisions and tactical decisions. We've spent considerable time reviewing asset allocation, represented by Modern Portfolio Theory (MPT) and the work of Nobel Prize winner Harry Markowitz; and we have also demonstrated our equal respect for focus investing as championed by Warren Buffett.

In general, people are accustomed to using labels that describe conditions and events as being solely one thing or another. An object is either big or small, hot or cold, near or far, good or bad. Yet we also recognize the value of relativity and how one's perspective is a significant factor with understanding the merits of an object or condition; we are mature enough to realize there are always subtleties and shades of gray in all matters we subject to our inquiry and inspection.

Given the degree of insight that comes with these layers of experience, does it make sense to exclude one theory of investing in exclusive favor of its opposing theory, knowing that both theories are credible and demonstrate significant merit for expanding our personal financial wealth? Will we limit our financial opportunities by choosing only one of the two options even though we can readily accept that both are likely to increase our fortune? Must we restrict ourselves to either/or when we can benefit materially from a wisdom that incorporates both/and? If both theories have proven value, why would we seek to limit the benefits they could provide our financial freedom?

In the pages that follow, a unique strategy will be introduced that creates the circumstances for acquiring wealth by employing the desirable features of both investment theories.

A QUICK RECAP:

Before we propel ourselves forward, a brief reminder is helpful since the Core Satellite Strategy portfolios offered by Synergy Asset Management are composed of a blend of these key elements.

Alpha Strategy: Alpha is when an investor seeks to earn a higher return than the benchmark for the asset class in which the security belongs. This is active investing.

Beta Strategy: Beta is when an investor seeks to mirror the benchmark return for the asset class in which the security belongs. This is passive investing.

Definition:

Alpha is the descriptor that describes a fund's excess returns when compared with the returns of a benchmark index.
Beta is the name of the descriptor that measures an investor's risk according to the market's average.

Asset Allocation Investing: Asset allocation is an investment strategy that involves diversifying, or spreading, investment funds among different types of asset classes to reduce return-rate volatility and risk. In traditional asset allocation, a range of best-diversified portfolio mixes of asset classes is determined, offering various expected return rates, each with the least possible volatility and risk. This range of investment elements is designed to achieve the efficient frontier, commonly shown as a curve on an efficient frontier graph.

To obtain the benefit of diversification, the most important step is to select several asset classes that are fundamentally different and, therefore, likely to vary above and below their expected return rates at different times. If, during a year, one asset class goes down, others are likely to offset that decline by going up.

The second step in the process is to apply a mathematical analysis called Modern Portfolio Theory, made famous by Harry Markowitz who won a Nobel Prize for this work. The analysis identifies the range of best-diversified mixes of the selected asset classes. The objective is to optimize the investment accounts through portfolio construction practices that are designed to minimize risk while maximizing returns.

Focus Investing: Focus investing, on the other side of the coin, advocates that the markets are inefficient, therefore offering an alpha investor the opportunity to find securities whose prices are below their true value. When purchased, huge profits are possible. Made popular by Warren Buffett, this investment style invests in only a few of the right assets, instead of scores of securities. The focus is on finding the best of the best securities, acquiring and holding them until their technical and fundamental indicators reach predetermined buy signals, and selling them once their true value is acquired.

EMBRACING ALL FOUR THEORIES AT ONCE...A PARADOX?

There are four theories, and they have characteristics in opposition. Alpha (active management) is a completely different investment style to Beta (passive management). Asset allocation is an investment strategy in direct conflict with focus investing. All four of these theories have advantages, and are proven pathways to financial success. How is it possible to develop a combined investment strategy that engages the elements of each?

A reasonable and prudent investor acknowledges that both sets of theories can be employed judiciously as circumstances suggest the application of either one or the other. At Synergy Asset Management we have developed portfolio models that comprise, to varying degrees, the harmonious application of these different strategies. We call these combinations of once disparate but now compatible investment styles our Core Satellite Strategy. As we have a variety of different Core Satellite portfolios, our clients can select the Core Satellite portfolio that is most appropriate to their financial goals on a range of conservative to aggressive.

Key:

You, or you and your financial planner, can design a portfolio that uses both asset allocation and focus investing. Though they are different strategies, they can work in tandem for risk control and accelerated returns.

What is a "Core Satellite Strategy" Model?

The term "Core Satellite Strategy" is composed of two essential elements:

1. A group of core investments that establish the main intention of the portfolio;
2. A supporting group of satellite investments which provide the additional emphasis of the portfolio, affording the opportunity for each portfolio model to achieve varying degrees of higher return with modified risk.

Essentially, an investor can pair a core investment with a satellite investment to create a desired outcome of any kind. The core investment is the nucleus of the portfolio, setting the primary expectation for performance. The satellite investment puts the spin on the portfolio, much like a side bet enhances the potential for additional gain. Think of the core satellite model as an ice cream sundae. Which do you prefer? A big scoop of chocolate ice cream, or vanilla? This is your core, because the sundae's flavor is significantly influenced by your choice of chocolate or vanilla. But then, what topping will you prefer? Would you like chocolate sauce, or would you rather have strawberry? Maybe you're partial to marshmallow or hot fudge...

Important:

A Core Satellite Strategy uses a core of investments as the portfolio's foundation, with several satellite investments to increase returns.

Let's consider a financial example. We could choose the S&P 500 as the core of our portfolio, and decide that it represents 60% of the portfolio. The bulk of our expectations are founded on the performance of the S&P 500. This is now our beta, our passive management core. However well or poorly the S&P 500 performs will determine a large part of the growth, stasis, or loss of this portfolio.

To augment the performance of this model portfolio, we can decide to purchase the efforts of four fund managers we believe are strong performers. We decide to buy an actively managed international stock, an actively managed bond fund, and we also think an aggressive REIT fund will be an excellent addition. These are the satellites, our alpha investments, representing the other 40% of the portfolio. We now have our solid passive core combined with three satellites that are seeking aggressive returns. This is a simple example of how to combine conflicting theories so your investments can benefit from optimized risk and return planning.

Asset Allocation Optimization

Before we explore a variety of asset allocation strategies, it's important to spend a few moments understanding how the asset allocation process is optimized. In this case, optimization simply means arriving at the best solution for the purpose desired. The following is an explanation of Figure N1, "Asset Allocation Optimization", which illustrates the global view of how a portfolio is optimized for investors.

Figure 36: Asset Allocation Optimization.

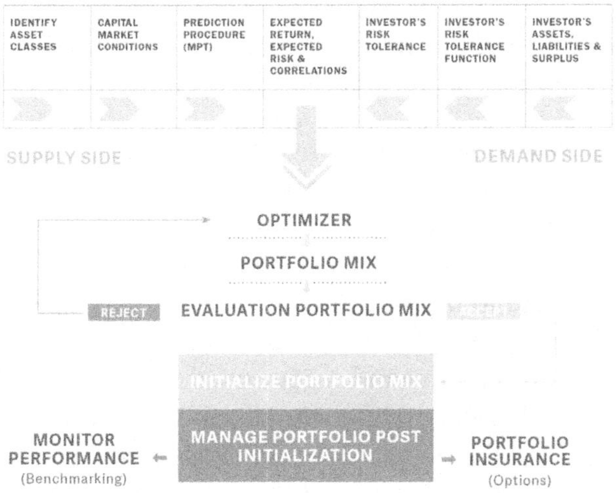

Once again, we have the metaphor of the two-sided coin. On the left is the supply side, representing the investment professional, and on the right is the demand side, representing the investor or client.

1. The investor is composed of the content identified within the three circles: risk tolerance, ability and willingness toward risk, and assets and liabilities.

2. The investment professional supplies the expertise to identify the portfolio-appropriate asset classes, the capital market conditions which include capital market assumptions, efficient frontiers, expected returns and risks in correlation, the investment term, and all the other details that help the professional arrive at a reasonable investment prediction using MPT, Modern Portfolio Theory.

3. The supply side and the demand-side converge in the central circle where the investment professional and the investor or client can consider the expected return, risk, and the correlations between the two.

4. Assuming approval, the expected return, risk and correlations are put into the mathematical blender called the optimizer, and

the optimizer identifies a potential portfolio mix of assets and their percentages.

5. The investment professional evaluates the portfolio mix and either accepts or rejects what the optimizer has suggested.

6. You may wonder why the investment professional might reject the conclusions of the optimizer, and that's because there are biases in the optimization process that, if left unconstrained, could derail the optimization process. The optimizer is constructed to provide the best of both worlds, which is a high return and low risk. An unconstrained optimization process will lead you astray and recommend two asset classes: small cap stocks and Treasury bills. Small cap stocks have traditionally been one of the highest producing asset classes, and similarly, Treasury bills have always been one of the safest asset classes. Obviously, this is unacceptable, and it is for this reason that the investment professional must modify the optimizer with constraints, rejecting the portfolio mix until a proper mix is finally presented.

7. Once the portfolio mix has been accepted, the investment professional or the investor purchases the initial investments for the portfolio. These purchases are in alignment with predetermined strategic and tactical allocations, which are discussed later in this chapter.

8. At this point, the professional or the investor monitors and manages the portfolio, and conducts a post-initialization assessment within a month of setting up the portfolio to confirm, through comparison with the appropriate benchmark, that the portfolio is performing as required. If it isn't, then

adjustments must be made to the portfolio until it is producing the expected results.

9. The portfolio is monitored according to a predetermined schedule and adjustments are made as circumstances require.

10. In addition, the portfolio can always be hedged with portfolio insurance as an assurance against significant loss.

This is the overview of the process when properly building an asset allocation portfolio. There is nothing haphazard about it; every step has been carefully considered so the investor's funds are thoughtfully and mathematically invested to achieve a particular result. In the next section, we will discuss the different kinds of asset allocation models, one of which might be a good choice for you.

Allocation Strategies

At Synergy Asset Management, we have a variety of unique portfolio models, classified into three categories of five portfolios each:

1. Risk-based.

2. Return-based.

3. Both risk and return-based depending on market circumstances.

Portfolio Goals

Our goal is to provide our clients with adaptive portfolios that are built to respond to all market conditions. This means we take advantage of Modern Portfolio Theory (MPT) as well as focused investing. Our three distinct groups of investment models are constructed to maximize long term portfolios. We are keenly aware of the interplay between risk and return and use our knowledge and experience to build these portfolios knowing that some asset classes pose risk-generating characteristics while other asset classes pose return-generating characteristics. Our variety of models are formulated to find the right combination of these two types of assets; in addition to our continual monitoring and periodic adjustment, these are the sources of our investment success.

1. **Risk-based:** This set of five portfolios, which we refer to as our Tugboat models, is risk-based, meaning that these portfolios are designed to limit downside volatility. These portfolios are for investors seeking downside protection from the unpredictable nature of the market. Tugboats motor steadily through the changing winds and tides.

2. **Return-based:** This second set of five portfolios are referred to as our Speed Boat models. The portfolios in this group have been designed to capture upside return. Investors selecting from this portfolio group have determined that upside growth is their priority, making it a race through the market's waters to capture as much growth as possible.

3. **Both risk and return-based:** We call this third portfolio group the Sailboat models because these five portfolios "sail" with the ever-adjusting "winds" of the changing market. These portfolios are also called our Focus Tactical Allocation (FTA) models because their purpose is to be tactically proactive as the market shifts, being defensive and protected in bear markets... and fully invested in bull markets.

Definition:

Risk-based: A strategy with a primary goal of protecting against loss.
Return-based: A strategy with a primary goal of increasing value.

The Tugboat and Speed Boat portfolios are built on Modern Portfolio Theory (MPT), which means that asset allocation is a key feature of their composition. The Sailboat portfolios are not based on MPT, but rather are built on our own unique and proprietary factors. The Sailboat models do not try to forecast the market's outcomes, nor are they based on the opinions of financial analysts. Our FTA models are devised from a custom blend of technical and fundamental facts, and these portfolios are dynamically monitored and adjusted as the facts change.

Building a Tugboat Portfolio

In this section you will gain insight about how the Dynamic Risk Model (DRM) portfolios are constructed so you can duplicate the concept, if you wish, when constructing your own portfolio. The Dynamic Risk Model is called this because it is actively monitored to prevent risk from exceeding the allowable range. Each of the five DRM portfolios has its specific threshold of risk, whether low or high, which cannot be transgressed. A description of each will be presented later in this chapter. For now, here is a step-by-step explanation of the process for building a Tugboat portfolio.

THE 5-STEP PROCESS:

Both the Tugboat and portfolios follow a 5-step process:

Step 1: Develop Asset Class Inputs

Step 2: Create Asset Class Models

Step 3: Analyze Investment Vehicles

Step 4: Construct the Portfolio

Step 5: Monitor the Portfolio

STEP 1: DEVELOPING ASSET CLASS INPUTS:

The first step is to analyze a global set of asset classes and apply a process that forecasts each asset class's expected return, risk measurement (standard deviation), and the relationships between the asset classes that correlate their interaction. It's essential to select several asset classes that are fundamentally different and are therefore likely to achieve different return rates at different times. This provides a balanced portfolio performance; the decline of one asset class will be offset by the increase in one or more of the other asset classes.

Of the 22 popular asset classes, only about eight of them are typically required to build a good portfolio. The Tugboat portfolios will normally add or delete asset classes on a monthly basis to optimize correlation relationships. Because the Tugboat portfolios are structured specifically to limit downside risk and preserve capital, exchanging asset classes is conducted as frequently as needed to sustain and improve the portfolios' value, keeping risk to a predetermined level.

Synergy Asset Management conducts robust forecasting methods based on historical data on returns, standard deviation, and correlation for each of the asset classes being considered for inclusion in the portfolios; we also employ additional analysis using our proprietary forecasting procedures to preserve wealth and build better portfolios.

Note:

The Tugboat Portfolios have a conservative core to protect the client's wealth, with satellite investments selected to increase varying degrees of return. This set of five portfolios range from conservative to aggressive and from a short time horizon to an extended time horizon.

In addition, the Tugboat portfolios are constructed using advanced multi-factor downside risk models. This means that because we are more concerned with the downside risk than the upside return, we adjust the periodicity to have a more informed and conservative picture for portfolio preservation. For example, we may use return and correlation expectations that are based on a rolling 120 months of data, but the data we use to forecast the threat of risk is likely to be measured with a faster signal such as a rolling 36 month data set. This is just one example of the data we watch and employ, and measurements that indicate skewness and kurtosis may be a source for yet other optimal data that advise our decision-making for our clients' portfolio defense. Because we are risk-averse in the Tugboat portfolios, our continual analysis emphasizes risk awareness and client protection.

STEP 2: CREATING ASSET CLASS MODELS:

Once the optimal number of asset classes have been selected and their expected return/risk characteristics have been forecasted, the Tugboat portfolio models are constructed using the Modern Portfolio Theory (MPT). This mathematical optimization process identifies the best-diversified combinations of the selected asset classes.

Regardless of the number of asset classes included in a portfolio, eight usually being the most mathematically appropriate, calculations will reveal the lowest possible variance of risk with the highest possible expected return, which is the highly desirable information we seek.

One of the reasons why Modern Portfolio Theory (MPT) is so highly employed is because the mathematical treatment identifies the combination of investments, having different expected returns and risks, that are likely to result in less risk as a whole than the weighted average risk of the combined investments, forecasting even less risk than the least risky asset class in the entire portfolio. This is achievable because of the dissimilarity in the patterns of return among the selected asset classes.

Mathematics for fun and profit!

The general mean variance optimization process is typically based upon log-normal historical data that relies on arithmetic expected returns, historical standard deviation as its risk measure, and historic correlation coefficients that match the periodicity of the returns data. This data is used to form a single period view of the efficient frontier.

At Synergy Asset Management, we build our portfolios with more sophisticated optimization techniques that do not necessarily rely on log-normal historic return data and other biases of general mean variance optimization. We also regularly conduct a variety of evaluation procedures including back-testing, sensitivity, and scenario analysis to ensure our models present stable recommendations through complete economic cycles. We do the homework!

Key:

A portfolio can be structured so it is risk-based, return-based, or both risk and return-based... Tugboat, Speed Boat, or Sailboat. Which is right for you?

STEP 3: ANALYZING INVESTMENT VEHICLES:

Having decided which asset classes we will use in the Tugboat portfolios, the next step is selecting the individual investments from the chosen asset classes. Synergy Asset Management's investment universe includes every security offered worldwide. When analyzing securities for inclusion, we employ both quantitative and qualitative factors. We also analyze the security using a combination of returns and holdings-based style analysis to determine which investments are best suited for implementation in our models for consistent and accurate performance as measured by our customized objectives and appropriate benchmark. Fundamental and technical analyses are used to guide the investment selection along with the examination of passive and active investment considerations. Our fundamental analysis tilts toward finding investment vehicles that stay close to their respective benchmark, which is appropriate for the Tugboat risk-averse portfolios.

Our review uses a "top down" investment selection process based on the hypothesis that the market is efficient. This focuses our research on passive investment vehicles like ETFs and/or index mutual funds unless we observe analytical evidence that we should rotate into active management.

Because the Tugboat portfolio style seeks beta, AKA a return close to the benchmark, it seeks managers whose funds or companies are quite similar to the selected benchmark. As we previously discussed in this book, designing a proper benchmark is important, and the Tugboat portfolios are monitored by comparison with an appropriate benchmark.

STEP 4: CONSTRUCTING THE PORTFOLIO:

This is where all the elements converge. We have previously selected the desired asset classes, built asset class models, and analyzed the individual investment choices; now we can construct the portfolio by purchasing the securities we've chosen. Our many insights, gained during our analysis, will guide us with setting strategic and tactical proportions. These decisions will result in a portfolio that is expected to maximize returns within the acceptable level of risk, and the result will be a finely tuned portfolio designed to meet its specific objectives...and ours.

1. Strategic decisions take a long-term view to investing and reflect investor-specific objectives and constraints based on the factors that compose our original market assumptions for expected risk, expected return, and expected correlations.

2. Tactical decisions are made when we believe that one asset class will perform better than another in the short term. As an example, we may believe that U.S. stocks will outperform U.S. bonds, or that international equities will outperform domestic equities; this insight could trigger a tactical decision with the holdings in the Tugboat portfolios.

Some Finer Points About the Tugboat Portfolios: These attributes are rarely found in asset allocation models:

- The Tugboat portfolios are pegged to a specific level of risk. These five portfolios range from conservative to aggressive and are equally spaced by two points of risk on the efficient frontier.

  Our Tugboat portfolios strive to maintain their specific risk target through all market conditions. As an example, the 8%-risk portfolio may have a return of 5% in one year, 4% in the next, and 10% in the third, yet the portfolio was aggressively managed so that it maintained an 8% risk level in all three years. The annual returns varied, but not the risk level. This type of portfolio is ideal for investors who want to be assured of the risk they are accepting. These investors are willing to receive whatever level of return becomes available while maintaining the guaranteed level of risk. The Tugboat portfolios are built for investors whose primary goal is to avoid risk.

- The Tugboat portfolios are strategically examined and rebuilt on a monthly basis and are therefore dynamic in nature. The important difference is that tactical decisions are usually made when the portfolio manager has new knowledge about an asset class and weights the portfolio in the direction of that information. With Synergy Asset Management, this activity is conducted monthly to ensure our clients' risk protection.

  For example, a Tugboat portfolio calls for a strategic allocation of 25% in short term, midterm and long-term U.S. bonds. Then new information suggests that interest rates will be rising, so the portfolio's 25% weight in U.S. bonds is tactically shifted to 100% short term bonds, protecting the portfolio in the new interest rate environment. The portfolio still contains its strategic 25% in U.S. bonds, but now the bond allocation is composed of only short-term bonds instead of the original blend of short term, midterm and long-term bonds. This is an example of the expertise that's applied to all Tugboat portfolios on a monthly basis.

STEP 5: MONITORING THE PORTFOLIO:

At Synergy Asset Management we embrace a dynamic approach to monitoring and adjusting our Tugboat portfolios. As time goes on, the market's continual change must be monitored, and the portfolios must be adjusted to maintain the optimal portfolio characteristics we've designed. Simplistic calendar-year rebalancing is insufficient and exposes the portfolios to the unnecessary risk we pledge to avoid. A monthly dynamic rebalancing is conducted as warranted to maintain the risk level.

Important:

The Tugboat Portfolios are evaluated on a monthly basis to ensure risk protection.

In conducting our monitoring process, we continually monitor and evaluate our portfolios on a monthly basis to determine the most appropriate portfolio strategies for the current market conditions. We apply back-testing strategies along with statistical procedures such as Monte Carlo analysis to guide our portfolio adjustments.

We rebalance the portfolios as little or as much as necessary to keep them on their designed track. We are always mindful of trading costs and taxes in our decision process. In fact, even though the goal is to strategically rebuild the Tugboat portfolios on a monthly basis, actual trading of the portfolios only occur when our analysis of the following five factors align with rational financial sense:

1. Asset weight drift from the policy target
2. Volatility
3. Correlation
4. Taxes
5. Trading costs

Our Tugboat portfolios are designed as risk-adverse investments, and we spare no effort to assure that our clients' funds are appropriately positioned for the most expertly designed downside protection...no matter how strong the market's tempests.

Note:

Dynamic Risk Models (DRM) (Tugboats!)

Conservative

The conservative model is designed for the cautious investor, one with a low risk tolerance and/or a short time horizon. It is targeted toward the investor seeking investment stability and liquidity from their investments. The main objective for this range is to preserve capital while providing income.

Moderate Conservative

A moderately conservative investor seeks both modest capital appreciation and income from their portfolio. The main objective of an individual within this range is to preserve the investor's capital, with minimum fluctuations.

Moderate

A moderate investor seeks relatively stable growth from their assets offset by a low level of income. The main objective of an individual within this range is to achieve steady portfolio growth while limiting fluctuations to less than those of the overall stock markets.

Moderate Aggressive

The moderately aggressive investor has a relatively high tolerance for risk and a longer time horizon. The investor has little need for current income and seeks above-average growth from their investment assets. The main objective of this range is capital appreciation, and the investor should be able to tolerate moderate fluctuations.

Aggressive

The aggressive investor has both a high tolerance for risk and long investment time horizon. The main objective of this model is to provide high growth without providing current income. Portfolios in this range may have substantial fluctuations in value from year to year, making this category unsuitable for those who do not have an extended time horizon.

Building a Speed Boat Portfolio

Also known as Speed Boats, the Strategically Designed Tactically Dynamic Models (SDTDM) portfolios are a good alternative to their Tugboat counterparts. The important difference between the Speed Boat portfolios and the Tugboat portfolios is that the Speed Boat portfolios are return-based models, not risk-based models.

The Speed Boat portfolios strive to capture as much upside return as possible, with an efficient amount of risk. Speed Boat portfolios are also asset allocation models, so they also have a nucleus of investments that determine the portfolios' core growth potential, and they also have satellite investments that are specifically selected to accelerate the portfolios' performance. Like Tugboats, Speed Boats are anchored to their core investment weight, but then may speed as far as possible with their satellite investments acting as their accelerator.

THE 5-STEP PROCESS:

Both the Tugboat and portfolios follow a 5-step process:

Step 1: Develop Asset Class Inputs

Step 2: Create Asset Class Models

Step 3: Analyze Investment Vehicles

Step 4: Construct the Portfolio

Step 5: Monitor the Portfolio

STEP 1: DEVELOPING ASSET CLASS INPUTS:

The complete set of worldwide asset classes are reviewed for their expected return, risk measurement (standard deviation), and the relationships between the asset classes (correlation). Analysis results in forecasts based on historical data and traditional time periods such as 120-day and 90-day technical cycles. When reviewing asset classes for portfolio selection, we are more interested in the return distribution on the right side of the efficient frontier chart.

With Speed Boat portfolios, changes to the original selection of asset classes, whether additions or deletions, are considered annually. This is because asset class selection for the Speed Boat portfolios is made for long term investment. With the Tugboat portfolios, the main focus is on reducing risk, so continual monitoring and readiness for adjustment is paramount to reduce the potential for risk/loss. This is not the case with the Speed Boat portfolios; since the main focus is on capturing return, the portfolios are composed of investments that are believed will perform as expected over the long term. The Tugboat portfolios are focused on the short term; the Speed Boat portfolios are focused on the long term. The Tugboat portfolios are risk-focused; the Speed Boat portfolios are return-focused.

STEP 2: CREATING ASSET CLASS MODELS:

After the asset classes have been selected for their potential to meet the performance expectations of the Speed Boat portfolios, they are then subjected to the optimization process so the best combination of asset class proportions can be calculated using historical data and mean variance. Historic standard deviation is used to measure the potential for risk, and historic correlation coefficients measure the potential for return. This data is used to form a single-period view of the efficient frontier so Synergy Asset Management can determine the best proportionate mix of the selected asset classes, providing the Speed Boat portfolios with the most potential for achieving their proposed returns. The Speed Boat models assume the manager can achieve alpha performance, which is a return in excess of the general market's return. Assuming that the market is not efficient, these portfolios are expected to exceed their appropriate benchmarks.

STEP 3: ANALYZING INVESTMENT VEHICLES:

During the analysis procedure, a bottom up investment selection process is employed. Because the underlying assumption is that the market is not efficient, we seek investments that are actively managed. In addition, fundamental analysis favors finding investments that do not hug their respective benchmark as represented with higher tracking error. Stated statistically, investment vehicles with a low R2 are chosen exclusively.

Note:

The Speed Boat Portfolios maintain their strategic equity and bond weights as the core investment, and use the satellite investments to drive higher returns.

Because these portfolios seek alpha, which is a return in excess of the appropriate benchmark, Synergy Asset Management searches for managers or companies that are fundamentally different from their benchmark and are successful with a competitive style or advantage. The result is an unconstrained set of active managers for each asset allocation selection.

STEP 4: CONSTRUCTING THE PORTFOLIO:

When constructing the Speed Boat portfolios, a strategic weight in equities and bonds is maintained; to this investment nucleus, tactical/dynamic decisions are made within the strategic asset classes. For example, a Speed Boat portfolio that is structured with 60% equities and 40% bonds will always maintain this 60/40 strategic weight. However, the portfolio managers may think it wise to dynamically optimize the equity or bond portion on a time continuum, such as quarterly, as changing conditions warrant.

As an illustration, here is a chart that demonstrates the asset allocation of a 60% equity and 40% bond portfolio over two quarterly periods:

Figure 37: Example of Optimizing a Portfolio.

Time Period 1		**Time Period 2**	
Equity		**Equity**	
Large Cap US Equity	20%	Large Cap US Equity	20%
International Equity	20%	International Equity	20%
Emerging Market Equity	20%	Small Cap US Equity	10%
Total Equity	**60%**	US Mid Cap Growth	10%
		Total Equity	**60%**
Bond		**Bond**	
US Treasuries	10%	US Treasuries	20%
Global Bond	10%	Global Bond	20%
US Corporate	10%	**Total Bond**	**40%**
Floating Rate	10%		
Total Bond	**40%**		

In both time periods, the proportion of equities to bonds is the same at 60/40. Note that the three equity sectors and four bond sectors in Time Period 1 have been adjusted to a different combination of equity and bond sectors in Time Period 2. The manager of this fictitious

Speed Boat portfolio decided to make the adjustments based on significant changes happening in the market and economy. This is an example of how a portfolio maintains its strategic intentions but can adjust tactically to suit market vicissitudes.

Note:

The Speed Boat Portfolios have an equity and bond core designed to increase the client's wealth, with satellite investments to accelerate return. This set of five portfolios range from 100% bonds to 100% equities, with three intervening combinations of bond and equity ratios for investors that want different portfolio performances.

STEP 5: MONITORING THE PORTFOLIO:

The Speed Boat portfolios are dynamically monitored, and they are evaluated quarterly to determine the most appropriate portfolio tactics for the current market conditions. Back-testing strategies as well as statistical procedures such as Monte Carlo analysis guide all portfolio adjustments. As you have seen from the chart example, our goal is to maintain strategic asset allocation weightings while tactically rebuilding the portfolios on a quarterly basis, as necessary. Actual trading of portfolio investments only occurs if the analysis of the following five factors indicates action is necessary:

1. Asset-weight drift from the policy target
2. Volatility
3. Correlation
4. Taxes
5. Trading cost

Here is a comparison chart that will help clarify the similarities and differences between Tugboat and Speed Boat portfolios:

Figure 38: Comparison of the Tugboat and Speed Boat Portfolios.

Tugboat	Speed Boat
Built on Modern Portfolio Theory	Built on Modern Portfolio Theory
Goal is to reduce negative compounding	Higher return participation
It is a Beta strategy	It is an Alpha strategy
Optimal global asset class universe	Optimal global asset class universe
Focus on downside risk	Focus on both up-side and down-side risk
Assumes markets are efficient	Assumes market are less efficient
Managers try to replicate benchmark	Managers try to beat benchmark
Quarterly tactical rebalancing	Maintains strategic weights; annual tactical rebalancing
Top down investment process	Bottom-up investment process
Passive ETFs	Active investment vehicles
Advanced optimization and forecasting techniques	Traditional optimization and forecasting techniques
5 risk-based models	5 return-based models

As you can see from this chart, the Tugboat portfolios differ from the Speed Boat portfolios in these significant ways:

1. Tugboats are risk-focused, and their goal is to preserve money by reducing negative compounding. The Speed Boat portfolios

are return-focused, and their goal is to achieve higher returns without regard to risk.

2. Tugboats are passive-focused portfolios because they have a beta strategy, and therefore their underlying assumption is that the markets are efficient. The Speed Boat portfolios are active-focused portfolios because they have an Alpha strategy, and therefore their underlying assumption is that the markets are not efficient.

3. This explains why the Tugboat managers seek to achieve the benchmark, and the Speed Boat portfolio managers seek to exceed the benchmark.

4. Tugboats are primarily focused on the downside risk, which means these portfolios are strictly risk-averse; their main goal is to not lose money.

5. Monthly tactical rebalancing is analyzed and considered for the Tugboat portfolios' investments; the Speed Boat portfolios are reviewed quarterly, and rebalancing is only considered within the context of long-term investing. This is discussed more completely in the next section of this chapter.

6. Tugboat portfolios employ the top-down analysis process while the Speed Boat portfolios employ the bottom up analysis process.

7. The Tugboat portfolios use passive ETFs and mutual funds for investment vehicles. The Speed Boat portfolios use actively managed investments.

8. Advanced optimization and forecasting techniques are used for the Tugboats because they are risk-adverse, and losses must be identified rapidly. Speed Boats use traditional optimization and forecasting techniques because they are long term and return-focused, so there is more flexibility with their trading range.

9. The Tugboat portfolios are based on a multi-period view because they use geometric return expectations which are multi-time

periods. The Speed Boats use arithmetic expected time period return data, which is a single-time period view.

Another good way to illustrate the difference between the Tugboats and the Speed Boats is by looking at the efficient frontier.

The Tugboats use a downside advance risk model on the X axis while the Speed Boats use standard deviation. Both of those axes are completely different, as you would imagine, and particularly because Tugboats are risk-based and Speed Boats are return-based.

Another essential factor to the composition of these portfolios is deciding on the length of time to employ when forecasting returns. The results will be vastly different if a 10-year period is used, or if a 15-year period is used. When analyzing the asset mix for the threat of risk, should a rolling 3-month period be used or a 10-year period? The periodicity of the data set makes a huge difference on the mathematical calculations, and the conclusions of these analyses tremendously influence the composition and weighting of the portfolios.

Then, too, periodicity is only one of the factors that must be calculated. Decisions must be made on which asset classes to use and how many. A determination must be made about which model is best for conducting the most appropriate measurement of potential risk... standard deviation or semi-variance? As well, when you arrive at the covariance matrix, there are several different methods for adjusting your initial results and advanced calculations are necessary to explore which composition offers the better solution. These advanced levels of investigation are far beyond the scope of this book, but it is an environment that financial planners and investment advisors inhabit regularly. Creating a portfolio that serves a specific design to achieve a calculated result for monetary protection and growth is a consuming activity.

When constructing the Tugboat and Speed Boat portfolios, a lot of significant decision-making is occurring behind the scenes. The resolution and commitment to the best selections from the barrage of choices is based on years of exposure to the market's performance, and experience with planning and projecting risk and return outcomes. Most people don't like statistics and aren't interested in mathematics at this level or in this category, but there is a lot to know and if you are interested in spending the time to learn these details, you will be able to effectively construct your own investment portfolio. If this is not something you want to spend time learning, a better choice is asking a professional financial planner to work on this information with you and for you.

The information we just covered provides an introductory insight to the composition of these two portfolio types, the Tugboats and the Speed Boats. If you wish more information on how these investment strategies and portfolios can serve you and your unique circumstances, please contact Synergy Asset Management.

Quarterly Versus Annual Tactical Rebalancing.

The reason why the Tugboat portfolios receive monthly optimization and rebalancing analysis while the Speed Boat portfolios are attended only quarterly is explained here.

Quarterly Tactical Rebalancing: Because the Tugboat portfolios' primary directive is to not lose money, risk management needs to be absolutely precise. If a particular Tugboat portfolio is designed always and only to be an 8% risk portfolio, then this portfolio must always be managed to restrain risk to 8%. On occasion this may require a lot of adjustment. Quarterly analysis is necessary to assure that the portfolio does not allow more than an 8% risk. If analysis is not conducted monthly, the portfolio may start to drift and increase in risk. The clients who have selected this portfolio have accepted the limit of 8% risk, but if regular analysis is not conducted and this portfolio's risk increases to 20%, there will be a lot of trouble and pain. Because the portfolio's risk is limited to 8%, accuracy can only be assured with quarterly analysis.

Notes:

Quarterly monitoring may indicate adjustment is necessary to limit the Tugboat portfolios' risk, but taxes and trading fees must be weighed in the calculations.

However, even if analysis confirms that the portfolio's risk is increasing, it may not be appropriate to adjust the portfolio because of the costs of taxes and trading fees. Generally, the tugboat portfolio is adjusted only two or three times per year, even though it's measured every month to determine if changes are necessary. Should analysis reveal that the portfolio is exceeding its 8% risk limit and rebalancing the portfolio would also add an extra 1% return, it doesn't make sense to execute the adjustments if the costs are going to be 2%. Rebalancing would not result in a better situation, so trades are only conducted as necessary and when the outcome makes financial sense. This is why the Tugboat portfolios are analyzed quarterly; it's to keep a close watch on the amount of risk and the preservation of capital, and make adjustments as soon as reasonably feasible.

Annual Tactical Rebalancing: The situation is different for the Speed Boat portfolios because the expectations are dissimilar. The Speed Boats are primarily focused on return, and their asset class optimization and investment selection have been designed to allow a reasonable trading range in order to capture upside growth. Risk is measured annually to ensure that the investments are within the portfolio's acceptable boundaries, but because of the quality of their original construction, adjustment is not anticipated to be as frequent as the Tugboat portfolios. Annual review is sufficient to identify any unexpected changes to the technical and fundamental data. The Speed Boat portfolios do not require as much precision as the Tugboat portfolios. If the market goes down 4% in one month, it may rise 4% in the next; if the investments had been traded, the portfolio would not have done as well. The Speed Boat portfolios fit a buy-and-hold strategy, accepting whatever risk comes so they can capture as much upside return as possible.

Keep in mind that in the Speed Boat example we used, the portfolio was set at 60/40, and it will always, always, always be 60/40. The composition of the investments that compose the equity portion (60) and the investments that compose the bond portion (40) may adjust as market circumstances change and as the manager believes is appropriate. The portfolio may be rebalanced annually as circumstances warrant, but the proportion of equities to bonds will always be 60/40.

By the way, 60/40 is only one of the five Speed Boat portfolio proportions. The five ratios in the Speed Boat portfolio set, expressed as equities to bonds, are: 80/20; 70/30; 60/40; 50/50; and 40/60. These ratios are maintained no matter what, based on the manager's quarterly analysis and subsequent decision to implement changes if necessary. The Tugboat portfolios are not built with strategic weights like the Speed Boat portfolios; Tugboats range from conservative to aggressive.

This explains why the Tugboat portfolios are analyzed quarterly for potential investment adjustments, and why the Speed Boat portfolios are reviewed only annually.

Figure 39: Strategically Designed Dynamic Models (SDDM) (Speed Boats!)

100% Bond
The 100% bond model is designed for the cautious investor, one with a low risk tolerance and/or a short time horizon. The portfolio allocation will remain 100% in bonds regardless of market conditions. It is targeted toward the investor seeking investment stability and liquidity from their investments. The main objective for this range is to preserve capital while providing income.

Income 40% Equity/60% Bond
The income model is designed for the cautious investor, one with a low risk tolerance and/or a short time horizon. It is targeted toward the investor seeking investment stability and liquidity from their investments. The main objective for this range is to preserve capital while providing income.

Income and Growth 50% Equity/50% Bond
This model provides stable growth offset by a low level of income. An investor in this category will have a higher tolerance for risk and/or a longer time horizon than the previous investors. The equity to bond ratio will remain constant even as market conditions change. The main objective of an individual within this range is to achieve steady portfolio growth while limiting fluctuations to less than those of the overall stock markets.

Balanced 60% Equity/40% Bond
This model is for the investor with a moderate risk tolerance and a longer time horizon than the previous investors. The investor seeks relatively stable growth offset by a low level of income. The equity to bond ratio will remain the same as market conditions change. The main objective of this range is capital appreciation, and the investor should be able to tolerate moderate fluctuations.

Growth 70% Equity/30% Bond
The aggressive investor has both a high tolerance for risk and long investment time horizon. The equity to bond ratio will remain the same even as market conditions change. The main objective of this model is to provide high growth without providing little current income. Portfolios in this range may have substantial fluctuations in value from year to year, making this category unsuitable for those who do not have an extended time horizon.

Aggressive Growth 80% Equity/20% Bond
This model is suitable for the investors with long time horizons and who can tolerate substantial market fluctuation. The main objective is to provide high growth with little to no income.

100% Equity
This is the most aggressive of all of the allocation models. This model is suitable for investors with long time horizons and who can tolerate substantial market fluctuation.

The next section introduces the third set of Core Satellite portfolios; the Sailboat portfolios are exceptional because they move whichever way the wind is blowing.

Building a Sailboat Portfolio

Sailboat portfolios, also known as Focus Tactical Allocation (FTA) models, are formulated to perform in both up and down markets. These portfolios are uniquely different from most of the models found on Wall Street and their goal is to be defensive and protected in bear markets, and fully invested during bull markets. The Sailboat portfolios do not try to forecast the market's outcomes, nor are they based on the opinions of analysts. Instead, the FTA models are built on a custom and proprietary blend of technical and fundamental facts, and are dynamically monitored and updated as the facts change.

The FTA models do not require the markets to be efficient, nor are investors in the market expected to behave rationally. Actually, we use these inconsistencies to our advantage and is one of the reasons we do not require our Sailboat portfolio models to remain fully invested during bear markets. FTA models anticipate performance consistency because their investment selections are based on the concept that the strength and weakness of the market's trend is more likely to continue in the same direction than it is likely to reverse its direction. This is a key technical component to the Sailboat portfolios.

The precise science behind Synergy Asset Management's FTA models is an intellectual property trade secret, however we can reveal that the core of the process focuses on measurements that mirror the continuous tug-of-war between supply and demand imbalances. In addition to supply and demand, a weighted blend of various fundamental factors/facts guides our portfolio construction.

Momentum: Researchers have identified a phenomenon called "momentum", and its history has been documented over a span of many decades. Momentum exists in both bull and bear markets. Momentum often predicts that a trending market will continue in the same direction in which it is trending. Our unique blend of factors/facts provides insight to current market trends, increasing the probability of being on the profitable side of the trade. Although there can never be a guarantee that the current factors/facts will achieve our desired end, in our view longer running trends are driven by longer term imbalances in supply and demand, and the fundamental facts that establish and maintain the trend will result in our investment success by following the trend and its steady momentum.

For example, in the stock market, higher performance has been documented as more inclined to continue than reverse. The same is also true for low performance; both trend performances demonstrate the increased likelihood of continuing rather than reversing.

No matter which direction the market is moving in, our FTA models continually benefit from the current factors/facts supporting the market's direction, and the portfolios are positioned to take advantage of the influences present in the market. It's important to remember that no attempt is made to predict future changes or the next Big

Thing; instead, our decision-making process relies on the careful measurement of actual, factual performance.

Category 4, Sailboats: We offer five "Sailboat" portfolios built on what we call Focus Tactical Allocation (FTA). FTA is a form of what many managers call tactical portfolio management.

As with our other portfolios, there are five risk classifications:

1. Conservative
2. Moderately Conservative
3. Moderate
4. Moderate Aggressive
5. Aggressive

Portfolio Construction: Once the market environment is understood, the Sailboat portfolios are constructed. The FTA models are implemented by selecting high-performing candidates from a deeply researched and continuously updated universe of electronically traded funds (ETFs) and mutual funds. Momentum, relative strength, rate-of-change, nearness-to-52-week-highs, and other measurements of performance characteristics are all combined to produce rankings of portfolio candidates.

Monitoring and Adjusting: Once high-performers are selected, low-performers are discarded, and the whole process is repeated at regular intervals, usually quarterly. This process of continuous self-renewal is intended to capture the profits of long-term winners without being hindered by the unnecessary inclusion of underperformers. Combining trend identification with portfolio construction gives us a simple-yet-complete strategy, providing guidance on when to be defensive and when to be aggressive.

REVIEW:

The Tugboat, and Sailboat portfolio strategies are excellent investment choices for investors who want to control their investments by having a strong core of strategically selected investments that provide the foundation of the portfolio's investment philosophy...

while also employing tactically selected investments that are likely to augment their portfolio's performance. These three portfolio styles, as explained, use varying asset allocation strategies to create their desired risk protection and return rates.

Note:

The Sailboat Portfolios have an equity and bond core designed to identify major market trends; our FTA models are implemented with high performing ETFs and mutual funds. Combining trend identification with portfolio construction gives us a simple-yet-complete strategy.

- FTA Conservative: The Conservative strategy seeks returns similar to the market but with increased downside protection.
- FTA Moderately-Conservative: The Moderately-Conservative risk range is appropriate for the investor who seeks both modest capital appreciation and income from their portfolio.
- FTA Moderate. The Moderate strategy seeks average capital appreciation potential along with above average downside protection.
- FTA Moderately-Aggressive: The Moderately-Aggressive risk range is designed for investors with a relatively high tolerance for risk and a longer time horizon.
- FTA Aggressive: The Aggressive strategy seeks above average price appreciation but tends to be more volatile and may provide less downside protection. The aggressive risk range is appropriate for investors who have both a high tolerance for risk and a long investment time horizon.

Some investors, however, prefer a focus investment strategy without the foundation of an asset allocation strategy. Focus investment portfolios can be composed entirely of equities if the investor is seeking the highest returns possible. Focus investment portfolios can also be composed entirely of bonds if the investor is seeking the best returns available from secure debt instruments. In addition, focus investment portfolios can also be constructed from alternative investment categories such as real estate, commodities, hedge funds, private equity, or currencies. The next section explains how Synergy Asset Management would build your focus equity portfolio.

We are shifting now from asset allocation models to focus models.

Building a Focus Equity Portfolio

The process for creating a focus equity portfolio differs from the process of creating an asset allocation portfolio. In an asset allocation strategy, the investor or financial planner analyzes the 22 asset classes to determine which ones are projected as likely to be the best selection for the portfolio's design. With a focus equity portfolio, the sole intention is to select only those equities that are forecasted to have the highest returns.

The 22 Asset Classes, Maybe

This is a good time to discuss the variety of asset classes available for inclusion in your portfolio. Depending on who you regard as your authority, you may find that there are really 15 asset classes, or 12 asset classes or...there are a number of different opinions on this. The reason we refer to 22 asset classes is because these are some of the more well known asset classes. As with everything, it is always wise to carefully study and reflect on the basis of a list such as this; by analyzing the assumptions and arriving at your own conclusions, you can use a resource to your advantage or, at the least, not be misled by it.

For our purposes at Synergy Asset Management, we work with a list of 13 asset classes. Our experience is that we find 13 asset classes is usually optimal. There are about 9 to 13 asset classes that you should probably be using all the time in your assessments of what to include in your portfolio. The additional nine that Morningstar identifies is more a matter of semantics and preferences than mathematically distinctive.

Here's an example of why a tighter list of asset classes makes more sense from a financial planner's viewpoint. If we analyzed the one-year, five-year, and 20-year Treasury bonds and determined they each had the same correlation coefficient, it wouldn't matter which one we employed in our portfolio because their performance and effect are equally the same. Why, then, should each of these Treasury bonds be listed as a separate asset class? The three of them behave exactly like each other; only if they had a uniquely different correlation profile would we need to consider their potential inclusion when constructing a portfolio with the desired outcome. I call this the Chocolate Chip Cookie Recipe.

THE CHOCOLATE CHIP COOKIE RECIPE:

Let's assume we're going to bake some chocolate chip cookies. We've got this really great chocolate chip cookie recipe and the recipe calls for...chocolate chips! Well, which brand of chocolate chips should we use? There is Brand A, Brand B, and Brand C. We want to make the world's best chocolate chip cookie, and our dilemma is which brand to choose. If the chocolate chips from all three brands are exactly the same and are only different because of their packaging, it doesn't make any difference which brand we use because the result will be the same.

If, however, one chocolate chip was a milk chocolate chip, and the other was an espresso-flavored chip, and the third chip had raspberry flavoring, then we know that the choice of which chocolate chip to use will have an effect on the flavor of the chocolate chip cookie we're baking. Applying this reasoning to our portfolio, when we use asset classes that perform the same mathematically, the optimization of the portfolio breaks down and we wind up with a confusing mess. So, if the asset classes are uniquely different, we may include them, but if they are the same, we choose only one.

Now let's return to the process of constructing a focused equity portfolio.

STEP 1: IDENTIFYING EQUITIES FOR RAPID GROWTH:

The first step is identifying equities that technically and fundamentally indicate their potential for immediate rapid growth and high returns. Risk protection is not an issue because the investor will remain invested in each of the selected equities only as long as the individual equity continues to earn the highest rate of return available among the entire universe of equities worldwide.

Therefore, the focused equity investor must be continually active, always searching for the best equities on the planet. As you're aware, this is an ever-shifting set; some equities are building their potential for explosive growth but are not quite ready yet, some indicate they have started their trend, some are in the middle of their trend, and some are peaking. The active focused investor must keep track of many equity candidates, and is always prepared to purchase the best performing equities when that moment comes...and sell investments whose time has passed.

STEP 2: ANALYZING THE EQUITIES:

Fundamental analysis and technical analysis were reviewed previously in Chapter 11; you may choose to review that section as a reminder. With fundamental analysis, the most appropriate method for a focus investor is the bottom up approach; as a focus investor you are seeking equities that are already performing well and have the potential to accelerate their performance. More information about analyzing equities is offered in Addendum 2. For now, however, the important detail to remember is that you must carefully conduct your analysis, so you know the equities you are studying have a strong capacity for rapid growth. As a focus investor you want to invest in the best of the best because the only equities that interest you are those which will reward your persistence with accelerated returns. This is the entire purpose of your focus investing.

STEP 3: SELECTING THE EQUITIES:

As an investor, your goal is to select only those equities that are earning the highest rate of return, or in which you have a strong legitimate reason to believe soon will. If one of the equities in your portfolio is earning 17 % return and you identify an equity that could bring a 21% return, you should consider whether it is worthwhile to sell the holding you have to purchase the better performing equity. Of course, you must take into account the cost of making this adjustment, calculating how it affects your fees and taxes. However, given your financial resources and your abilities to monitor the number of equities in your portfolio, you should always be seeking to acquire the highest performing equities available. This is what a focus investor does.

STEP 4: PURCHASING THE EQUITIES:

When you are certain you have analyzed every important detail relevant to making a new investment, and you know not only the details of entering this trade but also are committed to a rational plan for selling your holding under a set of specific circumstances you have chosen, you should initiate the purchase.

STEP 5: MONITORING THE PORTFOLIO:

Now that you have added an equity position which you are confident will perform the way you have projected, you must monitor the asset's performance daily and be ready to make a decision to exit your position when the equity reaches either the high or low level of the trading range you have established. Trading must be conducted according to the set of rules you instituted before entering your trade; this helps eliminate fear and greed, which can be immensely detrimental to your financial well-being.

Note: Two Focus Equity Strategies

Synergy Asset Management offers a variety of focused equity portfolios, the Focus Stock Strategy which concentrates on value and growth, and the Dividend Strategy whose purpose is to provide income along with value and growth.

Here are two examples of focused strategies designed for a specific purpose.

The **Focus Growth Strategy** seeks average capital appreciation along with above average safety. The investment time period would ideally be long term; however, this strategy will sell lackluster performers, and take profits when a stock hits our predetermined intrinsic value target without an upward revision to potential future fundamental performance factors.

The **Focus Dividend Strategy** is ideally suited for buy-and-hold investors. It contains well-established companies that often pay a dividend, and may be either close to their intrinsic value, or fully valued. The return expectation may be lower than the market expected return, have a lower capital gain expectation, higher income expectation, and lower volatility than the general market over the course of full market cycles. Additionally, we may execute a call option strategy given the right market conditions to enhance the potential income return.

Building a Focus Bond Portfolio

Creating a focus bond portfolio is somewhat similar to creating a focus equity portfolio. Because you are using a focus strategy, you are seeking the highest returns available. The difference is that you are using debt instruments, not stock/ownership instruments. The appeal of having a focus bond portfolio is not only that you are investing in a security that can provide high returns, but the income from these holdings could be either taxable or nontaxable depending on the type of bonds you buy. You may also find a focus bond portfolio is attractive because it provides a measure of balance when viewed as a single element in your overall investment portfolio collection.

STEP 1: IDENTIFYING BONDS FOR GROWTH:

As with identifying equities, you are now looking for bond investments that offer the highest rate of return. You are not concerned with the risks. Keep in mind that there are different types of bonds and you may choose to invest in only a specific category, such as Treasuries, corporate, junk, etc., in which case your risk and return scenarios will differ. Whichever category you choose, you are interested in bonds that are offering the highest rate of return. You want to use a bottom up approach because this is the most expeditious way to reveal the highest performing bonds.

STEP 2: ANALYZING THE BONDS:

Again, analyze the bonds that have caught your eye according to the technical and fundamental process you are comfortable with using. You will find more information about analyzing bonds in Addendum 2. The point of your analysis is to confirm which of the bonds you initially selected for review offer the highest rates of return, or have the potential to do so very soon. Again, you are seeking the best of the best.

STEP 3: SELECTING THE BONDS:

Once your analysis reveals the best bonds available in the bond categories you prefer, you need to make a selection decision. This should not be difficult because your final group has been closely analyzed, confirming their potential for high return.

STEP 4: PURCHASING THE BONDS:

Make the purchase, and as always, you want to enter this trade only when you have an exit plan.

STEP 5: MONITORING THE PORTFOLIO:

Monitoring the bonds in your portfolio should be a daily event so you can keep close track of how well your investment is performing. You want to be prepared to sell your position when your holding reaches either its high or low range of value, as decided by your exit plan. A focus investor is always ready to improve his or her portfolio by eliminating a position that is no longer productive, replacing it with a new position that continues to advance the portfolio's value. You always want the best of the best in your portfolio, and are ready and willing to make the changes, assuming that the issue of value loss, taxes and fees all make financial sense.

Note: The Focus Bond Strategy.

The Focus Bond Strategy seeks alpha opportunities from a universe of global bonds. This strategy is built on a thorough analysis of a variety of factors including economic analysis, general trends in fixed income and equity markets, yield curve analysis, credit analysis, spread analysis, risk adjusted returns, quality analysis, sector analysis, and total return projections. Event-driven factors, opportunistic and/or intrinsic value principals and a blend of bottom-up research with top down considerations are also considered.

At any given time, the active bond strategy may contain bonds in various sectors, such as government, municipal, corporate, agency mortgaged-backed, non-agency mortgage, cash and equivalents, and others, or it may contain concentrated sector allocations as well as various or concentrated industries. The quality of the portfolio strives to be investment grade.

Building a Focus Alternative Portfolio

As mentioned at the start of this section, an alternative portfolio might include investments in real estate, commodities, hedge funds, private equity, or currencies. A portfolio containing alternative investments could be appropriate for you if you are familiar with these investment types and are comfortable with conducting the fundamental and technical research they require.

STEP 1: IDENTIFYING ALTERNATIVE INVESTMENTS:

The same process will be conducted here as it was for equities and bonds. You will be examining specific alternative investment categories using a bottom-up approach to identify high-performing investment opportunities world-wide.

STEP 2: ANALYZING THE OPPORTUNITIES:

Using your fundamental and technical abilities, you will create a short list of the best opportunities currently available. More information about analyzing alternative investments will be discussed in Addendum 2.

STEP 3: SELECTING THE OPPORTUNITIES:

Once you have established your short list, you must now narrow the field to what you judge is the best of the best.

STEP 4: PURCHASING THE OPPORTUNITIES:

When you have completed your final analysis and have identified those investment opportunities that are most likely to earn the highest returns, it's time to make the purchases. As always, set your exit plan before purchasing.

STEP 5: MONITORING THE PORTFOLIO:

Alternative investments have the potential for being more volatile, and thus capable of larger and faster price movements. For this reason, you must keep a steady eye on your investments and be ready to sell your holdings when the sell signals you established are triggered.

REVIEW:

Whether you are interested in being a focus investor in equities, bonds, or alternative investments, the process is the same. You are seeking securities that are the highest performing, or have the potential for quickly becoming the highest performing, investments in your selected investment category. Once you have purchased what you believe to be the best of the best, monitoring your portfolio is critically important because the market does not stand still. Since you have chosen to be a focus investor, you are always actively reviewing opportunities to either improve your current portfolio or, similarly, are prepared to make changes when your investments either reach their sell signals, or other more lucrative investments appear.

Summary

The purpose of this chapter was to show how an investor can combine two dissimilar investment philosophies so the advantages of each can together contribute to limiting risk while increasing the value of an investment portfolio. These opposing philosophies have both proven their ability to generate profitable returns; even though their approach is different, a blending of their strengths can result in risk-resistant protection with wealth-building returns. A combination of these investment philosophies may have a place in your own portfolio design.

The Tugboat, Speedboat, and Sailboat portfolios represent examples of three different core satellite investment models with a total of 15 different combinations, each uniquely favoring a separate focus of either risk-based, return-based, or both risk and return-based abilities. These blended models were presented to help you consider how you might choose to structure your own portfolio. Optimizing your portfolio was also explained so you could observe how strategic and tactical decisions can work together to rebalance asset weights and more closely guide risk and return outcomes.

Whichever portfolio model you choose to follow, this chapter described the five steps to observe when constructing either a core satellite asset allocation portfolio or a focus portfolio. Because the intended outcomes for each of these portfolio structures are dissimilar, the elements an investor must identify and analyze are different as well. A core satellite asset allocation portfolio is best suited for a top down analysis approach beginning with the study of asset class performance. A focus portfolio's construction starts with a bottom up analysis for the highest performing securities and the selection of the best performers, pending the usual due diligence.

You may be most comfortable with the risk protection that is the standard expected outcome for a core satellite asset allocation investor, or you may prefer the celebrated returns that command the attention of a focus investor. Whichever philosophy is most attractive for your unique circumstances, you now have an investment insight of how to blend the best attributes of both by making your portfolio more effective with a combination of the two philosophies rather than limiting your opportunities to the benefits of only one or the other.

The bottom line is that the core-satellite approach provides access to the best of all worlds. Better-than-average performance, limited volatility and cost control all come together in a flexible package that can be designed specifically to cater to your precise investment needs.

Figure 39: Core Satellite Strategy Example

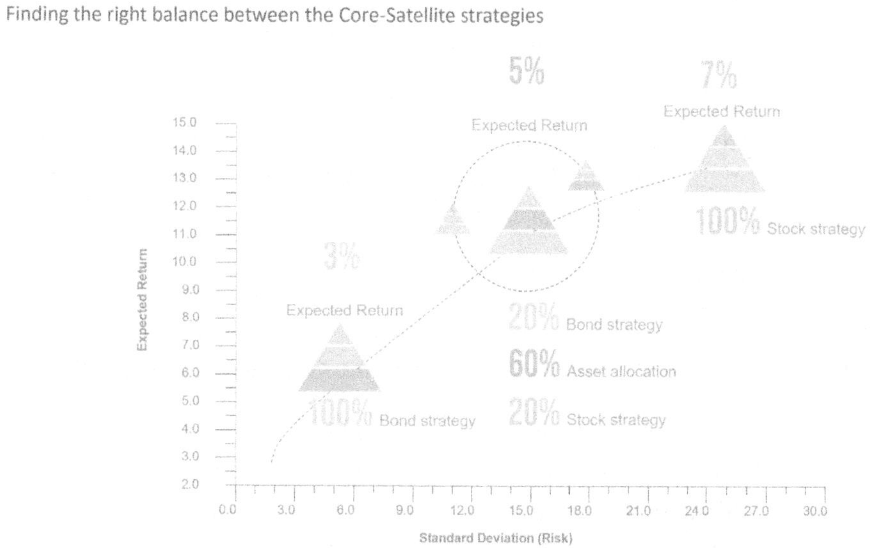

Chapter 15 Review Questions

1. Synergy Asset Management, LLC (SAM) offers 15 asset allocation portfolios. Which of the following is not a portfolio set offered by SAM?

   A. Tugboats.
   B. Motorboats.
   C. Speedboats.
   D. Sailboats.

2. Of the 22 asset classes, how many are typically required to build a good portfolio?

   A. 8.
   B. 10.
   C. 12.
   D. 14.

3. Calendar year adjusting is insufficient because the markets are in constant flux and an investor's portfolio may experience too much change. True or false?

   A. True.
   B. False.

4. What is the message of the Chocolate Chip Recipe concept?

   A. All assets taste like chocolate chips.
   B. Chocolate chip cookies are yummy.
   C. Oatmeal cookies are good, too.
   D. Including assets in a portfolio that duplicate each other does not add value and wastes an opportunity to either improve diversification, or save additional research time.

Chapter 15 Review Answers

1. Synergy Asset Management, LLC (SAM) offers 15 asset allocation portfolios. Which of the following is not a portfolio set offered by SAM?

   A. Tugboats.
   B. Motorboats.
   C. Speedboats.
   D. Sailboats.

   Answer: B. Motorboats. The Tugboat portfolios are risk-based portfolios, seeking to avoid risk. The portfolios are return-based portfolios, designed to capture upside return. The Sailboat portfolios are both risk and return-based portfolios, adjusting to the changing market, always avoiding risk and always seeking higher returns.

2. Of the 22 asset classes, how many are typically required to build a good portfolio?

   A. 8.
   B. 10.
   C. 12.
   D. 14.

   Answer: A. 8. Less than a third of all asset classes are necessary for building an effective asset allocation portfolio. As asset classes go through their cycles, the portfolio will undergo asset class rotation.

3. Adjusting a tugboat portfolio annually is insufficient because the markets are in constant flux and an investor's portfolio may experience too much change. True or false?

   A. True.
   B. False.

Answer: A. True. For Tugboat portfolios, an annual review and adjustment is much too untimely. Tugboat portfolios require a quarterly review while Speed Boat portfolios receive an annual review. Without a periodic review, a portfolio can become quickly unbalanced, increasing unnecessary risk.

4. What is the message of the Chocolate Chip Recipe concept?

   A. All assets taste like chocolate chips.
   B. Chocolate chip cookies are yummy.
   C. Oatmeal cookies are good, too.
   D. Including assets in a portfolio that duplicate each other does not add value and wastes an opportunity to either improve diversification, or save additional research time.

   Answer: D. Including assets that duplicate each other does not add value and wastes an opportunity to either improve diversification, or save additional research time. While it's true that chocolate chips, chocolate chip cookies and oatmeal cookies are all yummy, there is no point in having duplicate assets in your portfolio.

Closing Thoughts

The premise of this book is that the diversification...or not... of one's investment assets is a critically important debate every investor must have with themselves, and possibly with knowledgeable colleagues and, if they are fortunate enough, with their financial planner. The pro and con argument about whether or not to diversify is not as shallow as it seems because there are tremendous financial consequences at stake, which are dependent on the result of this important discourse.

The popular opinion in the markets is that diversification is the only sensible strategy. Though this sentiment may be largely the result of the losses many rueful investors suffered in the market downturn of 2008, support for the theory of diversification is currently widespread and vocal.

Indeed, this investment strategy is absolutely correct for many investors. Most investors are shy of capital loss, as they should be, and diversification of one's assets has been a reliable practice since the days of Aesop when the fictitious eggs were carried to market in a single basket.

And yet there are dangers in diversification. Investors must be educated on the subtleties of diversification so they can avoid less obvious causes for financial loss. Money is money, and it can be easily lost but sorely regained. At the start of this book the concept of negative compounding was presented; it is a mathematical fact that lost investment money requires a larger percentage of return with possible amplified risk and/or a longer period of time just to become even again with the original investment value. There are those among us who believe that the loss of investment time is even more painful than the loss of investment money, and to make matters worse, opportunities for other or additional investments are also sacrificed when resources are reduced. The pain of negative compounding is threefold.

While the popular belief may be that diversification and asset allocation are the wisest choices, there is a contrary opinion, based on factual evidence, that there is tremendous financial value in not following the tenets of the diversification model, focusing exclusively instead on investments that earn high returns, albeit not disregarding their inherent risks. A focus investor who has the time to carefully observe the global markets, and possesses the expertise to analyze investment candidates with the many available fundamental and technical tools can accelerate the return rate of his or her portfolio.

Of course, this takes a dedication to purpose and an investor with both time and knowledge. Should the investor lack either yet still remains excited by the prospects of greatly increased investment returns paired with contained risk, a professional financial planner with expertise in focus investing might be an alternative means for capitalizing on this strategy, and should be consulted for services. The cost for such services is likely to be inconsequential when compared with the potentially exorbitant benefits.

As explained earlier in the book, we do not live in a black and white world, and thankfully, when investing, we are not restricted to only choosing this or that. The dissimilar investment approaches of asset allocation investing, and focus investing are contrary to the other, but this doesn't mean only one must be exclusively employed in your portfolio. It is possible to combine the best elements of both and arrive at a portfolio design which respects the dangers of risk while simultaneously embracing the potential for healthy returns.

The Core Satellite portfolio models are a calculated blend of both asset allocation and focus investing, allowing the selective investor to enjoy the best aspects of both strategies, restricting risk to a precise measurement while augmenting the portfolio's ability to acquire higher returns. As illustrated, there is a comprehensive variety of asset allocation and focus investing portfolio blends in the Tugboat, and Sailboat models.

In order to fully understand the three choices inviting a decision by every investor, specifically whether to become an asset allocation/ diversification investor, or a focus investor, or an adherent of blending the strengths of both theories, this book began by introducing key concepts to establish or confirm a foundation of understanding. The progression started with a discussion of several basics every investor must know. Appreciating the tug-of-war between fear and greed is an emotional experience an investor can only truly grasp by being personally exposed to the avalanche of thoughts and feelings, whether positive or detrimental, when holding a trading position. Having once felt this rush of adrenaline, whether for flight or delight, an experienced investor will enthusiastically value having taken the time to create a predetermined, logical plan of action for exiting a trade.

This investor will also know better than chasing returns and losing the commodity of time; will sagely accept the importance of studying the most important technical analysis tools and becoming an ever-developing master of them; will take the time to develop and then refine their investment policy statement; will learn how to calculate the efficient frontier; and will regularly and at specific intervals monitor the investments in their portfolio to assure themselves there is sufficient evidence to enjoy a good night's sleep and the comforting thought of a potentially secure future.

By reading this book, you were able to determine whether you are better suited as a trader or an investor, and which niche of one or the other should be your intimate focus. Unless you already know your temperament and stomach for risk, you may want to explore the choices until the right role for you is clear. Achieving the highest return is not the best indicator of investment success; cash in your account is the only way to truly measure your progress. Setting meaningful goals and achieving them is the predecessor to a worthy end; establishing goals that represent an affordable future you have monetarily calculated, and working your way through the years to achieving them removes the fright and doubt of not knowing whether you are on track or not. This knowledge may allow you to enjoy your life as your wealth accumulates according to plan...rather than always being unsettled about the uncertainty of your unknown future. By calculating your RRR, your required rate of return, you can plan your financial future logically and mathematically, with much of the stress diffused.

Thereafter we discussed how an investor might choose to design their investment portfolio, as the values that are important to you and your family can be observed and reflected in the choices you make when selecting investments. If you favor a "green" environment, or wish to support education, or desire advances in medical research, or want to invest your money in space exploration, there are numerous investment opportunities you can consider. Once you establish your preferred niche, if any, this predilection now becomes part of your investment policy statement. Since your first priority is to build an affordable economic future for yourself and your family, it may be that focusing on a niche is a luxury you can't afford at this time, as much as you may wish to; this is certainly an idea you can revisit when circumstances change.

Another critically important concept that should be understood by every investor is how to select an appropriate benchmark to measure the portfolio's progress. As explained, many investors are quite casual in their choice, and while this may work well for many asset allocation investors who are seeking average returns, measurement must be much more precise for investors, asset allocation or focus, who wish to earn the best return for the risk they accept. As long as your money is at risk, which is true for every investment, a greater return for the same risk is preferred. Indeed, an investor is wise to have several different ways to measure portfolio performance because every measurement has its strengths and weaknesses, and it is only by analyzing the portfolio's growth through several different lenses that a true assessment of comparative performance can be more accurately achieved.

Considerable space was dedicated to elucidating the difference between the heads and tails of focus investing and asset allocation, Alpha and Beta, active and passive management, hunter and gatherer. Some investors have the time, the training, the experience, and the willingness to dedicate themselves to the intention of acquiring the highest returns as rapidly as the changing markets will allow. Some investors will seek the services of a professional financial planner to do this work for them, and they are willing to pay the service fees for the rewards they anticipate. Other investors are more comfortable with the slow and steady accumulation of wealth the markets offer by mirroring the market indices, and are willing to accept the munificence of the markets without the tireless intensity of the focus investor's continual activity of analysis. The antidote for one is the poison of the other...or is it? There is a third choice, as you know. The question truly does not need to be "diversification...or not" because you have seen it is possible to marry the best elements of both by combining strategic and tactical calculations that carefully bind risk and return to a portfolio formula designed to capture as much downside protection and upside expansion as an investor might choose.

Having read this book, you now possess a good but basic introduction to Modern Portfolio Theory and the benefits of Harry Markowitz's Nobel prize-winning work, which includes making an asset allocation model that indicates which investments to combine so the several different expected returns can offset the corresponding risks they represent. Working with this model, it's easy to understand the importance of rebalancing the portfolio from time to time so the original intention of your portfolio, which is essentially to modify risk while allowing modest gains, can be achieved over time.

Similarly, the theory of focus investing received equal attention, and in the discussions which followed, the process of conducting a top down analysis versus a bottom up analysis were described with sufficient detail to guide an investor when conducting his or her own investment selection. Having read about the top down and bottom up approaches, an investor can more clearly determine their own preferred bias toward being either an asset allocation investor or a focus investor. This is very helpful when defining the level of risk they are willing to accept and the return they are willing to enjoy, should they choose to participate in the third alternative which is the blending of both.

We conclude where we began, but now you are informed enough to answer these questions, questions you must answer to arrive at a decision you are required to make.

- Are you inclined to be a passive or active investor?
- Are you willing to be an investor who values average risk for average return?

- Are you eager to commit yourself to work for higher than average returns?
- Are you open to considering the blend of controlled risk combined with the potential for accelerated return?
- Are you proficient enough to calculate the required rate of return (RRR) that mathematically defines your financial goals?
- Are you truly capable of analyzing investment securities and creating a portfolio that sits on the efficient frontier of the risk you are comfortable taking for the return you are desirous of having?

Whether you do this financial planning work yourself, or get assistance, or turn everything over to a professional financial expert, you can now see that designing and managing a portfolio requires knowledge, time, and personal dedication to properly supervise your investments on a regular or day-to-day basis. If you realize you don't have the time or lack the necessary depth of knowledge or experience, you can always engage a financial professional to the degree that is appropriate. The professional's role can either be limited to certain tasks or could be complete service.

Portfolio duties can be organized into four categories:

1. Managing your portfolio in whole or in part.
2. Observing and evaluating your portfolio's performance.
3. Reporting information about your investments' performance, their continuing alignment with your investment policy, the degree of progress toward attaining your portfolio's goals, and the impact of taxes.
4. Advising on making changes that should be made to your investments or your investment plan.

Money is too dear to invest haphazardly; if you are willing to invest but know you don't yet know enough, you should make an appointment with a fiduciary advisor who can help with your portfolio's design, and the selection decisions that are the most appropriate for your comfort level, your unique set of circumstances, and the financial future you envision.

You now have in your hands the information you need to decide the right course for you. There is always more to learn and more to do, but now that you have read this material, you have all you need to decide if you want diversification...or not. You also now have the extraordinary benefit of a third choice, a middle path, a bearing that blends the best of both, that may provide a more treasured ride upon the market's tides as you set your compass for the joys that financial freedom brings.

Joe M. Maas

March 2024

Addendum 1
Investment Instruments

This addendum provides an informative overview of the many different types of investments available for investors. The first section focuses on the investments that are regarded as traditional while the second section describes alternative investments that may appeal to investors who want to diversify their holdings, or who have professional insight with these categories.

Traditional Investments

There are essentially three main categories for traditional investments: stocks, bonds, and cash. All of the following 10 types of traditional investments belong to one of these three main categories, or a mix of them.

1. Stocks

There are many different types of stocks; they vary by classification, by the type of ownership, by their global location, by their response to business cycles, and by their public or private availability. While the variety of many types of stocks may be formidable, the availability of such a great number of choices allows investors to more precisely build the type of portfolio they wish.

COMMON STOCKS:

These are the types of stocks that are generally owned by the public, and the shares represent pro rata ownership of the company. Most common stocks include voting rights; some common stocks offer the payment of dividends while others do not.

PREFERRED STOCKS:

This type of stock pays a fixed rate of return through dividends, making preferred stocks more similar to bonds in their nature than common stocks. No matter how well the stock does, the fixed rate of return does not increase. The benefits of owning preferred stock is that, even though preferred stockholders do not have voting rights, their claims to the company's assets are paid before common stock shareholders are paid. Owners of preferred stock also receive their dividends before shareholders of common stock.

UNLISTED SECURITIES:

As its name implies, unlisted securities are not listed on organized stock exchanges such as the NYSE. These stocks are available instead by over-the-counter (OTC) trading. Unlisted securities are generally regarded as high-risk investments because they are harder to research and trade.

PENNY STOCKS:

This type of stock is also regarded as high-risk. Penny stocks sell for less than five dollars per share, as defined by the Securities and Exchange Commission. These stocks are often issued by young companies with limited performance history, or companies that are experiencing difficulty with some aspect of their business, such as unstable earnings or legal issues; they may be difficult to sell when the shareholder wishes to release them.

SIZE OF STOCKS:

Stocks are often categorized by the size of the company, which is typically measured by the value of all the outstanding shares of its common stock. Many analysts evaluate a company by its size, and these values are highly variable. Be sure to notice the assumptions that determine how a company is being categorized.

A. **Large cap stocks.** Stocks from large cap companies are considered liquid investments because they are traded frequently and in large volume on the stock exchanges. The bid-ask spread is usually very tight because so many traders are buying and selling the stocks. Large cap companies are capitalized at $10 billion or more. Stocks from large cap companies often pay dividends, and their prices are the least volatile of the equities on the market. Within this group of large cap companies are 30 companies in the Dow Jones Industrial Average (DJIA); these are called blue-chip stocks because of their consistent performance.

B. **Midcap stocks.** The market capitalization for midcap stocks is between $2 billion and $10 billion. These stocks are also quite liquid and also have tight bid-ask spreads.

C. **Small cap stocks.** Stocks in this category are capitalized between $200 million and $2 billion. Small cap companies are typically young companies that may have faster growth rates than either mid or large cap companies. Because of their nature, they are regarded as higher-risk investments when compared to larger capitalized companies, and as a group they are less liquid as well. Individual investors own a higher percentage of small cap stocks than institutional investors because of these reasons.

D. **Microcap stocks.** Companies with capitalization between $20 million and $200 million are seldom purchased by institutional investors because their shares are even less liquid, which increases trading costs. Microcap stocks are traded on smaller stock exchanges or over-the-counter (OTC). The appeal of microcap companies is that they may specialize in unusual products or services, and with some success they may grow into small cap companies with higher value.

STOCKS KNOWN BY THEIR STYLE:

Stocks can also be categorized by their type of performance, and some investors prefer a certain style over others. Again, it is wise to examine the underlying assumptions of why a company is categorized as having a particular style, as there is a degree of bias by the analysts who define the stock's category.

Aggressive growth stocks. Companies that issue stocks in this category are companies that are rapidly growing, and the appeal of strong and accelerated returns is attractive to investors who are willing to take the risk. These stocks usually do not offer dividends because they are reinvesting their profits into the company.

Growth stocks. Companies with above-average growth, but with growth that is not as alluring as aggressive growth companies, are categorized as growth stocks. Many growth stocks offer modest dividends, though it is also likely that profits may instead be reinvested in the company.

Value stocks. The appeal of value stocks is that they are considered to have more value than their stock price reflects, and therefore represent a bargain. Investors in value stocks believe that eventually the price of the stock will increase to match the underlying value. The lower valuations are generally ascribed to an inefficient market, declining sales, and limited expectations for business performance. The purchase of value stocks has been championed by Warren Buffett.

Income stocks. Companies that offer dividend yields are income stocks. Income stocks' dividend payments are similar to the fixed interest rates paid by bonds, but some investors prefer the additional advantage of the potential for an income stock to appreciate, thus increasing dividend payments.

CYCLICAL STOCKS:

There are some investors who prefer to purchase stocks from companies that are at different phases of the business cycle, hoping to acquire increased returns as a company moves from its slow cycle to its growth cycle. Examples of this kind of cyclical behavior are companies that offer products or services that are seasonal, or when the economy is more able to sustain the purchases of new technology or luxury items.

There is also investor interest in companies that are not cyclical and whose earnings are predictable, such as with companies that provide essential services like medical products, or food products; these companies' products and services are continually needed, even when the economy slows down.

OTHER TYPES OF STOCK:

There are a number of other types of stock you may be interested in knowing about; here's a description of each.

Origin of issue. Stocks that are issued by a corporation whose headquarters is outside the United States are considered international stocks. These stocks are subject to currency exchange rate fluctuations, as well as the politics and economies of the countries in which they are situated. The accounting practices and regulations under which these companies operate may also be significantly different than those of the United States and thus may increase an investor's risks...and returns.

American Depositary Receipts (ADRs) Another way to invest internationally is by purchasing ADRs, which are negotiable certificates representing the shares of an overseas company's stock. ADRs are issued by a United States bank, and are denominated in U.S. dollars; they are traded on the U.S. stock exchanges and offer an alternative to investing directly in foreign securities.

Subscription rights Investors who are shareholders of a corporation could elect to secure the right but not the obligation to purchase new shares of common stock, usually at a discount, before they are offered to the public.

Warrants This is another device for acquiring the right but not the obligation to purchase securities from a company at a specified price before an expiration date.

New issue stocks. Some investors are drawn to investing with companies that are making their initial public offering (IPO). These are called new issue stocks because they are being offered by a company that has been newly accepted by a trading exchange. This type of stock helps the company raise capital to finance growth or meet expenses. It is sometimes difficult to acquire these stocks because there is a limited quantity and demand can be high; additionally, brokerage firms might limit the availability to only their preferred clients.

2. Bonds

Bonds are debt instruments issued by a company or government agency wishing to raise money for a particular purpose. A company may sell bonds to expand its business; a government agency may issue bonds to build a bridge or renovate schools. Bonds offer a fixed return for a set period of time; there is a broad range of both returns and investment periods. Here is a short overview of the possibilities.

GOVERNMENT BONDS:

There are three distinct types, differentiated by the length of time the debt is offered.

A. **Bills.** These securities mature in less than one year.

B. **Notes.** These debt securities mature between 1 to 10 years; the length of time is fixed by the issuing agency.

C. **Bonds.** Bonds are debt securities that mature after a 10-year period.

When the United States government issues debt instruments, they are known as Treasuries, so there are Treasury bills, Treasury notes, and Treasury bonds. Other national governments can issue bonds, but the investor should be careful because international bonds have their own particular degree of risk.

Municipal bonds. Also known as "munis", municipal bonds are issued by states, cities, and counties. A benefit of purchasing the debt is that they are free from federal tax, and these municipalities are often solvent entities. Yields may be lower because of the benefit of tax-free returns, but they may be an important part for your portfolio if they serve a purpose in your investment design.

CORPORATE BONDS:

Companies can offer bonds as well as stocks; companies may sell their debt to make purchases, expand a workforce, purchase auxiliary companies, etc. Companies can also issue debt over varying periods of time. A short-term bond matures in less than five years; an intermediate bond matures between 5 to 12 years; a long-term bond matures after 12 years. Corporate bonds are known to have higher yields because the risk with a company is greater than the risk with a government agency. When purchasing a corporate bond, diligence is needed to determine the company's credit quality; the higher the quality of the company's credit, the lower the interest rate that is offered.

Convertible bonds and callable bonds. Variations of corporate bonds include convertible bonds which allow an investor to convert the bond into stock, and callable bonds which permit the company to redeem their bonds before the bonds mature.

Zero coupon bonds. With this type of bond, an investor loans a portion of the bond's eventual value, receiving the principal and the interest at the end of the term. For example, a 5-year zero coupon bond with a $1,000 par value is trading at $700; the investor pays $700 for a bond that will be worth $1,000 in five years.

3. Cash

Cash investments refer to short term obligations that provide interest; cash investments typically provide low levels of risk, and low returns. There are several types of cash investments including bank accounts, money market funds, and certificates of deposit (CDs). Investors often turn to the cash market when markets are in a downturn or as a haven from financial turmoil.

A. **Money Market Funds.** Most money market securities have a six-month maturity term, or less. Though commonly regarded as a safe investment, they are not FDIC insured. Money market funds offer a reasonable interest rate and generally serve as a safe haven for temporary cash storage. Because money market securities are traded in amounts of $100,000 or higher, most investors must participate through money market funds rather than money market securities.

B. **Certificates of Deposit (CDs).** Traditional CDs offer a fixed interest rate for a predetermined period of time. The range of maturity could be one month, and up to five, 10, or even more years; interest rates typically increase as the term of investment increases. The interest is paid when the maturity is reached; an early withdrawal results in a reduced interest return and may include penalties. CDs are typically issued by banks; they are FDIC insured up to $100,000. When purchasing a CD, the interest rate is indicated by the annual percentage rate (APR), and the yield is conveyed by the annual percentage yield (APY). The APY is always larger because it is the calculation of the interest rate on the principal as well as the compounding of the interest over the term of the CD. Because CDs are fixed interest investments, if interest rates rise after the purchase of a CD, the investor cannot receive the higher rates without exiting the CD and accepting the fee for early withdrawal. Once maturity has been reached and the CD is cashed out or rolled over, the investor can then reinvest at a higher interest rate, if continued investment is desired.

C. **U.S. Treasury Bills.** T-Bills are also a low risk and low return investment vehicle; U.S. T-bills are guaranteed by the federal government and are offered at three-month, six-month, and 12-month terms. T-bills are sold at discount from their face value and then redeemed at maturity for their full value. T-bills are highly liquid and are offered in amounts beginning at $10,000. Investors can also purchase T-bill investments through T-bill mutual funds.

D. **Commercial Paper.** There is a variety of commercial paper available from companies with high credit ratings, which implies their low risk. In essence, these are promissory notes, and they are issued in a wide range of denominations. They offer a modest interest rate.

4. Mutual Funds

A mutual fund is a company that pools the funds of its investors for the purchase of securities from a collection of companies; mutual funds often focus on a particular category of the market, explained below. Investors own shares in the mutual fund by paying the current net asset value (NAV) for the number of shares they wish to purchase. The NAV is the value of one share of the fund, in addition to a sales charge, if applicable, known as the sales load. Mutual funds are not guaranteed or insured; before you invest in a mutual fund, you should carefully read the prospectus to find out the fund's goals, risks, fees, and expenses.

The value of the shares fluctuates as market conditions change, and shares may be worth less than their original cost when sold; they may also increase. Risk is modified to some degree because a mutual fund is the collection of many different securities; if any particular company or groups of companies underperform, the fund's value may still increase because of the performance of the other securities in the fund. Your costs may be lower than what you would normally pay if you were purchasing the securities on your own because the fund acquires and eliminates large amounts of securities at a time, saving costs. If the fund is actively managed, you may also benefit through the services of its professional investment manager, who is continually considering selection and timing decisions. Be aware, however, that some funds have very high expenses that can significantly impact your portfolio's net return; annual expenses may further reduce your net, and it's also possible that a fund manager can make investment mistakes that decrease the fund's profitability. It's quite important to pay attention to the fees and expenses because they can have a substantial effect. Normally there are sales loads, transaction fees, 12b-1 fees, and management fees. The costs of the fund are required to be in the fund's prospectus; you can use this information to compare with other mutual funds you are interested in knowing more about.

There are many different kinds of mutual funds. Usually a mutual fund will specialize because of its investment objectives, and thus will purchase different types of securities. Knowing what the fund's objective is will also help you decide if the fund is aligned with your own financial objectives. Here is a brief overview of the different kinds of available mutual funds:

A. **Stock funds.** Stock mutual funds might focus on the size of companies such as large cap, mid-cap, and small cap companies, or they may specialize in a geographic region, by industry sector, and in the type of stock such as preferred versus convertible.

B. **Bond funds.** There are also a wide variety of bond mutual funds that may specialize in the level of risk, the level of return, the length of term, and the many different types of bonds. As interest rates rise, bond prices usually diminish, but as interest rates decline, the bond's value may increase.

C. **Money market funds.** Again, there are many different types of money market investments, and some funds specialize in types of money market funds, lengths of term, and level of risk. Money market funds are generally safe, but there are fluctuations in their NAV.

D. **Natural resources funds.** These are funds that invest in companies engaged with activities in coal, natural gas, oil, timber, chemicals, and metals. These companies may be domestic or international.

E. **Precious metals funds.** Mutual funds specializing in precious metals are investing in the production of metal resources such as platinum, gold, and silver. These companies may also be domestic or international.

F. **Commodities funds.** Commodities are typically agricultural products like corn, wheat, soybeans, etc.; some funds also invest in natural resources including metals like copper; a few funds may also be focused on currency investments.

G. **Real estate funds.** Real estate funds normally invest in REITs, real estate investment trusts; these funds may also invest in related industries such as construction and real estate management companies.

H. **Open-end and closed-end funds.** Most mutual funds are open-end funds, which mean the fund will buy back your shares when you wish to close your position. Some funds are only closed-end funds, which mean that the number of shares is set at the time of the initial public offering and does not vary. When you want to eliminate your position, you can only sell your shares to another investor, as the fund company will not buy them.

I. **Actively and passively managed funds.** Portfolios can be either actively or passively managed. Active management is known as alpha; its philosophy is focus investing which seeks a higher than average return. Passive management is known as beta, seeks average returns and is based on the philosophy of diversification and asset allocation.

J. **Diversified and non-diversified funds.** There are also levels of diversification among mutual funds. To be considered a diversified fund, a mutual fund can have no more than 25% of its assets in a single security, and of the rest of its assets, no single asset can have more than 5% of the fund's value. A non-diversified mutual fund could have up to 50% of all its assets invested in a single security; also, non-diversified funds often have less than 40 securities in their portfolio.

K. **Growth and value funds.** Two common categories for mutual funds are growth funds and value funds; growth funds seek companies that are quickly growing, and value funds seek companies that appear to be strong companies that are momentarily undervalued, and thus a potential bargain.

L. **Tax-free, tax-deferred and tax efficient funds.** Some mutual funds specialize in securities that fit one of these three categories; they are issued by the federal, state or local governments. In some cases, the fund may minimize a shareholder's tax liability by eliminating federal tax altogether through tax-free investments, or may choose to minimize trading to limit the potential for capital gains taxes. There are many varieties from which to choose, and careful selection is necessary for the most efficient alignment with your portfolio.

5. ETFs

ETFs are exchange-traded funds traded on the stock exchanges, like stocks. An exchange-traded fund can hold a variety of assets such as stocks, bonds, and commodities.

One of the primary benefits of ETFs is their diversification potential. Investors gain exposure to a wide array of assets within a single investment vehicle, mitigating individual stock risk. In addition, ETFs often have lower expense ratios compared to mutual funds, contributing to cost-efficient portfolio management. Another benefit is that ETFs offer intraday tradability, giving investors greater flexibility with making swift adjustments to changing market conditions.

6. Real Estate

Real estate investments are a popular alternative, or an additional element, to an investment portfolio. Investing in commercial or residential real estate offer the following potential benefits:

- Portfolio diversification
- Protection against inflation
- Increased capital gains
- Monthly income
- Potential tax credits
- The pleasure of ownership

Real estate provides diversification for a traditional investment portfolio, and Synergy Asset Management is licensed for brokering real estate to ensure that your real estate assets work effectively with your other investments, helping you attain your financial goals as efficiently as possible.

7. Options

When you trade options, you are purchasing the right to buy or sell an underlying asset for a specific amount by a specific date. You do not have to purchase the underlying asset, but you have the option to do so if you wish. This is what is meant by having the right but not the obligation.

As an example, if you wanted to buy a farm but knew you didn't have the cash to purchase it for three months, you could speak to the owner and offer an option to buy the farm for $2,000 at some point during the next three months. As the deadline comes closer, you realize that another farm down the road is a better choice for you. You will lose the $2,000 you paid for the option to purchase, but you used the window of time to your advantage. If you had not found a better farm, your option to buy was helpful because it secured the first farm when you weren't ready to purchase it. This example explains why options are called derivatives; the value of the option is derived from the underlying asset. In this case, the underlying asset was the first farm.

8. Futures

Buying and selling futures contracts takes place at a futures exchange where commodities and financial instruments are sold at a fixed price based on the potential for the underlying asset to be valued at a specific dollar amount by a specific date in the future. Commodity futures can be agricultural, such as corn and soybeans; they can be natural resources such as oil and gold; they can also be international currencies such as the U.S. dollar or the Swiss franc. If the underlying asset performs close to or exceeds the specific contract level by the specific date, the futures trader earns a profit for holding the contract; otherwise the contract has no value and the futures trader has lost a portion or all of his or her original investment.

9. Money Markets

Discussed above, money markets are cash instruments with maturity terms of six months or less. As noted, money market securities are traded in units of $100,000 or higher, and money market mutual funds are a more reasonable way for most people to invest in them.

10. Certificate of Deposit (CD)

Also detailed at length above, certificates of deposit are issued by banks as a safe cash investment that is insured by the FDIC up to $100,000 per account.

Alternative Investments

Aside from the traditional primary asset classes of stocks, bonds, cash, and the other investment products mentioned above, there are three alternative investments that could bring an additional level of profitability and risk control to your portfolio. The markets often use the term "alternative" with broad flexibility; alternative investments could include natural resources, a specific style of investing, or even refer to geographic regions. Because of their unique nature, if you possess specialty knowledge about a specific asset class, you should consider working with a financial planner who can provide the expert advice you'll need when selecting alternative assets for your portfolio. In the next segment, we're going to take a detailed look at real estate, private equity, and hedge funds, which could be good choices for your portfolio.

1. Real Estate

There are a number of reasons why including real estate could be an advantage to your portfolio. Depending on your circumstances, any of the following may be a prime consideration.

Diversification. As an asset class, real estate performs differently than stocks, bonds, and cash, and this is one of real estate's attractive features. The value of real estate depends on its location, and whether it is residential, commercial, raw land, or developed property. This distinction makes real estate a potentially worthy addition to your portfolio because it is not always in synch with the financial markets, providing the opportunity for value appreciation during economic turbulence.

Inflation. With the inflation rate between 2% and 3% per year, real estate can be an excellent means for keeping pace with the constant erosion of the dollar's value. Often, real estate prices rise along with the price of commodities. It's true that real estate values can fall, too... and no investment is ever risk-free. Even so, real estate has a strong history of value appreciation.

Capital gains. When property increases in value, either through site development or neighborhood improvements, real estate can become a lucrative investment. Purchasing property or shares of property in areas that may appreciate in value could substantially benefit your portfolio.

Income. Should you decide to become a landlord, you would receive revenue from rental or lease payments to offset operating expenses and debt.

Tax credits. In some instances you may be eligible for tax credits. And, in the larger picture, purchasing real estate may provide a tax advantage through the interrelationship of your other financial circumstances. A Synergy Asset Management representative can help you review your options, consider the best choices with you, and help ensure that your investment allocations fit your overall financial strategy, based on the goals you've selected. Portfolio allocation is customized to your unique circumstances, with a diversification that builds growth steadily while preserving your wealth against loss.

Ownership. Owning a primary residence or vacation home can have the dual advantage of enjoying your ownership and benefiting financially.

REASONS FOR NOT INVESTING IN REAL ESTATE:

Depending on your individual circumstances, there are several features of real estate investing that suggest caution.

Lack of liquidity. It's not easy to sell physical property quickly if you need the cash; buyers may not be available, or require time to finance the purchase. You may be able to acquire a loan with the property as collateral, but would incur interest on the debt. If, however, you own shares in an REIT or a real estate-focused mutual fund, your shares can be liquidated fairly quickly.

Initial costs. If you are purchasing real estate directly, there are a number of costs that require cash outlay, such as a down payment, legal fees, insurance, etc. Depending on the size, condition and your intentions for the property, expenses can be reasonable or exorbitant.

Depreciation. Real estate has always seemed to grow in value, yet there have been several real estate market downturns. Real estate is a cyclical market, though investments typically experience low price volatility.

Property issues. When directly purchasing real estate, there are a number of details that warrant review. Some of the issues to consider are the potential for natural disasters like flooding or earthquakes, hazardous materials, eminent domain, rent control laws, pests, etc.

With careful forethought and research, many of these potential detriments to investing in real estate can be circumvented. At Synergy Asset Management, we have real estate specialists who can guide you with personalized service, so your investments have the greatest likelihood of growth with a reasonable amount of risk. In our experience, one of the greatest benefits of working with a financial representative is the reassurance of knowing you have a knowledgeable professional on your side.

YOUR REAL ESTATE INVESTMENT POLICY STATEMENT:

Just as important as having an Investment Policy Statement (IPS) for your financial markets' portfolio is creating your Real Estate Investment Policy Statement (RIPS) to establish a clear understanding of your investment intentions.

Your Real Estate Investment Policy Statement will:

- Establish reasonable investment and financial goals
- Create the framework for a well-diversified real estate portfolio that projects acceptable returns
- Identify the required rate of return (RRR) needed to achieve your goals
- Set the criteria for making investments, such as commercial properties within a specific price range, or undeveloped real estate in prime locations
- Determine the frequency for portfolio review, and detail the criteria for evaluating your progress toward your goals
- Calculate your tolerance for risk, preventing overexposure and potential loss

Synergy Asset Management uses sophisticated and robust analysis to evaluate all types of commercial and residential real estate. We analyze your goals and the current economic and real estate outlook, and recommend the property type best suited for your investment.

SELECTING A COMMERCIAL REAL ESTATE FIRM:

Investing in commercial real estate can be complex. Finding the right team of experts to help you acquire or divest your commercial real estate investments is critical. Synergy Asset Management offers the experienced services you need to secure a quality real estate investment, or sell a property that needs to be released. Our advisors are credentialed and trained in commercial real estate investment to capably guide your decisions. We have expertise in all facets of commercial real estate such as accounting, financial analysis, tax analysis, and valuation, so we can supply the depth and perspective you need.

Real estate contributes valuable diversification to a traditional investment portfolio, and our tailored service will enhance and protect your portfolio. Our priority is to ensure that your real estate assets are complementary to your other investments and that all the elements in your portfolio work together efficiently to achieve your financial goals. As a real estate broker, we can guide and manage the entire process of any real estate transaction. From helping our clients negotiate the finer points of the deal, to being confident with the final settlement statement, we are here to ensure a smooth transaction. All our support can be provided in-house, without our clients having to engage several firms, agents, or advisors. We offer a simple solution to an otherwise complex process.

When you seek advice, select and work with a Certified Commercial Investment Member (CCIM) who has the training and experience to professionally guide your real estate decisions. We recommend you hire a CCIM who is independent and not associated with any investment company, so you receive only unbiased recommendations. Your CCIM should also be fee-based, not commission-based, so you know your advisor's priority is solely focused on your best interests.

2. Private Equity

Private equity is an ownership interest in a company, but this type of investment is not listed on a public exchange. Purchasing private equity requires a very large investment amount, sometimes a minimum of as much as $1 million, and requires a long-term focus because the level of profits an investor anticipates usually do not occur right away, if ever. Most often, private equity is for pension funds and institutional investors, and independently wealthy investors.

This investment is attractive because returns can be highly profitable, although so are the risks. Private equity investors usually participate through a limited partnership. There are many tax issues created by this relationship, so consulting with your tax expert is absolutely necessary. Because this investment is independent of the markets, there are fewer restrictions; however, this independence could also make the investment vulnerable to a calamitous mistake that might destroy the company and your investment. Should you choose to exit your position, you may find it difficult because there is a lack of liquidity.

3. Hedge Funds

The term "hedge funds" comes from the ability of these funds to protect their value against a market downturn by selling short positions. Hedge funds are private investments which manage money for wealthy individuals and institutions. Like private equity, hedge funds are organized as limited partnerships and require a very high minimum investment; investors are restricted on the ability of selling their position. There are stipulations on the requirements for an investor, one of which is that an investor is usually required to have a personal value of at least $1 million, not including their primary residence.

Hedge funds use a variety of interesting techniques to increase their return and minimize their risk. You may be interested in knowing that hedge funds can:

- Buy an investment that has the potential to offset losses in other investments (hedge)
- Borrow shares and sell them immediately, attempting to cause a price drop so the shares can be replaced at a lower cost and generate a profit.
- Buy and sell the same security simultaneously to take advantage of different prices (arbitrage)
- Invest with borrowed money to try to maximize profitability (leverage)
- Make large investments in a few securities that are anticipated to be highly profitable (concentrate positions)
- Invest in distressed or bankrupt companies, derivatives, and privately issued securities

Some of the negative attributes of participating in a hedge fund is that hedge funds are often difficult to research and compare with other investments, management fees are typically very high, and hedge funds may lack liquidity, making it troublesome to exit your position and thus possibly lose your entire investment.

Summary

This addendum presented a general overview of 10 traditional investment vehicles, and three alternative investment vehicles. Most investors are well-served by the wide variety of traditional investment categories and the astounding universe of thousands of investment choices. Investors may also be attracted to investing in real estate because of their own personal or business experiences or because they are receiving professional advice from a licensed real estate investment broker. Private equity and hedge fund investments are for those investors with a large amount of capital resources who are attracted to the benefits of high returns and willing to take calculated risks.

Addendum 2

How to Analyze an Investment Security

Introduction

As explained in this book, there are generally two different ways to engage in the security evaluation process. The first method is with a top down approach, and the other is the bottom up approach. Both of these approaches work well for fundamental and technical analysis. Asset allocation investors should use the top down approach and work from the global to the specific. On the other hand, focused investors who are eager to select the best performing investments, will be more productive if they select the bottom up approach and work from the specific to the global.

The following pages present an overview of how to analyze stocks, bonds, mutual funds, and real estate for investment.

How to Analyze a Stock

Before investing in the stock of a company, the investor needs to know how much the stock is really worth and understand the risks involved. It's also imperative that the investor identifies the best time to buy the stock, have a strong opinion about how long to hold the stock, and determine a high and low target price for exiting the position and selling the stock.

While there are several ways to evaluate investments, the two most basic methods are fundamental analysis and technical analysis.

Fundamental analysis. To perform a fundamental analysis of a company, the investor needs to investigate the company's products or services, the various aspects of its current financial condition, the efficiency of its operations, and the quality of its management's performance. Most of this information is available through the company's annual reports and forms filed with the Securities Exchange Commission (SEC).

An investor should study the company's earnings per share (EPS) to detect whether or not the company is growing, and the price/earnings (P/E) ratio to gain an understanding about the value of the stock from the perspective of other investors. Two other important factors are the current ratio to learn if the company is able to pay its debts, and the company's debt-to-equity to examine the company's vulnerability during an economic downturn.

Technical analysis. Technical analysis relies heavily on charts that represent various elements of information such as moving averages, price, momentum, volume, stochastics, etc. Charts help analysts study patterns that may indicate future stock price movements.

STOCK INVESTMENT THEORIES:

As you might imagine, there are many stock investment theories. Here are a few of the more popular.

Dow Theory. The Dow Theory is based on an analysis of the market and a prediction of its general direction. This theory analyzes three different trend cycles, looking for patterns that indicate whether the market will move higher, sideways, or lower. Because this theory relies heavily on industrial and transportation stocks, critics question this theory's validity today because of the significant changes in our economy since this theory was first proposed. However, as with any theory, there is a lot that can be learned by studying various characteristics of this insightful theory.

Elliott Wave Theory. The Elliott wave theory claims that the markets move in waves based on investor sentiment. In general, there are five waves for a bull market and five as well for a bear market, with intervening waves of different intensity. Elliott wave analysts believe they can predict the market's performance by analyzing the wave patterns.

Odd-lot Theory. This theory claims to predict stock prices by the purchase and sale of small quantities, or odd lots, of securities. An odd lot is a quantity of less than 100 shares of a company's stock. The underlying belief is that small-time investors often mistake market activity, and therefore contrary buying and selling could be profitable.

Dogs of the Dow Theory. With this theory, investors purchase equal amounts of the half-dozen to dozen stocks with the highest dividend yields. These stocks are held for 12 months, and then they are sold to purchase the new set of high-performing dividend yield stocks. It's important to note that the dividend yield rises when the stock price falls, assuming dividends remain steady, so buying stocks with the highest dividend yields means that the investor is purchasing blue chip stocks representing strong value whose prices have temporarily dropped but will recover...making them excellent investments available at a discount.

Random Walk Theory. This curious theory states that since all investors have the same information, predicting the price of the stock is impossible. Patterns and trends are meaningless and coincidental and therefore passive investing to keep trading costs low while seeking the market average is the most sensible way to invest and achieve steady returns.

RESEARCH RESOURCES:

There are many resources available online and in books and magazines. Specific resources include the SEC's EDGAR database, and the Hoover online database. Delayed and real-time stock price quotes are available on the Internet in many locations.

A Suggested Process for Analyzing a Stock.

Here is a good process to follow when analyzing stocks to include in your portfolio. Before purchasing a stock, you should know the company inside and out.

1. PROCESS SUMMARY:

   A. Examine 10 years of summary financial statements

      1. Balance sheet

      2. Income statement

3. Cash flow statement

B. Look for trends, red flags, and abnormalities.

1. Read the most recent 10-k filing and the last two years of annual reports.
2. Pay special attention to the following sections:
    - Company
    - Industry
    - Risks
    - Competition
    - Legal issues
    - Management discussion
    - Footnotes
3. Pay attention to any mention of loan guarantees, contractual obligations, and any large cash outflows in upcoming years.
4. Read the most current quarterly report (the 10-Q) to see if anything has changed since the annual report.
5. Read the two most current proxies' statements to better understand executive compensation (Form DEF-14A).
6. Perform a company valuation, or have your financial planner do one.
    a. Discounted Cash Flows (DCF)
    b. Relative valuation: Check the valuation trend and the historical valuation range. How much upside is in the stock?

C. Basic Company Analysis

1. Growth
2. Profitability
3. Financial health
4. Risks/ the bear case
5. Management

D. Growth

1. How fast is the company growing, from what sources, and how sustainable is that growth?
   - Sales growth drives earnings growth
2. Four sources of growth:
   - Selling more goods or services
   - Raising prices
   - Selling new goods or services
   - Buying another company

E. Profitability

1. How much profit is the company generating relative to the amount of money invested in the business?
   - ROE
   - ROA
   - DuPont Analysis
   - Free Cash Flow (Cash flow from operations – capital spending)
2. We desire high ROIC %, high free cash flow, high ROE.

F. Financial health

1. We want manageable debt and fixed costs.
   - Review leverage ratio = assets/equity
   - Debt to equity ratio
   - Times interest earned ratio
   - Current and quick ratio
2. Free cash flow to total debt.

G. Risk / the bear case

1. List all the potential negatives from most obvious to least likely. What could go wrong with the investment thesis?
2. Why would we want to sell the stock rather than buy it?

H. Management

1. Compensation
    a. Proxy statements
    b. Salary vs. bonus vs. restricted stock vs. options
        - Prefer big bonus over big salary
        - Prefer restricted stock grants to generous option packages
    c. Executive loans abuse; forgiven debt
    d. Executive perks
    e. Is a founder still a large shareholder?
    f. Do executives have 'skin in the game'?
2. Character
    a. Does management hire friends and family?
    b. Is the board independent or stacked with family?
    c. Is management honest about their mistakes?
    d. Does the CEO have a cult of personality?
    e. Is the company able to retain high quality talent?
3. Operations
    a. High ROE and ROA, or increasing , without the use of excessive leverage?
    b. Organic growth vs. M&A /Acquisition growth
    c. Does management execute on its strategy?
    d. Is the company transparent with information?

2. RED FLAGS:
    1. Declining cash flows
    2. Serial changes
        - Frequent one-time charges
        - Write downs
        - Restructuring
    3. Serial acquisitions
    4. CFO or auditor departures

5. Stuffing the channel; shipping out more product than customers request.
6. Account receivables (ARs) not tracking sales. AR and sales growth should be close.

3. OTHER ISSUES TO LOOK FOR:
    1. Large or unreasonable gains from investments
    2. Pension pitfalls
        - Underfunded
        - Overfunded
    3. Pension padding
        - Booking excess gains as profit
    4. Cash flow reduction from stock option exercise
        - Cash flow statement
            — Tax benefits from employee stock plans, or
            — Tax benefit of stock options exercised
    5. Full warehouses
        - Inventories rising faster than sales
        - Temporary build up for new product launch is acceptable
        - Producing more than selling; demand dried-up or poor forecasting
    6. Change in assumptions
        - Financial statements
        - Accounting
        - Depreciation methods
        - Allowance for doubtful accounts
    7. Expensing vs. capitalizing

4. SUSTAINABLE COMPETITIVE ADVANTAGE (ECONOMIC MOAT):

    Note 1: Economic moats allow companies to retain above average levels of profitability for many years. Longer periods of excess profitability lead to better long term stock performance.

Note 2: Primary question: How does the company manage to keep competitors at bay and earn consistently above average profits? If you can answer this question, you have found the source of the company's economic moat.

Note 3: Four common steps to analyze an economic moat:

a. Evaluate historical profitability.
b. Why is the firm able to hold off the competition?
c. Estimate how long the firm will be able to hold the competition off.
d. Analyze the industry's competitive structure.

a. Evaluate the historical profitability:

1. Does the firm create free cash flow?
2. What are the firm's net margins?
3. ROE
4. ROA
5. ROIC and WACC

b. Why is the firm able to hold off the competition?

1. What is their strategy?
2. Why can't a competitor charge a lower price?
3. Why do customers accept a higher price?
4. What value does the product or service bring to the customer?
5. Why do customers use the firm's product over a competitor?

Building sustainable competitive advantage:

1. Differentiation
   a. Real: superior technology or features
   b. Perceived: trusted brand or reputation
2. Cost advantage

a. Driving down costs allows for lower pricing for similar product

3. High switching cost
   a. Lock customers into firm's product or service
4. High barriers to entry
   a. Lock competitors out

c. Estimate how long the firm will be able to hold off the competition.

1. Depth: How much money can a firm make?
2. Width: How long can the firm sustain above average profits?
   - A few years
   - Several years
   - Many years

Porter's 5 Forces:

1. Rivalry among competitors
2. Barriers to entry: threat of new entrants
3. Negotiating power of customers
4. Negotiating power of suppliers
5. Threat of substitute product or services

d. Analyze the industry's competitive structure.

1. Cycles
2. Number of players
3. Profitability of industry
4. Growing
5. Dying

Margin of safety: valuation and pricing.

1. Don't pay too high a price
2. Buy stock for less than it's worth
3. Include a margin of safety

- Small cap
- Midcap
- Large cap
- Risk

4. Historical P/E and trend
5. Valuation, valuation, valuation
6. Buy when markets are down, and people are pessimistic

Long-run view: Buy the company, not the stock.

1. Long term commitment
2. Long term capital gains
3. Minimize trading cost

Sell rules.

1. Know when to sell: establish at the time of purchase
2. Constantly monitor the stock
3. Stop loss pros and cons
4. Reasons to sell
   - We made a mistake in our evaluation
   - The fundamentals have deteriorated
   - The stock has risen excessively above its intrinsic value, and the new valuation does not support a sufficient upside margin of safety
   - We have a better investment opportunity
   - Our position is too big for the portfolio

Stock Analysis Review

Analyzing an equity can be accomplished using fundamental and technical analysis, which examines the many different elements of a company's ability to perform its mission and gain a profit. Five stock investment theories were presented to illustrate the variety of theories an investor could choose to study and apply. A method for analyzing stocks was offered in a detailed outline as a suggestion for how an investor might choose to proceed; looking for red flags was also itemized in the outline, as well as achieving insight about the company's competitive advantage.

Also, a reminder to the investor to always include a margin of safety was noted, as well as a brief review of the sell rules discussed in depth in an earlier chapter. As always, an investor should only proceed when he or she is confident in his or her academic knowledge, and should be cautious until a sufficient degree of experience has been earned; otherwise, it is strongly recommended that the investor hire the services of a professional financial planner in whole or in part to guide the investor with decisions that can produce a healthy return for a reasonable risk.

How to Analyze a Bond

When you are thinking about investing in bonds, there are six elements that require your careful analysis. They are the rate of return, the yield, the tax you can expect to pay on the interest, the maturity date, the bond's rating, and the bond's call features. Here is some introductory information on each of these six items.

THE RATE OF RETURN:

Investors purchase bonds because they want the fixed income bonds generate. When people think of bonds, they usually think of holding the bonds until maturity, but some investors don't. As with any investment, there is some degree of speculation, and some bond investors buy bonds with the calculated expectation that the price of the bonds will increase, allowing them to cash out their position with early profits. If this does not become the case, the investors are still earning a fixed return on their investment.

When analyzing a bond, the APR or annual percentage rate is the return you receive for the risk you are accepting by purchasing the debt of a government agency or the debt of a private or public company. The APR is different from the APY.

THE YIELD:

The annual percentage yield (APY) is the return you are expected to receive if your investment is held to maturity. The yield is higher than the return because the yield includes the published return as well as the monthly interest generated by the money in the account.

THE TAX ON THE INTEREST:

The cost of the tax on bond interest is a key concern for bond investors. Generally, bonds issued by state or local governments are free from federal taxation, and sometimes from state taxes as well. Tax-free bonds typically offer a lower interest rate than taxable bonds, so when analyzing the effect of taxes on a potential bond investment, it is wise to consider your entire financial circumstances; it might be smart to invest in a tax-free bond if you are in a high tax bracket, whereas if you are not, the lower interest rate offered by a tax-free bond may not be sufficient incentive for you to invest.

THE MATURITY DATE:

As you know, there is a wide range of maturity dates for different bonds. Some bonds are offered for only a three-month period and long-term bonds can be offered for as much as 30 years. The longer the maturity date, the higher the interest rate, typically. Because the price of bonds fluctuates, there are sometimes anomalies. Deciding how long you intend to hold your bond investment is a key factor in your deliberations.

THE BOND'S RATING:

The credit rating of the bond is another significant element to consider when analyzing the value of including bonds in your portfolio. Bonds with a low credit rating often pay higher interest rates because of the increased risk from the underlying company, which could go bankrupt and default on the bond; credit risk can be substantial, and your risk could be high. On the other hand, bonds issued by the United States government are considered highly reliable, so the interest rates are normally among the lowest available; the trade-off is a safer investment for a smaller return.

THE BOND'S CALL FEATURES:

You should also be clear on the call, or conversion, feature. In some cases, bonds can be redeemed, or called, by the issuing entity prior to the maturity date. A bond can be called if interest rates fall and the issuer wants to call in their debt and then reissue new debt at a lower interest rate, thus creating less interest payment cost for the company. Be sure to read about these details in the terms and conditions so you understand what could potentially occur. Also, some bonds allow conversion into the common stock of the company, and this might be an attractive alternative for you, should this opportunity develop.

Bond Analysis Review

Bonds offer their own unique opportunity to engage with the market and generate returns for your portfolio. Investing in fixed-income instruments could generate safe returns and may offer strategies for limiting taxation. In all cases, if you are interested in the bond market, enhance your expertise by first doing some additional reading to better understand the complexities and the benefits of including bonds in your investment portfolio, or consult with your investment advisor.

How to Analyze a Mutual Fund

Investing in mutual funds may provide your portfolio's access to industries or sectors that might otherwise require a great deal of time researching fundamental and technical information. However, you should conduct a careful analysis of the mutual fund to assure yourself that the fund will perform as you anticipate. A fund's return is important, but other factors must come under your scrutiny. They include the fund's investment objective, the risks derived from the underlying securities, and the amount of fees and expenses required to participate; these are a few of the elements reviewed below.

THE FUND'S INVESTMENT OBJECTIVE:

Perhaps the most important place to begin when analyzing a mutual fund is determining the fund's investment objective. Because you are looking for an investment that will provide either the kind of return you seek, or because you wish to diversify your portfolio in a certain manner, knowing the mutual fund's objective will clarify whether this fund is an appropriate candidate for your purpose. The three basic investment objectives are growth, income, and capital preservation, and some mutual funds may offer a combination of these. There are many subdivisions within each of these three basic types, so every investor will need to read the prospectus to more accurately determine the degree of the fund's intentions and its relation to the investor's own investment philosophy and goals.

THE UNDERLYING SECURITIES:

The securities held by the mutual fund may represent an investment across asset classes to help the fund achieve its objectives, or the fund may specialize in a particular industry niche. If you are analyzing a balanced fund, for example, you will find it interesting to note the ratio of stock securities to bond securities, or if you are selecting a commodities fund, you may be intrigued to note the different sectors represented by the securities in the fund. Every mutual fund investor should carefully read the information about the market sectors the mutual fund manager is authorized to purchase. Having a good idea about what will be included in this mutual fund will further help you determine if the fund is an appropriate fit for your own portfolio.

THE FUND'S INVESTMENT STYLE AND STRATEGIES:

Find out if the fund will be actively or passively managed so you know if this mutual fund is seeking alpha or beta returns, important information for your decision-making process. Another key consideration is whether the fund manager proposes growth investing or value investing as this also provides insight about how the fund is being managed and its alignment with your own purpose and goals. With this information you may be more capable of understanding the length of time the manager considers when making his or her decisions on the fund's capacity for returns. Remember to also check if the fund is an open-end fund that allows you to purchase and sell your shares directly, or a closed-end fund that restricts sales to only other investors.

MEASURING PERFORMANCE:

Determine if the mutual fund has been achieving its performance goals. While past performance is no assurance of future results, there are several popular metrics that can give you a good understanding of the fund's ability for continuing its successful practices. When looking at the fund's prospectus, study the historical performance in the one-year, five-year, and 10-year representations. There will be a comparison of that performance with an appropriate benchmark index to show you how the fund performed; take into consideration whether or not the economy was experiencing a bear or a bull market at that time. Peaks and valleys may be indicative of market cycles that are particular to the industry or sector, providing you with more insight to the timing or level of risks the fund may incur.

Your assessment should also include a review of the fund's historical volatility; this can be gauged by looking at the standard deviation of the fund's returns from its own average, and against the volatility of its benchmark index and the overall market as well. Finally, noting the management team's length of service will explain to what degree the historical performance is relevant to the current manager's decision-making. Is the manager newly appointed and does that raise a question about this fund's future performance, or was this manager a member of the original investment team and thus can take some credit (or blame) for the fund's historical performance?

IMPACT OF TAXES:

Taxes are a significantly important consideration because of the substantial impact they can have on your net. Capital gains taxes could have a disturbing effect on your bottom line for that year, so you should find out when capital gains or dividends are paid to shareholders; it could be wise to delay your investment purchase until after those disbursements are made, which typically occur near year-end. Continuing this line of thought, if you're planning to sell your mutual fund shares, you might be able to minimize your taxes by divesting prior to the distribution date. It is highly recommended that these issues are resolved with your accountant or tax advisor. Taxes are predatory, and your best defense is having the information you need to make the best decision for your financial health.

FEES AND EXPENSES:

The costs to purchase, participate, and sell mutual fund shares can also have a significant negative effect on your investment's net, so you should identify your costs if you are going to be a shareholder in the fund. These costs vary among the funds; because some funds have a higher turnover rate than others, trading expenses could be higher than those of other funds that are also attractive to you. There are shareholder fees, sales charges, redemption fees, and operating expenses that are likely to come out of your account's net. A helpful tool is to check a fund's expense ratio. This reveals the fund's annual costs as a percentage of its total assets; you can use this tool to compare the expense costs with other funds. Another helpful tip is to determine if a quantity purchase would provide a breakpoint that reduces your sales fees. It's quite important to take these fees and expenses seriously because they can significantly diminish your returns and thus reduce your most important asset, which is the time you have available for investing and reaching your financial goals.

RATING SERVICES:

Doing your own research is the best way to increase your knowledge and effectiveness as an investor. There are a number of mutual fund rating services, available for free online or by subscription, that provide a large amount of viable information. Your library may have a subscription service you can use as well. Then again, if you don't have the time to spend doing what really should be careful ongoing research and analysis, your money is too valuable to leave to chance; your best decision may be to take advantage of the services of a professional financial planner who can provide you with a set of appropriate choices you can then review and discuss before making your final decision.

Mutual Fund Analysis Review

Investing in mutual funds can provide you with access to investments in an industry or sector, or an investment style or strategy, which may be a good fit for your portfolio's investment goals. Knowing the goals of the mutual fund quickly gives you an indication of whether the fund is an appropriate candidate. Measuring the past performance of a mutual fund provides insights on the fund's ability to weather bear markets, rise with bull markets, and how it compared with an appropriate benchmark index. While past performance can never predict future accomplishment, there are indicators to help you make an investment decision that recognizes the potential degree of risk you will incur by purchasing shares. A fund's expenses can have a significant impact on your investment's return, so a careful review and comparison of expenses among other funds of similar type is a good procedure for making choices that retain as much of your net return as possible.

Addendum 3
Glossary

Absolute benchmark: The benchmark used to assess your investment's performance toward achieving your financial goals.

Active management: Account management in which the manager attempts to capture a higher return than an appropriate benchmark.

Aggressive investor: An investor who actively seeks high returns.

Alpha: The excess return of a fund against an appropriate benchmark.

Alpha strategy: An investment strategy that seeks alpha returns.

Annuity: An investment that provides payments at prescribed intervals; annuities are typically issued by insurance companies.

Asset: A property of financial value.

Asset allocation: The distribution of money into different asset classes, such as small cap, midcap, and large cap funds, plus others.

Asset class: A group of securities with similar characteristics.

Asset rotation: The rotation of assets that are not performing well for those that are.

Attribution analysis: A tool that allows an investor to determine which assets have affected the portfolio by being either overweight or underweight.

Benchmark: A point of reference used to measure performance.

Beta: The return of an asset as compared to its benchmark.

Beta strategy: An investment strategy that seeks beta returns.

Bond: The debt of a company or government agency that promises repayment with interest; bonds are usually issued in $1,000 multiples.

Bottom up research: Analysis conducted to determine the worthiness of an investment by starting with the specific and progressing toward the universal.

Certificate of Deposit (CD): A certificate from a bank authorizing a specified interest rate return for a sum of money after a set period of time; premature withdrawal creates penalties.

Compounding: Earnings generated from previous earnings.

Conservative investor: An investor who prefers risk protection over return.

Conservative strategy: An investment strategy that prioritizes risk over return.

Constraints: Limitations.

Correlation: The mathematical relationship between two or more elements.

Credit risk: A debt instrument's degree of risk, indicating the level of default risk for an investor.

Current ratio: A company's ability to pay its debts; the higher the ratio, the more likely the company is able to meet its liabilities.

Custom benchmark: A benchmark that is custom designed to accurately reflect the investment strategies and specific asset allocations of various asset classes and ratios in a specific portfolio.

Debt-to-equity ratio: A company's debt in relation to its equity. The higher the ratio, the more vulnerable the company might be to economic downturns.

Derivative: A security that derives, or receives, value from another asset.

Diversification: Investing in several different types of asset classes to reduce risk while also increasing the opportunity for growth.

Dividend: The payment by a company to its shareholders from profits; this is usually a quarterly payment.

Dow Theory: The Dow theory analyzes three different trend cycles looking for patterns that indicate whether the market will move higher, sideways, or lower.

Downside protection: Protecting against the risk and loss of wealth.

Dynamic rebalancing: The rebalancing of a portfolio on a regular basis to prevent the portfolio from an imbalance of asset allocations as prescribed by the Investment Policy Statement (IPS).

Earnings per share (EPS): A company's after-tax income divided by the number of shares. If there is an increase in this figure over a period of time the company is growing.

Efficiency ratio: Ratios that measure the financial health of a company such as inventory turnover and average collection period.

Efficient frontier: The efficient frontier is a strategy for investing your funds based on the most growth with the least risk according to your unique circumstances.

Elliott wave theory: The Elliott wave theory claims that the markets move in waves based on investor sentiment. In general, there are five waves for a bull market and for a bear market, with the intervening waves of different intensity. Elliott wave analysts believe they can predict the market's performance by analyzing the wave patterns.

ETF: Exchange traded fund; a marketable security that tracks a set of assets and trades like a common stock.

Factor model: A mathematical model that measures how the elements of a portfolio may be influenced by a variety of economic factors and the changes those factors may experience.

Fiduciary advisor: A professional who has fulfilled the certification requirements of the Certified Financial Planner Board of Standards.

Focused investing: A specific style of investing in which the primary interest is the accelerated increase of a portfolio's wealth. This is accomplished with an active alpha management that consistently selects the best performing securities, and retires holdings that decline as soon as it is financially reasonable to do.

Focused investor: An investor who engages the market with a focused investment style.

Frictional cost: The costs associated with a transaction such as commission, associated fees, interest, or tax costs.

Fundamental analysis: a method for studying a security's potential monetary value by examining the underlying influences (fundamentals) of the security, such as economic and political conditions, competitive advantage, sales revenue, financial reserves, experience of its management, etc.

Fundamental index: The measurement of key components of a company's performance rather than only the market value of the company's shares

General mean variance optimization: The process of finding the best combination among a set of securities to achieve the highest return with the least risk.

Growth equities: Companies whose price per share is anticipated to grow at a faster rate than the average rate of the market.

Growth investor: An investor who seeks growth equities for investment.

Hedge fund: A private fund, organized as a limited partnership, which manages money for wealthy individuals and institutions.

Kurtosis: A description of a probability distribution's shape.

Inflation risk: The degree of exposure and risk a security may have to an increase in the rate of inflation.

Initial stop: A stop-loss placed on a security, ordering the security to be sold at a specific market price, if possible. The stop is fixed, and can only be changed by a further order from the investor.

Interest risk: The exposure and risk a security may have with a change in interest rates.

Investment Policy Statement (IPS): A written statement detailing an investment plan's philosophy, objectives, responsibilities, asset classes and investment choices, evaluation of performance, and criteria for making changes to investments and service providers.

Investment risk: The degree of risk an investor accepts by purchasing a security.

Large cap stocks: Stocks issued by large companies, typically with over $10 billion in assets.

Leverage ratio: A measurement of a company's ability to repay its debt.

Liquidity ratio: The ratio of a company's liquid assets compared with its liabilities.

Log-normal: A data set in which the random variable of a logarithm is distributed normally.

Macro screening: A process used to discover the variety and impact of external forces affecting the value and growth of the candidate company.

Market cap index: An index composed of companies that are capitalized within a specific category, such as large cap, midcap, and small cap companies.

Market risk: The degree of risk a security may experience with changes in the market, such as with volatility or inflation.

Mean variance: The degree of difference between a mean and a variance when analyzing the potential return of the security.

Micro screening: A process used to analyze a company's internal data such as market share, experience of the management, production capabilities, sales forecasts, price to earnings ratio, the amount of stock owned by the company's senior management, etc.

Midcap stocks: Stocks issued by mid-sized companies, typically with between $2 - $10 billion in assets.

Moderate-balanced investor: An investor who favors an investment strategy of contained risk and moderate returns; typically, an investor nearing their time horizon for investing and who wants to maintain investment safety.

Modern Portfolio Theory (MPT): An investment theory by Harry Markowitz that attempts to maximize a portfolio's return for a specific limitation of risk. Mr. Markowitz received a Nobel Prize for his work.

Momentum investing: An investment strategy based on following an investment's momentum.

Momentum trend: The direction of an investment's momentum, going up, down, or sideways.

Money market fund: A mutual fund that earns interest by investing in short term debt such as Treasury bills.

Moving stop: A stop, or order to sell, that moves in tandem with the movement of an investment's price.

Mutual fund: A fund created by an investment management company that invests pooled investor money for a particular performance goal.

Negative compounding: The idea that returning to a breakeven point after experiencing an investment loss requires either more time, or a higher and therefore riskier rate of return, or both.

Noise: As applied to the market, the term refers to the excessive amounts of data that may confuse or distract an investor.

Odd-lot theory: This theory claims to predict stock prices by the purchase and sale of small quantities, or odd lots, of securities. An odd lot is a quantity of less than 100 shares of a company's stock.

Options trader: A trader who specializes in buying options on an underlying security giving the trader the option but not the obligation to purchase the security.

Passive management: An investment management style in which an investor purchases securities that match a benchmark index, participating only passively as the portfolio and index rise and fall according to market influences.

Price/earnings (P/E) ratio: A ratio that measures the price of a company's stock in relation to its earnings per share (EPS). Generally, a higher ratio indicates the willingness of investors to pay more for the stock because of the increased possibility that earnings will increase rapidly. This ratio is only useful when used to compare companies in the same industry.

Personal financial pyramid: A tool that describes a philosophically ideal distribution of a person's investments.

Phantom stop: A stop-loss trigger point that exists only in the investor's mind, not as a market order.

Private equity: Equity in a company that is not available for investment by the general public.

Profit margin analysis: The analysis an investor conducts to determine whether a company should be included in the investor's portfolio because of the equity's potential risk and return.

Profitability ratio: These are ratios that help determine the potential profitability of a company, such as return on equity (ROE) and return on assets (ROA).

Qualitative driver: A non—numeric factor used to determine the value of a security, such as the analysis of the company's industry, or its management, or its competitive advantage.

Quantitative driver: A numeric factor that measures the value of the security, such as ROA, ROE, sales growth, margins, etc.

Real estate: Land and permanent fixtures such as buildings; natural resources are included.

REIT: A Real Estate Investment Trust is a fund that invests in real estate and possibly allied industries such as real estate management companies.

Relative benchmark: A benchmark that is similar to a particular portfolio, thus making the benchmark a valid tool for the portfolio's comparison.

Required Rate of Return (RRR): The minimum annual percentage an investment must earn to achieve the investment's goal for growth. The RRR is different for different investments, and for different people.

Risk tolerance: The amount of risk that is acceptable for your investments given your personally unique situation.

ROA: Return on Assets is a ratio indicator that measures the percentage of a company's profits compared to its total assets. Generally, an ROA over 5% is considered good.

ROE: Return on Equity identifies the profitability ratio of a company. The ROE shows how much profit each stockholder's dollar has generated. Look for historic stability and trends.

ROIC: Return on Invested Capital is a metric that expresses financial performance by measuring a company's profit based on the company's total investment dollars. This shows shareholders and interested parties the ability of a company to employ its money to generate returns.

SAMURAI: An acronym composed of seven components which are often used in gauging whether a benchmark is appropriate: Specified in advance; Appropriate; Measurable; Unambiguous; Reflective; Accountable; Investable.

Scenario analysis: A process for projecting possible outcomes for a set of investment scenarios.

Semi-passive strategy: A strategy whose purpose is to diversify investment funds among the different types of asset classes so return-rate volatility and risk are reduced.

Sensitivity analysis: When a single variable is adjusted to determine how this one modification might affect the performance of his or her investment.

Skewness: A mathematical measure of a probability distribution related to a random variable and its mean.

Small cap stocks: Stocks issued by smaller companies, typically with under $2 billion in assets.

Speculator: An investor who is willing to take high risks for high returns.

Static rebalancing: The process of rebalancing a portfolio to its original percentage mix.

Stock: A security that represents an investor's ownership in a company, granting the investor a portion of the company's assets and earnings.

Stop loss: A market order to sell a position at a price set by the investor, if possible.

Strategic: Having a large influence, being comprehensive.

Strategic decisions: Decisions that have a significant impact on a direction or outcome.

Systematic risk: The risk of the system itself, as in the inherent risk of the market system.

Tactical: An influence that supports a larger purpose.

Tax-deferred: Money that is earned by a tax-deferred account and taxed only upon withdrawal.

Tax-free: Money that is earned by a free account and is not taxed.

Technical analysis: A method for studying a security's potential monetary value by forecasting its future price through a study of its market data, particularly its history of price and volume.

Time horizon: The amount of time available for achieving a specific goal.

Top down research: Analysis conducted to determine the worthiness of an investment by starting with the universal and progressing toward the specific.

Trader: A person who purchases financial assets in a financial market. The key difference between an investor and a trader is that an investor normally holds a position longer than a trader.

Trailing stop: A stop-loss order put in place by the investor to trail a security's price by a set amount.

Unsystematic risk: The risk is accepted by an investor in order to participate in the purchase and sale of securities.

Upside capture: The profits an investor wishes to secure by investing in securities.

Value drivers: The factors that make the purchase of an investment attractive to an investor.

Value equities: Stock securities that are regarded as undervalued by the market, and thus attractive to value investors who believe they are purchasing these securities at a discount.

Index

A

B

C

D

E

F

N

O

P

Q

R

W

Y